中 国
历 史 与 文 明

The History and Civilization of China

CONTENTS

Chapter I.

The Sun Rises in the East

--the Pre-historical Age

The Chinese nation is rich in history. China is one of the birthplaces of mankind, and it is an important cradle of the world's civilization.

The Yellow River

I. Legends of Remote Antiquity

The Distribution of the Archaeological Relics of the Old Stone Age in China

According to Chinese mythology, it was Pan Gu, Creator of the Universe, who separated heaven and earth. He then turned different parts of his body into the sun, the moon and the stars in the heavens, and into mountains, rivers, land, soil, grass, trees, wind and clouds on earth. Man was created out of earth by the goddess Nüwa. Later, Chaoshi, chief of a tribe, learned to make shelter from the weather by use of wood, as such Man learned how to build a home. Suiren, the giver of fire, got fire from wood by friction, and as such Man learned how to use fire. Meanwhile Fuxi domesticated animals to provide a source of meat for Man, and Man learned how to go hunting and fishing, and began to develop household animal husbandry. It is also said that Fuxi cultivated the primitive people by persuading them to establish marriage relations. By observing the skies and the earth, he also invented Eight Trigrams and created Han script so that Man ceased to keep records by tying knots in strings. When it came to the age of Shennong, he invented plough-like farm tools for turning over the soil and then taught his men how to farm. At the same time, he discovered many medical herbs by personal experimentation. He also taught his men how to weave and make pottery, and set up markets so that people could barter. At that time, there were no rules or laws, and no rewards or punishments. People cooperated with each other, and all men were socially

Huang Di

Painted patterns on the pottery, Neolithic

Pottery jar, Neolithic, the jar is 16.5cm high, the stand is 12.5cm high, unearthed at Cishan, Wu'an, Hebei province

Painted pottery ewer of the Liangzhu culture (3300-2200 BC)

Painted pottery basin with dance scenes, Neolithic, of the Zongri culture (c. 3300-2050 BC), height: 12.5cm, diameter: 22.8cm, unearthed at Zongri, Tongde, Qinghai province

Painted pottery basin with design of fish and human face, Neolithic, diameter: 50cm, unearthed at Banpo, Xi'an, Shaanxi province

Painted pottery basin with design of fish and frog, Neolithic, diameter: 30.4cm, unearthed at Jiang Zhai, Lintong, Shaanxi province

Huang Di (Xuanyuan) Tomb in Huangling County, Shaanxi province

Painted pottery bowl with engraved symbols, Neolithic, diameter: 34.2cm, unearthed at Jiang Zhai, Lintong, Shaanxi province

5

第一篇

日出东方

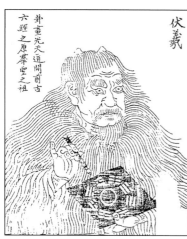

Fuxi, one of the three sage "kings". Legend has it that he invented Eight Trigrams and created script

Shennong, also called Yan Di, is the creator of farming. Legend has it that he discovered many medical herbs by personal experimentation and knew pharmacology very well.

Cang jie, legend has it that he is the creator of Chinese characters

Shennong with ancient plough, Han Dynasty stone relief, Wuliang ancestral hall

Pottery human face, Neolithic, 5.5cm high, unearthed at village ruins in Zhaobaogou, Chifeng, Inner Mongolia Autonomous Region

The painting of Fuxi and Nuwa, Tang Dynasty, artist unknown, silk scroll, 220cm high, 116.5cm wide

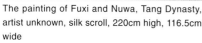

Pottery horn of Dawenkou culture (4300-2500 BC), 39cm long, unearthed at linghe, Ju county, Shandong province

was named Jiang. The tribe he led first lived in Shanbei and later moved eastwards along the Weihe River and the Yellow River to areas now belonging to Shandong province. The Miao Tribe lived in the Yangtze-Huaihe Valley and were led by San Miao. Another tribe, called Jiuli Tribe was active in Shandong and central Anhui province, with Chiyou as the chief.

While expanding westwards, Jiuli Tribe extended its territory by invasion. And there were constant encroachments by Jiuli Tribe on Huang Di's Tribe and Yan Di's Tribe. Consequently, a fierce battle broke out between the Yan-Huang allied forces and Jiuli Tribe on the outskirts of Zhuolu. Jiuli Tribe was defeated and Chiyou was hacked to death. Part of his Tribe joined Huang Di's Tribe and Yan Di's Tribe. The rest moved southwards to areas now called as Jing and Chu. Gradually they were amalgamated into Miao Tribe. Later, three fierce battles broke out between Huang Di's Tribe and Yan Di's Tribe in Banquan (now belonging to Huailai county, Hebei province), the result of which was that Yan Di was defeated. The two tribes were further merged and settled down in the Central Plains together with part of Jiuli Tribe. Since then Han people all respect and revere Huang Di, looking on him as the common ancestor of the whole nation and calling themselves as the scions of Yan-Huang or scions of Huang Di.

equal. People could identify their mothers but not their fathers because of the lack of marriage relations. But females played a dominant role in the society, so that age was called matriarchal society. Gradually many tribes entered the era of the patriarchal society, among which were two famous tribes in the upper reaches of the Yellow River. One had Huang Di as its chief. The other was headed by Yan Di. Huang Di's name was Ji alias Xuanyuan. Huang Di's Tribe originated in what is known today as Shanbei. They then came to the southeast valley of the Yellow River and settled in today's Zhuo Lu, Hebei province. Yan Di, who was presumably the descendant of Shennong,

Warring States, painting on silk, 28cm high, 20cm wide, unearthed at Chenjia Dashan Chu Tomb, Changsha, Hunan province

Polished embossed black pottery plate with a bird-shaped post, height: 23.4cm, diameter: 36.2cm

Painted pottery bowl, diameter: 29cm, unearthed at Huquan village, Hua county, Shaanxi province

Squared pottery bowl, 11.7cm high, unearthed at Hemudu, Yuyao, Zhejiang province

Black pottery food vessel with two loop handles, 13.9cm high

Painted pottery pitcher with a human face on its mouth and a flat bottom, Neolithic, 31.8cm high, unearthed at Dadiwan, Qin'an, Gansu province

Gourd-shaped painted pottery pitcher with design of fish and birds, Neolithic, 29cm high, unearthed at Jiang Zhai, Lintong, Shaanxi province

Pottery gui of Longshan culture (2500-2000 BC)

Owl pottery tripod, 23.3cm high, unearthed at Huquan village, Hua county, Shaanxi province

第一篇

日出东方

II. Ancient Society Discovered by Archaeological Excavation

(Old Stone Age: From 1.7 million years to 10 thousand years ago)
(New Stone Age: From 10 thousand to 4 thousand years ago)

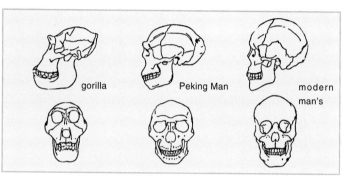

comparison of gorilla, Peking Man and modern man's skulls

gorilla　Peking Man　modern man's

Shandingdong relics, Zhoukoudian, Beijing

Where did mankind come from? Where did the Chinese nation come from? The research discoveries from archaeology and palaeoanthropology have revealed the path of how the ancestors of the Chinese nation were civilized . It has been borne out that the remote ancestors of mankind originated in China by the 45-million-year-old fossil of Zhaishu Ape discovered in Shanxi, 8-million-year-old fossil of Lama Ape and 1.7 million-year-old fossil of Yuanmou Man. Old Stone Age to New Stone Age witnessed the birth of the civilization of the Chinese nation.

About 1.7 million years ago, Yuanmou Man had already learned how to make stone artifacts, 800,000 years ago, Lantian Man inhabited in Lantian County, Shaanxi Province. These ape men have been believed to be the first to walk erect, though somewhat stooped. Stone artifacts made by them were rough and clumsy. Peking Man, who inhabited in Zhoukoudian 500,000 years ago, had already learned how to make and use simple tools: tools made of wood and bone. From Jinniushan Man 280,000 years ago to Dali Man, Dingcun Man, Maba Man, Changyang Man and Xujiayao Man, the evolution from apeman into Homo Sapiens was finally achieved. In the late Old Stone Age, Homo Sapiens, such as Hetao Man, Shandingdong Man (Upper Cave Man), Liujiang Man, Zuozhen Man, Xiacaowan and Ziyang Man, had already acquired the new skills of polishing, drilling and so on and applied these skills in the making of stone artifacts. In addition, bows and arrows made during that time have also been found.

In the Old Stone Age, mankind evolved gradually from apeman into modern man. The whole period of the Old Stone Age was marked with the making of stone implements. In the New Stone Age, Neolithic Man began to settle down and practise the slash-and-burn method of farming, and more complicated stone implements appeared at this time. The world's earliest manufacturing plant of stone implements was discovered in Site of Dayao Culture (or: Site of Ancient Dayao Cultural relics). With the aid of sharp stone implememts, Man started to go hunting and gathering and improve the means of fishing. He also learned to make pottery and wooden tools, and to weave, thus promoting production.

In the early days of human race, in order to rise to the fierce challenge of nature, man had to live in groups primitively without marriage relations. In the late period of Old Stone Age,

Colored pattern of Yangshao culture

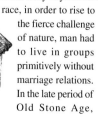

The restored house at the Banpo relics of Yangshao culture

Millstone and bar, Neolithic, the millstone is 56.5cm long, the bar is 41.5cm long, unearthed at Cishan, Wu'an, Hebei province

The Distribution of the Archaeological Relics of the New Stone Age in China

Legend

- ★ Majiayao Culture
- ● Yangshao Culture
- ○ Dawenkou Culture
- ◎ Qingliangang Culture
- ▥ Qujialing Culture
- ■ Hongshan Culture
- ▲ Longshan Culture
- □ Qijia Culture
- △ Daxi Culture
- ▨ Liangzhu Culture

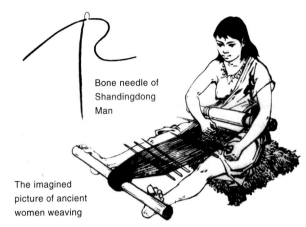

Bone needle of Shandingdong Man

The imagined picture of ancient women weaving

clan societies were taking shape. About 100,000 years ago, these clan communes gradually entered the era of matriarchal society. About 6,000 or 7,000 years ago, the matriarchal society reached its zenith in the Yellow River Valley, the Changjiang River Valley and the Pearl River Valley. During this time, females played a dominant role: Family property was inherited by the maternal side, and positions in the family hierachy was determined by the maternal side. System of exogamy was established.

Site of Jiang Zhai Relics in Lintong County, Shaanxi Province, established about 4,600-3,600 years ago, is a relatively well preserved ruins of village in the Yellow River Valley and is also to date the largest site of village ruins in the New Stone Age which was excavated in China. It has revealed the social structure and life style in the Matriarchal society.

In the late New Stone Age, males played a dominant role in various productive activities eventually. Gradually all tribes entered the era of the patriarchal clan society. Family property was inherited through the paternal line and positions in the family hierachy was determined by paternal line. Hunting and fishing was then second only to primitive agriculture and household animal husbandry in man's productive activities in which women had been engaged. Males were the primary primitive agricultural producers, while women played a secondary role, being confined to laboring chiefly with the household such as weaving. An important symbol of the partriachal society was the appearance of a more firm and enduring system of monogamy in marriage relations. Joint graves of adult men and women began to appear in the late period of Dawenkou Culture. The male was invariably in the middle with a female on either side facing upward or facing the male. This phenomenon showed that the marriage form had taken dramatic change.

The imagined picture of farming in the New Stone Age

Reproduction of the Jiangjun rock painting in Lianyungang, Jiangsu province

Pitchfork-shaped bone ware, 15.8cm high, unearthed at Jiahu, Henan province

Bone flute, 22.2cm long, unearthed at Jiahu, Henan province

第一篇

日出东方

III. The Discovery of Beauty

The distant view of Hongshan on the south side of Yingjin River in Chifeng, Inner Mongolia

Man's pursuit of beauty dates back to the primitive society. In the early Stone Age, colourful culture began to bud . Different tribes created their own unique culture with distinctive features. In their upper caves, together with the remains of upper Cave Man were not only the used tools and the remains of consumed animals, but also many painstakingly made ornaments such as perforated animal teeth, pebbles, polished bird bones and stone beads. All these ornaments revealed primitive man's pursuit of beauty.

Colorfully painted pottery and black pottery were symbolic of the development of civilization. Excavated from Site of Yangshao Culture were, among other things, beautifully hand-made terra-cotta and red pottery. On these pottery there were painted animals, plants and geometric designs. On the pottery made by Banpo Man, there were black or red patterns of whirlpool, wave, geometry, flower, deer and fish with a human face, and so on. The shapes and patterns of some of the painted pottery were elegant.

Hongshan Culture, which was located in Liaoning province, is the greatest discovery of the Stone Age. One small pottery statue of a woman was discovered in Xishuiquan, Chifeng county. It was moulded with brown clay, with breasts projecting, waist slim, the lower part of the body taking on the shape of a trumpet. In Dongshanzui, Kazuo, some pottery statues of naked women with broken heads were excavated, whose bodies presented some features of pregnancy. These statues might be *the Goddess of Birth'* worshipped by people of that time.

Hunting and gathering were also important themes of what primitive Man expressed. Primitive paintings are those mainly carved in or painted on rocks. Among the most famous rock paintings are the Cangyuan Rock Paintings in Yunnan, the Huashan Rock Paintings in Guangxi, the Jiangjun Rock Paintings in Lianyungang, the Hutubi rock paintings in Xinjiang, the Gangcha Rock Paintings in Qinghai and the Heishan Rock Paintings near Jiayuguan. These rock paintings portray the social economy and productive situation, as well as the group organizations of primitive Man. Some of them also describe religious activities, villages, wars and dance scenes. There are rock paintings of birds, fish and stone axes drawn with a simple and unaffected style. They present a clear theme and create some vivid images. The origin of some basic brush techniques of Chinese modern painting like line-drawing and color-filling drawing can also be traced to these rock paintings.

Various materials like bones, teeth, pottery and stone were used for carving arts. The bird-shaped bone knife of the Hemudu culture, the hollowed-out ivory canister of the Dawenkou, and the relief head portrait of Yuanyang Pool discovered in Gansu, all maintain high artistic level. The rim of the colored pottery bottle unearthed in Miao Di Gou is a round-carved head portrait with the hair pulled down. The eyes, mouth and nostrils were all open work. The transitional relation between the head and the body was roughly incarnated. The bottle can be regarded as a masterpiece of the remote antiquity period.

Music and dance have the same

The symbols on the pottery of the Majiayao culture

The painted patterns on the pottery of the New Stone Age

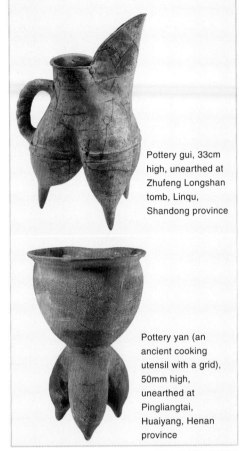

Pottery gui, 33cm high, unearthed at Zhufeng Longshan tomb, Linqu, Shandong province

Pottery yan (an ancient cooking utensil with a grid), 50mm high, unearthed at Pingliangtai, Huaiyang, Henan province

long history as that of human beings. A colored pottery basin of the New Stone Age was unearthed in Datong County in Qinghai Province. On the inside wall of the basin are vivid paintings showing dancing scenes. The current unearthed primitive musical instruments include Pottery Xun (egg-shaped and holed wind instrument), a bone whistle, pottery drums and pottery bells as well as those made of bamboo, wood, silk etc. With the birth of musical instruments, people began to realize the relations among different tones and developed a musical scale. One Pottery Xun excavated in Wantong County can play four different tones. More than ten bone flutes were unearthed in Wuyang, Henan. Most of them have seven holes which can play seven tones. Some of them can still work today.

Jade figure, the late Neolithic Age, 8.1cm high, unearthed at Lingjiatan, Hanshan, Anhui province

Jade figure, the late Neolithic Age (c. 30th-26th centuries BC), 9.6cm high

Pottery statue of a naked woman in her shoes

第一篇

日出東方

4. Towards Civilization

Jade pig-dragon, Neolithic, Hongshan culture (c. 3th century BC), 7.9cm high, 5.6cm wide, unearthed at Niuheliang, Lingyuan, Liaoning province

Stone owl, 2.5cm long

Phoenix-shaped jade pendant in fretwork (c. 25th-21st centuries BC), unearthed at Li county, Hunan province

Primitive culture is the early foundation of Chinese civilization. Different clans, pursuing their productive activities in different natural environments created differently featured primitive cultures.

The Yellow River Reaches were the cradle of Chinese Shu (millet)-Mai (wheat) agriculture. The comparatively complete agricultural tools and animals like chicken unearthed in the relics of the Pei Ligang culture in Henan and the Mount Ci culture in Hebei, the two cultures established seven or eight thousand years ago, indicating that China is the first country in the world to rear chicken.

The Hemudu culture in Zhejiang was the origin of rice planting agriculture. The carbonized paddy unearthed was identified to have been artificially planted and was the earliest in the world. Two categories of paddy were also identified as japonica rice and indica rice.

Primitive weaving was a kind of handiwork in its earliest form. It referred to the techniques employed in bamboo-ware making. In the New Stone Age, methods of weaving the hand-made cloth included plain weave and hanging weave. The earliest silk was found among remains unearthed in the Liangzhu culture in Huzhou, Zhejiang Province. The only weaving tool at that time was the spindle.

Religious consciousness also appeared during this period. Religious concepts and consciousnesses like phallism, worships of the sun and many other gods were embodied in rock paintings, carvings, construction of houses and graves. The Hongshan culture in Liaoning Province is the most important representative of the New Stone Age culture. The stone-made construction groups discovered at the mouth of Mount Kazuodong and the goddess temple relics discovered in Niuheliang are mainly square-like and half-crypted. The goddess temple, several stone-grave groups, and a walled square or castle covering an area of about 40,000 square meters, were where the ancient people offered sacrifices to the gods and their ancestors.

Some exquisite potteries for sacrificial purpose with peculiar designs were found in the goddess temple. They suggest that there were a large number of sacrificial activities in the temple and comparatively advanced primitive organizations began to appear at that time. The jade pig-dragon, jade pendant of semi-circular-shaped with two dragon heads, and the remains of the jaw of a colored pig-dragon were the earliest discoveries in the images of dragons of remote antiquity in archeology. Jade was made into many decorations or figurines like sea turtles and small birds. Found near the stone constructions for sacrifices, these figurines stand for symbols of religion or were made for religious purpose.

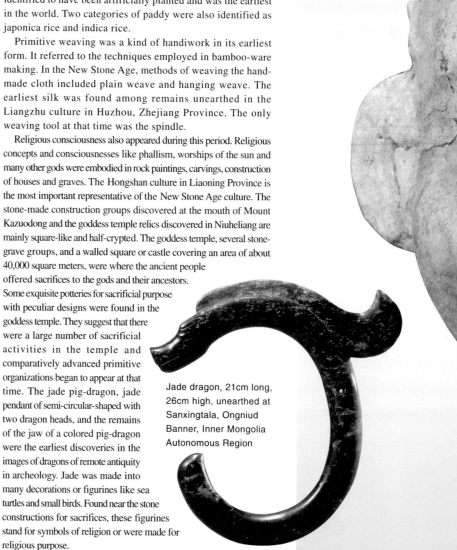

Jade dragon, 21cm long, 26cm high, unearthed at Sanxingtala, Ongniud Banner, Inner Mongolia Autonomous Region

Jade eagle, 8.4cm long, unearthed at Lingjiatan, Hanshan, Anhui province

Jade cong, 4.5cm high, unearthed at Liangzhu, Yuyao, Zhejiang province

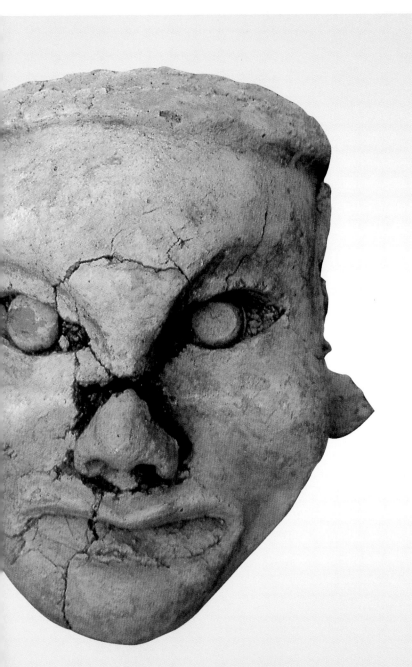

Double body animal-shaped pottery jar, Neolithic, 32cm long, unearthed at Karuo, Changdu, Tibet

Painted pottery dou-vessel of Dawenkou culture (4300-2500 BC), 29.3cm high, unearthed at Dawenkou, Taian, Shandong province

Pottery pitcher with human head (c. 40th-30th centuries BC), 21cm high, unearthed at Dafen, Jiaxing, Zhejiang province

Clay statue of goddess, unearthed at the Goddess Temple in Niuheliang, Lingyuan, Liaoning

第一篇

日出东方

夏

Chapter 2

Bronze Age

--the Xia, the Shang and the Zhou

The Xia, the first dynasty in China.
The Shang, the beginning of
written history.
The Zhou's unification of China, an
important phase for the
establishment of the Chinese
nation.

Relics of Sanxingdui, Guanghan, Sichuan province

1. The First Dynasty -- The Xia

(Approximately from 2070 B.C. to 1600B.C.)

The Situation of Xia Dynasty

1 Siyu	2 Qi	3 Taikang				
		4 Zhongkang	5 Xiang	6 Shaokang	7 Zhu	8 Huai	9 Mang
10 Xie	11 Bujiang	14 Kongjia	15 Gao	16 Fa	17 Lugui Jie
	12 Jian	13 Yinjia			

Shun Di

According to the legend, Yu the Great won people's trust because of his great feats in water control in the 21st century B.C. He was later chosen as chief of his clan. Since Yu was titled in a place called Xia, his clan was thus named. Yu the Great organized his people to develop agriculture and went on punitive expeditions

against the Sanmiao Tribe in the south. He invited many tribe chiefs to come to Mount Tu and held a conference. He made inspection tours to the south and hunting expeditions in the North. He also divided the state into nine administrative districts and used bronze to make weapons and develop the treasure of the country. In his late years, Yu the Great recommended Gaotao to succeed him. However Gaotao unexpectedly died before Yu, and Boyi was then chosen to succeed him. However, after Yu's death, Qi, Yu's son, relying on his family' great strength, seized the position of king and established the first country in China, the Xia. As a result, the principle of the aging monarch relinquishing power to someone better qualified rather than his own son was violated and a new hereditary system came into being. In ancient times, this was considered to be the beginning of a system of whereby the ruler "takes all under heaven as his family possession".

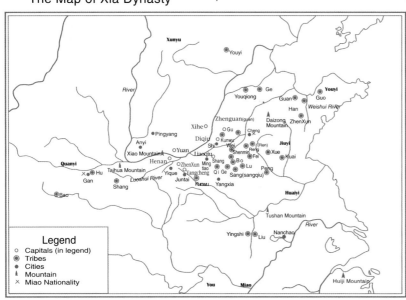

Da Shun (respectful term of address for Shun) ploughs in the field, brick carving, Jin Dynasty, unearthed at Jishan, Shanxi provinceh

The sites of late Xia's palaces are scattered amongst the Erlitou relics in Yanshi, Henan Province. The construction was built on a grand rammed-earth platform. The platform is a square with a length of 108 meters from east to west and a width of 100 meters from south to north. It covers an area of about 10,000 square meters. The state institution of the Xia was relatively simple. The king was the highest ruler of the state. Xishi and Heshi were assigned to be in charge of observing celestial bodies and the four seasons. Muzheng, Chezheng, and Paozheng were responsible for administrative affairs. Prisons called "Xia Tai" were established. Xia divided the state into nine administrative divisions and nine governors were appointed accordingly. Xishi and Heshi worked out a

The Map of Xia Dynasty

Legend
○ Capitals (in legend)
◉ Tribes
● Cities
▲ Mountain
✕ Miao Nationality

Bronze he-pot (a tripod for warming wine) of the late Erlitou culture (1700-1400 BC), unearthed at Erlitou, Yanshi, Henan province

Yu of Xia Dynasty

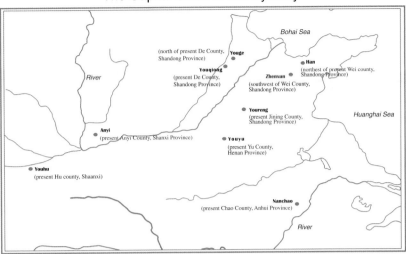

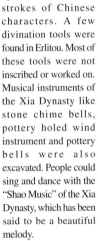

calendar called "Xia Xiao Zheng", which divided the year into 12 months. They also recorded the monthly configuration and movement of the stars, appropriate farming activities in different living states of plants and animals in different months.

Agriculture was the Xia's main industry. The Xia people lived on the loess plains of the Yellow River formed by alluvial deposits; therefore, they began to use primitive wooden and stone tools in cultivation. They knew how to dig channels for irrigation and how to irrigate the earth by wells. With the development of agriculture, there was an oversupply of foodstuff and this led to the development of a brewing industry. It became a fashion for the Xia people to drink wines.

As regards to the production of pottery, stonewares and bronze wares, there were also achievements in the Xia dynasty. Potteries were watered before they were taken out of the kiln. Therefore, most of the potteries were black or gray in color and hard in texture. Besides the basket pattern, the diamond pattern and the rope pattern, there were other exquisite patterns like the nailing pattern, the feather pattern and the lining pattern. Bronze metallurgy was a newly developed industry and the techniques were fairly advanced. The relics of large-scale palaces found in Erlitou, Yanshi of Henan Province correspond with information recorded in the historical documents. There are more than 20 kinds of signs inscribed on the wares unearthed from the Erlitou and Dawenkou cultural relics. These signs already represented the forms of

Bronze ornamental plate with animal mask motif inlaid with turquoise, Xia Dynasty (about 21st-16th centuries BC), unearthed at Erlitou, Yanshi, Henan province

strokes of Chinese characters. A few divination tools were found in Erlitou. Most of these tools were not inscribed or worked on. Musical instruments of the Xia Dynasty like stone chime bells, pottery holed wind instrument and pottery bells were also excavated. People could sing and dance with the "Shao Music" of the Xia Dynasty, which has been said to be a beautiful melody.

The picture of celebration for Da Yu's success in curbing floods (Da Yu is a respectful term of address for Yu), stone inscription, Emperor Yu pavilion in Kaifeng, Henan province

Pottery he-pot, Xia Dynasty (1700-1400 BC), unearthed at Erlitou, Yanshi, Henan province

Da Yu Mausoleum in Shaoxing, Zhejiang province

17

第二篇

青铜时代

2. The Shang

(approximately from 1600 B.C. to 1046 B.C.)

Emperors in Shang Dynasty

1 Zitang	2 Taiding	5 Taijia		8 Xiaojia	11 Zhongding	14 Zuyi (Zhongzong)
	3 Waibing	19 Yangjia	6 Woding	9 Yongyi	12 Wairen	
	4 Zhongren	20 Panyin	7 Taikang	10 Taiwu	13 Hechanjia	
		21 Xiaoxin			24 Zugeng	26 Bingxin
15 Zuxin	17 Zuding	22 Xiaoyi	23 Wuding (Gaozong)		25 Zujia	27 Kangding
16 Wojia	18 Nanyin					
28 Wuyi	29 Jiaoding	30 Diyi	31 Dixin (Zhou)			

The Situation of Shang Dynasty

Legend
- ◉ Capitals in Shang Dynasty
- ● ○ States owned by Dukes
- [Yin] Ancient place names
- Xunyu nationality
- (Qufu) Place name nowadays

The Shang dynasty traced its origin to an ancient tribe on the lower reaches of the Yellow River. The tribe was one of the Yi tribes in the east worshipping black birds. From its beginning to King Tang, The Shang tribe moved its center of activities eight times until Tang settled in Bo. When Xia's power gradually diminished in its late times, Shang colluded with nine Yi tribes and defeated Xia at Mingtiao (present-day Fengqiu in Henan. Jie, Xia's last king fled to Nanchao (present-day Chaohu in Anhui). The Chiefs of three thousand other tribes supported Tang to be the king. He then established the Shang dynasty in approximately the sixteenth century B.C.

The influences of the Shang reached far broader than the Xia. Kings of the Shang made use of the former sites of Xia's palaces and built their own palaces and temples in the south of Erlitou village, Yanshi of Henan Province. These buildings were the earliest known temples and palaces in China. The patterns and styles of these buildings exercised far-reaching influences on the later ages. The Shang relics unearthed in modern Zhengzhou covered an area of 25 square kilometers. There were city walls, rammed-earth construction sites and various workshops inside.

In the middle of the relic site was a 7-kilometer-long city wall. The relic of palaces covered an area of more than 60,000 square meters. Pottery inscriptions of the characters "Bo" and "Bo District" unearthed in the relics indicate that these palaces were where the early Shang's temples

Chengtang

Ivory cup inlaid with turquoise, Shang Dynasty (c. 16th-11th centuries BC), 30.3cm high, unearthed at Fuhao Tomb, Anyang, Henan province

Bronze tiger with two tails, Shang Dynasty (c. 16th-11th centuries BC), 53cm long, unearthed at Xingan, Jiangxi province

Foundation ruins of a Shang building in Dongbeidi, Xiaotun, Anyang, Henan province

Bronze mao-spear, from Qijia to Kayue culture (c. 20th-11th century BC), 61cm high, unearthed at Shenna, Xining, Qinghai province

第二篇　青铜时代

Foundation ruins of the west part of a Shang palace, Yanshi, Henan province

Relics of a Shang palace on the north bank terrace of the Yellow River

The Distribution of the Relics of Shang Dynasty

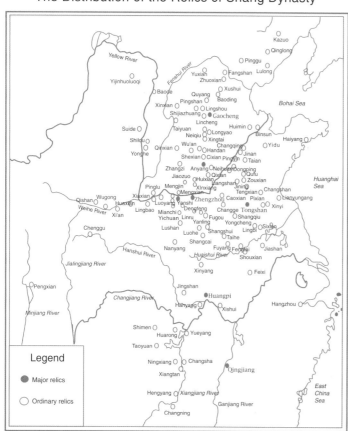

Kazuo
Qinglong
Pinggu
Yellow River
Fenshui River
Yuxian
Fangshan
Lulong
Zhuoxian
Yijinhuoluoqi
Baode
Xushui
Quyang
Baoding
Xinxian
Pingshan
Lingshou
Bohai Sea
Shijiazhuang
Lincheng
Gaocheng
Suide
Huimin
Taiyuan
Longyao
Binsun
Neiqiu
Haiyang
Shilou
Xingtai
Yidu
Qinxian
Wu'an
Changqing
Yonghe
Shexian
Handan
Jinan
Cixian Pingyin
Taian
Zhangzi
Anyang Neihuang Dongping
Jiaozuo
Qixian
Qufu
Pinglu
Huixian
Zouxian
Mengjin
Xinxiang
Jining
Huanghai
Xiangshan
Tengxian
Sea
Qishan
Wugong
Xiaxian
Zhengzhou
Caoxian
Changshan
Lianyungang
Huaxian
Luoyang Yanshi
Pixian
Xinyi
Weihe River
Lingbao
Dengfeng
Tongshan
Xi'an
Mianchi
Changge
Shangqiu
Chenggu
Yichuan
Linru
Fugou
Yongcheng
Sixian
Lushan
Yanling
Lingbo
Luohe
Shangshui
Taihe
Nanyang
Shangcai
Fuyang Fengtai
Jiashan
Hanshui River
Huaishui River
Shouxian
Jialingjiang River
Xinyang
Feixi
Jingshan
Pengxian
Huangpi
Changjiang River
Hanyang
Hangzhou
Minjiang River
Xishui
Shimen
Yueyang
Huarong
Taoyuan
Ningxiang
Changsha
Qingjiang
Xiangtan
East
China
Hengyang Xiangjiang River
Sea
Changning
Ganjiang River

Legend
● Major relics
○ Ordinary relics

Elephant-shaped Zun, the late Shang Dynasty, 22.8cm high, 26.5cm long, unearthed at Liling, Hunan province

and the state were located.

In order to defend against natural disasters, Shang moved its capital many times. It was not until the 14th century B.C. that King Pan Geng moved the capital to Yin (the north western of An Yang in Henan) and settled down. From then on Shang lasted 255 years with 12 kings from 8 generations. Since the time of its move to Yin, Shang experienced its golden era under King Wuding. King Wuding launched many military expeditions against the surrounding tribes and states. He conquered Tu Fang and Gui Fang in the north-west, and achieved victories in the wars of the Hanjiang River basin in the south. Therefore, Shang's territory was increasingly expanding. King Wu Ding was succeeded by several kings who were mostly pleasure-seeking and paid little attention to state-affairs. The last king, Zhou was known in history as a notorious tyrant. Building luxurious places and gardens, he led a life of debauchery. Taking advantages of the opportunity, King Wu of Zhou, a small country at the foot of Mount Qi in Shaanxi Province launched an eastern expediton against King Zhou in 1046 B.C..Soon his army took over Chaoge (present-day Qi County in Henan), the capital of Shang. King Zhou burned himself to death and the Shang Dynasty came to an end.

In the Shang society, the king enjoyed the highest power. Before King Pan Geng moved to Yin the younger brother could succeed to the throne from his elder brother, or son from his father. It was after King Pan Geng moved to Yin that the system of hereditary from father to son was established. Lower in rank than the king were the nobles. According to historical documents, there were about 20 noble families in the Shang Dynasty. However the common people were the most important creators of wealth. They not only undertook heavy productive labour, but also had to serve in the army. They were ruled over and worked as slaves at the bottom of society. They were engaged in various kinds of hard labour; they could be wilfully killed and even buried alive with the dead or killed and offered as sacrifices to ancestors. Many relics of slave-sacrifice

Si Yang Fang Zun (four-sheep quadripod), the late Shang Dynasty, 58.3cm high, diameter of diameter of rim 52.4cm long, unearthed at Ningxiang, Hunan province

have been found among Yin ruins. The methods of killing included beheading, dismembering and burning. The killed were mainly captives, servicemen and a few concubines.

The Shang people began to grow plants like He (grain), Shu (sticky millet), Mai (wheat), Ji (millet) and Dao (paddy). In animal husbandry, they reared horses, cows, sheep, dogs and pigs. The Shang handicrafts industry included production of bronze wares, pottery, bone wares, jade and lacquer. Bronze metallurgy was the most highly developed of all handicrafts. Bronze consisted of copper and tin. In the Shang Dynasty, bronze weapons were widely used and huge tripods and quadripods appeared. The famous large rectangular *Si Mu Wu quadripod* and *Four-sheep quadripod* can be regarded as the best examples of the bronze culture. Besides the common gray and red pottery, there were also more advanced white and hard pottery. The pottery made of Gaoling earth became the primitive porcelain. Provinces like Henan, Hubei, and others in the low reaches of the Changjiang River became the prime productive areas of primitive blue porcelain. The Shang people already had linen and silk textiles. Cowries shells that were unearthed indicate that the Shang businessmen had already traded with the eastern coastal areas.

Si Mu Wu quadripod, the late Shang Dynasty, 133cm high, diameter of rim 110cm long and 79cm wide, unearthed at Anyang, Henan province

第二篇

青铜时代

Relics of Sanxingdui, Guanghan, Sichuan province

Bronze double-faced human figures, Shang Dynasty (c. 16th-11th century BC), unearthed at Xingan, Jiangxi province

Bronze human head sculpture, 41.2cm high

Bronze human head sculpture, 46.7cm high

Bronze bird, Shang Dynasty (c. 16th-11th century BC), unearthed at Sanxingdui, Guanghan, Sichuan province

Profile of a bronze human head sculpture, Shang Dynasty (c. 16th-11th century BC), unearthed at Sanxingdui, Guanghan, Sichuan province

Bronze figure, Shang Dynasty (c. 16th-11th century BC), 262cm high, unearthed at Sanxingdui, Guanghan, Sichuan province

Animal mask sculpture, Shang Dynasty (c. 16th-11th century BC), 65cm high, unearthed at Sanxingdui, Guanghan, Sichuan province

Golden-faced bronze head sculpture, Shang Dynasty (c. 16th-11th century BC), 48.5cm high, unearthed at Sanxingdui, Guanghan, Sichuan province

第二篇

青铜时代

3. Oracle-bone inscriptions

Some examples of oracle-bone insacriptions			
oracle-bone inscriptions	regular scripts	oracle-bone inscriptions	regular scriapts
鼎	眾	目	臣
戈	刍	妻	妾
牧	牧	役	役
古	工	婢	婢
羊	羌	奚	奚

Chinese characters first developed during the Yangshao era six thousand years ago. According to the legend, characters were created by Cang Zhe, the official of Huang Di, who was inspired by the footprints of birds and beasts. The signals and patterns inscribed in the pottery of the New Stone Age could be regarded as the earliest forms of the Chinese pictograph.

Oracle-bone inscriptions were the popular Shang characters which were inscribed on the tortoise shells and animal bones. The Shang society was superstitious. They worshipped the universe and offered sacrifices to ancestors. They also believed that everything was controlled in the unseen world by gods. Therefore, they asked God's favour and practised divination for things ranging from national affairs to the private life of nobles, from wars, sacrifices, agriculture and weather to luck, hunting, illnesses and giving birth. Diviners were specially appointed. These diviners claimed themselves to be the heralds of the gods in the other world and exercised great influences on the political situation and society.

Since the Shang oracle bone inscriptions were mainly used for divination, they were also called divination characters on oracle-bones. The number of characters on one piece of oracle bone varied from a handful to over a hundred. The total amount of the characters amounted to 1.5 million on the 0.15 million shells unearthed, among which there were more than 5000 different characters. Less than half of these characters have been deciphered.

The oracle-bone inscription was fairly mature. The six ancient categories of Chinese characters, namely pictographic characters, self-explanatory characters, associative compounds, phonetic loan characters, pictophonetic characters (with one element indicating meaning and the other sound), mutually explanatory characters, were all present. Complete sentences also came into being with a basically fixed word order. In oracle-bone inscription there were thirteen numbers including 1 to 10, one hundred, one thousand, and ten-thousand. The decimal system was used and the 4-digit-number was found with the largest one as thirty thousand. There were also concepts like odd numbers, even numbers, and multiples.

"Hao" and "Haoqiu" inscribed in the pottery

Oracle turtle shell, the late Shang Dynasty (14th-11th centuries BC), 19.5cm long, unearthed at Nandi Xiaotun, Anyang, Henan province

Oracle bone, Shang Dynasty, 19.5cm long, unearthed at Xiaotun, Anyang, Henan province

Ten characters known as "Heavenly Stems" and twelve other known as "Earthly Branches" were used to name the days in a circle of 60 days. From these inscriptions we know that the Shang people used a lunar calendar which was combined with the solar year through the addition of intercalary months. Special terms were used for counting the time. Inscriptions on oracle-bone demonstrated advanced calligraphy techniques which became the origin of Chinese calligraphic arts. The culture was embedded in the characters, and the appearance of characters opened a new era for the development of human thoughts and civilization.

The evolvement of Chinese character

Oracle-bone inscriptions	Characters carved on bronze wares		Characters in Warring States Periods		Small seals	Regular scripts
						馬
						隹
						游

The evolvement of Chinese character

第二篇

青铜时代

4. The Zhou

(From 1046 B.C. to 771 B.C.)

Emperors of Western Zhou Dynasty

| 1 King Wu,Jifa | 2 King Cheng | 3 KIng Kang,Zhao | 4 King Zhao,Xia | 5 King Mu,Man | 6 King Gong,Xihu |

| 8 King Xiao,Pifang |

| 7 KIng Yi, Jian | 9 King Yi,Xie | 10 King Li,Hu | The Period of Joint Administration | 11 King Xuan,Jing | 12 King You,Gongnie |

Emperors of Eastern Zhou Dynasty

| 1 King Ping, Jiyijiu |
| 2 King Heng, Lin |
| 3 King Zhuang, Tuo |
| 4 King Li, Huqi |
| 5 King Hui, Lang |
| 6 King Xiang, Zheng |
| 7 King Qing, Renchen |

8 King Kuang, Ban	10 KING Jian, Yi	13 King Dao, Meng	17 King Ai, Quji	
9 King Ding, Yu	11 King Ling, Xiexin	14 King Jing, Gai	18 King Si, Shu	22 King Lie, Xi
	12 King Jing, Gui	15 King Yuan, Ren	19 King Kao, Wei	23 King Xian, Bian
		16 King Zhending, Jie	20 King Weilie, Renwu	24 King Shenliang, Ding
			21 King An, Jiao	25 King Nan, Yan

Bird-shaped You (a small-mouthed wine vessel),
King Cheng of Xi Zhou, 23.4cm high

The people of the Zhou era were also an ancient tribe with a long history. The tribe was famous for its agriculture. The earliest ancestor Qi, was an agricultural official of Yao. He was worshipped as the god of agriculture because of his outstanding abilities in this area. Together with Xia Yu, Shang Qi, Qi became Shun's official and assisted Shun to control water. His great-grand son Gongliu started a settlement in Bin. Ten generations later, Father Gu Gongtan led his people to Zhouyuan (present-day north-western part of Shaanxi). Father Gu Gongtan led his people to develop farm production; build houses, temples, palaces, city walls and had the city administrated under officials. All of these laid the foundation for the rise of the Zhou. Father Gu Gongtan was later honored as the Great King. He was succeeded by his young son Ji Li, during whose reign the Zhou became a strong country in the west. Ji Chang, Ji Li's son, later became the celebrated King Wen of the Zhou. Ji Chang honoured talented people and enlisted their services, and made great efforts to govern his country, thus winning the support of many tribes and becoming the head of western tribes and states.

Four years after King Wen's death, King Wu attacked King Zhou of the Shang and vanquished Chaoge and overthrew the Shang Danysty. King Wu established the Zhou Dynasty with the capital built in Hao Jing (the south west of Xi'an in Shaanxi province). In history, this dynasty was called Western Zhou.

King Wu divided his country into three parts called as Bei, Yong and Wei and assigned three governors to administrate them. When King Wu died, his brother, Duke of Zhou Ji Dan acted as regent for seven years until King Cheng came of age. Wu Geng, the son of King Zhou of the former Shang Dynasty rebelled against the Zhou in collaboration with the other two brothers of King Wu, Guan Shu and Cai Shu. The Duke of Zhou led his forces in an eastern expedition and saved the Zhou Dynasty.

In order to control the newly conquered broad areas, Kings of the Zhou began to set up many fiefdoms under their control. When the Duke of Zhou was acted as regent in charge of the country, he established the rule that the King's eldest son born of his wife should be made the heir to the throne. Thus the throne was transferred through generations of oldest sons. This was the major lineage. The other sons born of, his wife and of his concubines became heads of the minor lineages. The vassal lords with the royal surname belonged to minor lineages in relation to the king, but in their own states, they established the same kind of lineage system as a major lineage and many minor ones. The vassals awarded their land and people to his family and favorites. These people were called Dafu (the title of a senior official), who were in charge of sacrifice, administration or military affairs. Within a Dafu's own fief, he also maintained a system under which the first son of his wife was his legitimate heir representing the major lineage. Therefore, the clan relationship system, with the king as the center was greatly strengthened. The Duke of Zhou also built the City of Luo Yi, (now Luoyang city in Henan) and called it "Cheng Zhou". Many people who remained loyal to the Shang were forced to move out and troops were stationed to watch them. The Duke of Zhou built another city about 15 kilometers west of Chengzhou.

The early Western Zhou Dynasty was marked by political stability and economic prosperity and was at its peak during the reign of King Cheng and his son King Kang. This period is known in history as 'Golden Years of Cheng-Kang'. King Kang's son, King Zhao made remarkable achievements in the wars against Country Chu. King Mu, powerful and ambitious was said to have toured the regions from Hao Jing to Mount Yin in the north and arrived at Mount Kunlun in the west. He was met with a warm reception in Yao Chi from the Country of West Queen and was entertained with a great banquet. He left behind a much-told tale about the communications between the central plains and western regions. The eleventh king of Zhou, King Li was cruel and ferocious. He mercilessly exploited the capital residents and further more, he suppressed all public discussion with harsh punishment and draconian laws. As a result, people dared

Yue Ren Shou Men Ding, the middle Western Zhou Dynasty, 17.7cm high, diameter of rim 9.2cm x 11.9cm

Jade deer, Western Zhou Dynasty (11th century-771 BC), 8.8cm high, unearthed at Baoji, Shaanxi province

Bronze he-pot, the late Western Zhou, 34.6cm high

Houji

King Wen, Jichang

King Wu, Jifa

not to talk meeting each other in streets when met on the road; they only dared to communicate with their eyes. For the capital residents it became unbearable and they raised an army in revolt. They attacked the royal palace and banished the king in 841 B.C. The Duke of Zhou and the Duke of Zhao

第二篇

青銅時代

The sketch-map of patriarchal clan system on Western Zhou

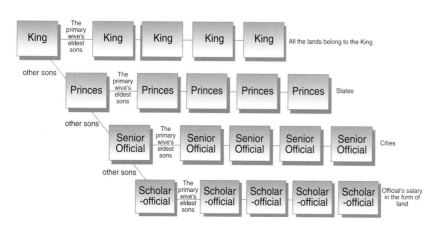

Hou Ma Meng Shu, 16.6-17.9cm long

Gold belt ornament, Western Zhou (11th-771 BC), the outer diameter of the rings 3.7-4.35cm, the animal mask 2cm high, cemetery of Guo Dukedom, Sanmenxia, Henan province

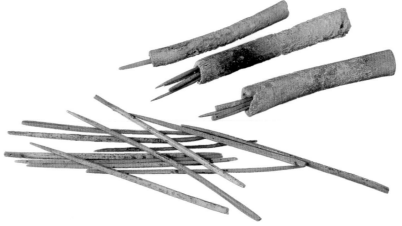

Bone needles and Holder, needles 8.4-3cm long, holder 9.4-8.5cm long, unearthed at Tianshui, Gansu province

Agate jewellery, Western Zhou, unearthed at Liulihe, Fangshan, Beijing

Relics of the capital city wall of Yan Dukedom in Western Zhou, Liulihe, Fangshan, Beijing

The Duke of Zhou, Jidan

took charge of the government together. This period was called the 'Gonghe' (republic administration) in history and 841 B.C. became the first year of 'Gonghe'. The last king of Western Zhou, King You, was a self-willed, self-indulgent and cruel ruler. He dismissed Queen Shen and the crown Prince Yi Jia and made his favorite concubine Bao Si queen. queen Shen attacked the king in collaboration with the Quanrong tribe. As the vassals no longer trusted King You, they refused to send him reinforcements. King You was killed at the foot of Mount Li (present-day Lintong in Shaanxi). Western Zhou came to its end in 770B.C. The dynasty had lasted for 257 years under 12 kings of 11 generations.

The society and economy of Western Zhou achieved further developments. Agriculture remained the most important industry. At the same time, handicraft industries like textiles, brewing, metallurgy and baking were much advanced. Bronze metallurgy is an outstanding example. After the middle period of Western Zhou, a method was invented for casting several wares with the same mold, thus increasing the production rate by several times. Many delicately-made bells tripods and quadripods, tripods and quadripods are still well preserved. There were no patterns on Xia's bronze wares and only very simple patterns on early Shang's bronze wares. Those patterns were mainly mono-layer and with a few double ones, so they looked clumsy. The patterns on the bronze wares of the late-Shang were more complicated, beautiful and vivid, so were the bronze wares of the Early Western Zhou. Animal patterns were the most frequently used. There are a variety of patterns including phoenix, birds and elephants. The style of these patterns was lucid, vivid and simple. Most of the bronze wares in this dynasty also had inscriptions. The number of the words varies from less than ten to several hundred. These inscriptions recorded wars, award-granting sacrifice, lawsuits and trade of slaves. They are very valuable historical documents.

King Cheng, Jisong

The restored picture of a palace in Western Zhou

King Kang, Jizhao

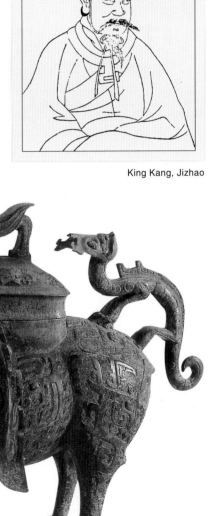

Deng Zhong Xi Zun, the middle Western Zhou, 38.8cm high

第二篇

青铜时代

5. The Bright Light of Ritual and Music

Jade kneeling man, Shang (1600-1046 BC), unearthed at Fuhao Tomb, Yinxu, Anyang, Henan province

According to the legend, the Duke of Zhou worked out a set of rites and composed music. Western Zhou had already established a patriarchal clan system, a system of enfeoffment, a social estate system, hereditary system as well as a system of protocol and penalty. With the patriarchal clan system as its foundation, Zhou's protocol combines the God's will, monarchical power, clan relations and political constructions together to establish the consistent protocol institutions and imperial ceremonial music system. The sacrificial vessels and their combinations were different for different nobles. Common people were forbidden to apply the noble's protocol. School education in Western Zhou had ritual and ceremonial music as its foundation. Four other kinds of the so called "six-art-form education" were also taught, namely, shooting, horse-riding, calligraphy and mathematics. The education focused on the raising of moral standards. A system of moral principles with the protocol as its foundation was set up to regulate people's daily life.

Music was also used as a tool for strengthening the rein. The kings of the Xia, the Shang and the Zhou dynasties communicated with the gods through wizards by means of music and dance. *Wu Yu*, the ancient dance prayer for rain became an important ceremony. Grand Xia of the Xia Dynasty was composed to praise Yu's feats in water control. *Grand Huo* of the Shang Dynasty was composed to flaunt their martial achievements. Governors also regarded music as their great enjoyment. King Jie of Xia Dynasty had more than 30,000 musicians who played music loudly at the city gate every morning. King Zhou of the Shang made Musician Shijuan compose new melodies. He enjoyed the voluptuous music, drank and amused himself throughout the whole night until dawn.

Complete royal music came into being in the Zhou Dynasty. Royal music synthesized the music of earlier generations and set up a strict status system. Royal music included *Yun Men Da* Juan of King Huang's time, *Grand Xian* of Yao's time, *Grand Qing* of Shun's time and *Grand Xia, Grand Huo* as well as *Grand Wu* which was used to praise King Wu's victories over King Zhou. The royal music also absorbed folk music and dances and those of the Yi tribes. The musical instruments used in the royal music included eight types: gold, stone, pottery, leather, silk, wood, gourd and bamboo. Nearly 70 kinds of musical instruments belonged to these eight types including the bell, the large bell, the chime stone, the seven-stringed plucked instrument, the twenty-five-stringed plucked instrument, the vertical bamboo flute and the reed pipe wind instrument. There were already twelve swings and seven tones in the musical scale of that time, which reflects the high technical level. In order to publicize royal music, special music organizations were set up by the state and administrated by music officials. The number of musicians amounted to more than 14,000. According to *Li Ji* (the book of ceremonial rites and regulations), scholar-bureaucrats should receive an education in music and dance from an early age. Western Zhou was the golden age for royal music.

Liangqi Bell, the late Western Zhou, 53.5cm high, the inner distance 31.8cm, unearthed at Fufeng, Shaanxi province

Gong with animal mask motif, the early Western Zhou, 22.9cm high

The inscription on bronze gui-vessel marked Fu

Bronze gui-vessel marked Fu, King Li of Western Zhou, 39cm high, diameter of rim 43cm, unearthed at Fufeng, Shaanxi province

The decorative patterns on the bronze of Shang Dynasty

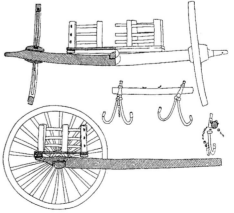

Bronze double-faced drum with animal mask motif

The structural drawing of a cart of Shang Dynasty

第二篇　青铜时代

Chapter 3

Chasing the Deer on the Central Plains, Seeking Control of the Empire

--Spring and Autumn, and Warring States Periods (from 770 B.C to 221 B.C.)

Zhou Dynasty came to an end, large numbers of powers came into being. This was an era of harsh contention. All states spared no efforts to make them prosperous, numerous thinkers constantly provided their own strategies as to how to govern the states. Only by conforming to the historical trend and taking the nerve to practise new laws, would success be likely to come off in the contention.

Dujiangyan--Qingcheng Mountain Dujiangyan, Sichuan province

1. The Rise and Decline of Five Big States

The Situation of Princes Striving for Supremacy

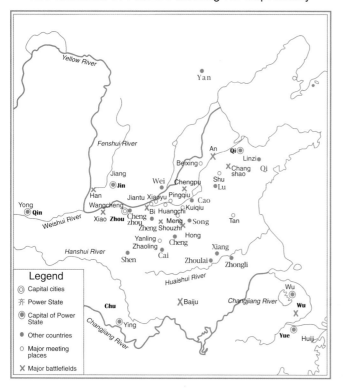

Legend
- ◎ Capital cities
- 齐 Power State
- ◉ Capital of Power State
- ● Other countries
- ○ Major meeting places
- X Major battlefields

In 770B.C, King Ping of the Zhou moved the center of political power eastward to Luoyi (present-day Luoyang), and Eastern Zhou Dynasty came into being. Eastern Zhou Dynasty could be divided into Spring and Autumn Period (770 B.C-476 B.C) and Warring States Period (475 B.C.-221 B.C.). The term "Spring and Autumn Period" was derived from a historical book of Lu State "*The Spring and Autumn Annuals*", which kept a record of this period.

Since moving the capital eastward, the influence of the Zhou Dynasty was severely impaired and the political status declined so sharply that it was reduced from a dominator governing all the states to a vassal clinging to big states. Therefore, all the vassals didn't take orders from King of the Zhou any more. Instead, they went on punitive expeditions at will, contending for the control of the empire. In this way, the formalities and rites collapsed, the original political order was thrown into confusion.

The first overlord was Duke Huan of state Qi. With the help of an intelligent statesman Guan Zhong, he facilitated the development of agriculture, industry and commerce in the state of Qi through mintage, price-controlling, administration of the production of salt and iron, removal of customs and market taxes. As a result, the strength of his state was greatly enhanced. Meanwhile, he advocated the union between the government and the military forces so that he built up strong armed forces. He called on allied states to resist the Di and Rong people with the slogan "Resist barbarians and keep loyal to King of the Zhou". In 651 B.C., Duke Huan held a conference with the vassals at Kuiqiu (today's Lankao, Henan Province), where he was

Bronze rectangular jar, Spring and Autumn Period (770-476 BC)

Duke Huan of Qi and Guanzhong, stone relief in the Wuliang memorial hall in Jiaxiang, Shandong province

Royal Tripods, Altar Table and Bells, Spring and Autumn Period
(6th century BC), unearthed at Xichuan county, Henan province

nominated as the leader of all the states on the Central Plains.

Duke Wen of Jin state took over Duke Huan's hegemony after his death. As soon as Duke Wen ascended the throne, he rectified the internal affairs and enhanced the armed forces. In 632 B.C., Duke Wen united state Qin and Qi to rescue Song with the determination to seek hegemony over the Central Plains against state Chu. They defeated Chu at Chengpu (today's Pu County, Henan Province). The victorious encounter enabled King Wen to summon the vassals to Jiantu (today's Yingze County) and held a conference at which he was recognized as an overlord on the Central Plains. When King Wen died, the friendship between Jin and Qin came to an end, and wars went on year after year leading to the decline of the supremacy of Jin. Chu, a state in the upper reaches of the Changjiang River gained great strength with the

Cylindrical vessel supported by three rhinoceros, Warring States Period (late 4th c. BC), bronze, H 58.5cm, unearthed at Pingshan county, Hebei province

Agate ear ornaments, Warring States Period (475-221 BC), bronze ring: d.2.1cm, agate bead: d. 1.2cm, unearthed at Zichang County, Shaanxi province

第二篇

逐鹿中原

The Situation of the Spring and Autumn Period and the Distribution of Five Powers

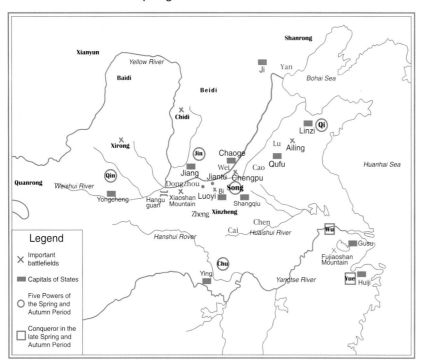

Qibei bronze sword of the King of State Yue, Warring States Period (475-221 BC), 64cm long, unearthed at Anqing, Anhui province

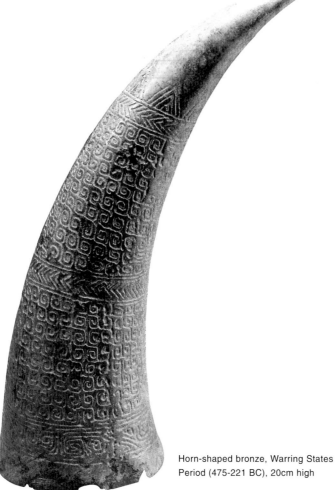

Horn-shaped bronze, Warring States Period (475-221 BC), 20cm high

Bronze mao-spear with cicada motif, Warring States Period (475-221 BC), unearthed at Pengzhou, Sichuan province

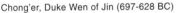

Chong'er, Duke Wen of Jin (697-628 BC)

King Zhuang of Chu, Mi Lu

management of King Wu and King Wen. In the middle of Spring and Autumn, the territory of Chu expanded to the drainage area of the Huaihe River. At the time of King Zhuang of Chu State, Jin was once defeated and hegemony came to King Zhuang. Then state Wu, in the lower reaches of the Changjiang River grew stronger that it frequently defeated Chu. After beating State Yue, State Wu went to north and knocked Qi down, contending for power with Jin. The wars between them shook the Central Plains. However, it didn't take long for the state Yue to gather strength and annihilate Wu at one swoop. Later, Yue met Qi and Jin in the north and was made an overlord there.

The contention for hegemony among the vassals enabled the overlord to give orders to the vassals in name of the sovereign and enjoy the tribute of smaller states. The overlord was also entitled to mediate the dissension among the states. Though the wars contending for hegemony brought tremendous disasters to the people, it facilitated the cultural communication between the minor nationalities like Di and Rong to some degree. In the wars, small states were constantly annexed, gradually forming the scene of big states striving for power.

Bronze mythological animal, the late Spring and Autumn Period (second half of 6th c.-476 BC), 48cm high

第三篇

逐鹿中原

2. Seven States Striving for Power

Engraved pot with dragon-shaped decoration, 63cm high, diameter of rim 15cm

Through long-standing wars, dozens of states in the Spring and Autumn Period were annexed to seven states-Qin, Chu, Yan, Qi, Han, Zhao and Wei. This period was called the Warring States Period in history.

During the earlier stages of the Warring States Period, state Wei was the most powerful among the vassals. Marquis Wen of Wei put Li Kui, a talented man in charge of reforms together with Wu Qi, Ximenbao and other talents in charge of the armed forces and localities. In this way, Wei took the position of supremacy. When Prince Hui of Wei ascended the throne, the state had come to the height of power and splendour. However, he was so arrogant that he belittled the enemies and made foes everywhere.

In the middle of the Warring States Period, other states like Qi and Qin grew up, posing threats to Wei. King Wei of Qi appointed Zou Ji as the prime minister, who undertook lots of reforms on the politics, Qi thus soon became powerful. As King Wei of Qi had long been dissatisfied with Wei's hegemony, he determined to challenge the power of Wei. In 354 B.C., King Hui of Wei launched an attack on Zhao. The following year, King Wei of Qi appointed Tian Ji as general, Sun Bin as military counselor and sent the troops to fight against Wei in order to rescue Zhao. Finally their troops defeated Wei at Guiling (to the northeast of today's Heze County, Shandong Province). In 341 B. C., King Wei of Qi chose Tian Ji and Tian Ying as general, Sun Bin as military counselor to lead the troops in fighting against Wei to rescue Han. Again, they gave Wei a severe blow at Maling (to the southwest of modern Fan County, Henan Province). From then on, Wei gradually declined, making space for Qi's ruling over the east.

At the beginning of the Warring States, Qin was too weak to attract other states' attention. Therefore, Duke Xiao of Qin put Shang Yang in charge of many reforms with emphasis on farming and military arts. Due to his effective reforms, honesty prevailed everywhere and Qin became more and more powerful years on. When Prince Huiwen ascended the throne, he appointed Zhang Yi from Wei as the prime minister and adopted the strategy of "setting up allies with some states such as Han and Wei to separate other states". In this way, he aroused much conflict and abruption among the six states and he lost no chance to defeat the enemy and develop its power. Gradually, Qin seized hold of lots of land from Wei, Han and Chu, turning itself into a great power controlling the situation of Central Plains.

The Capital Cities in the Spring and Autumn Period and the Warring States Period

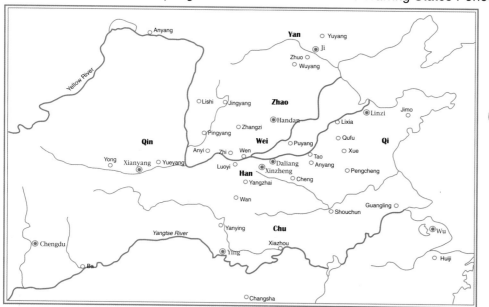

Round dragon-shaped topaz pendant in fretwork, d.6.4cm, 0.5cm thick

Bronze dragon and phoenix stand with gold and silver inlay

Bronze lamp with a silver-headed bronze human figure, Warring States Period (475-221 BC), 66.4cm high, unearthed at Pingshan, Hebei province

第三篇

逐鹿中原

Gold and silver-inlaid bronze stand in the shape of tiger swallow deer, Warring States Period (475-221 BC), 51cm long, unearthed at Pingshan, Hebei province

Ware in the shape of the Chinese character "shan", 119cm high, 74cm wide

Chu used to be powerful at Spring and Autumn Period. However, during the Warring States, its power gradually declined due to the nobles' despotism and the faction among the nobles. But Chu still remained a big obstacle for Qin to swallow up the six states. In 318 B.C., under the leadership of King Hui of Chu, Wei, Zhao, Han, Yan, Chu as well as other states formed an alliance to attack Qin. However, they were defeated in the end. Qin sent Zhang Yi to Chu to persuade Chu into breaking off the alliance with Qi and be friends with Qin instead. As a result, Qin would give up land of six hundred li (a Chinese unit of length) to Chu. However, Qin later broke the agreement so that Chu launched an attack on Qin in 312 B.C. Unfortunately, Chu was defeated at Danyang (today's Xixia, Henan Province) and captured Hanzhong area. Later, Chu launched a counterattack, and was defeated again at Lantian (today's Shaanxi Province). In 278 B.C., General Bai Qi of Qin seized Chu's capital Yin so that Chu had to move its center of political power.

Yan was the weakest among the seven states. When Prince Zhao of Yan ascended the throne, he recruited talents such as strategist Yue Yi and diplomat Su Qin. They made great efforts to achieve prosperity and resurgence. In 284 B.C., Yan united Qin, Chu, Zhao and Han to attack Qi. They captured Qi's capital Linzi as well as other 70 cities. From then on, Qi never recovered from the setback.

Han lay in the center of the Central Plains with Wei on the east, Chu on the south, Qin on the west and Zhao on the north. Being threatened by these big states, Han never grew strong. In 355 B.C., Marquis Hanazhao appointed Shen Buhai as the chief minister to carry out reforms. However, as soon as Shen Buhai died, Han ceased to move forward. Besides, the threat from Qin was especially severe. At the early stages of the Warring States Period, Zhao often united Han and Wei to attack other states and expanded its territory towards the north where the minor nationalities inhabited. Zhao also built the Great Wall to resist the invasion of the northern enemies. King Wuling of Zhao carried out military reforms by organizing a powerful cavalry and clothing the cavalry men in the style of nomadic peoples, making it easier for them to ride and to shoot their arrows. In this way, Zhao grew stronger. The victories battle over Qin under the leadership of Zhao She-a great general, in Queyu (today's Heshun, Shanxi Province) demonstrated Zhao's strength. In 262 B.C., Qin fought with Zhao for the land of Shangdang at Changping (to the northwest of today's Gaoping County, Shanxi Province). This war lasted three years and finally General Bai Qi lured the Zhao forces into

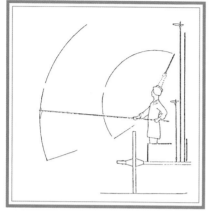

Sketch of war chariot in the Warring States Period

Return the jade intact to the State of Zhao, stone relief

a trap, thus defeated the Zhao forces and buried alive 400,000 men of Zhao altogether, including General Zhao Kuo. After this war, the main forces of Zhao were annihilated so that no single state among the six was left to be strong enough to fight against Qin.

Bronze Zun in the shape of mythological animal, Warring States Period (475-224 BC), 53.7cm high, unearthed at He county, Huangxi province

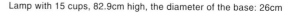

Lamp with 15 cups, 82.9cm high, the diameter of the base: 26cm

Lacquer Dou, with 24.3cm high

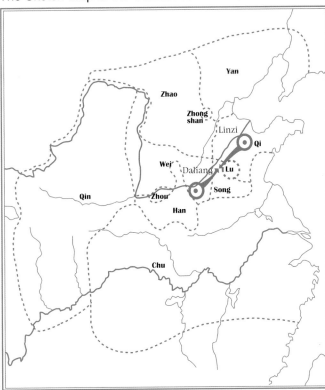

Yan

Zhao

Zhong
shan

Linzi

Qi

Wei

Daliang　Lu

Qin

Zhou　Song

Han

Chu

Gold-laid mythological animal with two
wings, Warring States Period (475-221 BC),
40cm long, unearthed Pingshan, Hubei
province

Crystal cup, Warring States Period (475-221 BC),
15.4cm high, unearthed at Shitang village, Hangzhou,
Zhejiang province

第三篇

逐鹿中原

3. Teacher of Thousands of Generations-Confucius

Confucius, Kongqiu (551-479 BC)

He advocated the idea that "the benevolent should hold love for others", and proposed "virtuous rule". Besides, he emphasized that "benevolence" and "formalities and rites" should supplement each other and "rites formalities" should be based on "benevolence". The nature of "formalities" was to maintain social orders, getting every subject under control according to the principle that officials should be loyal to the emperor and sons should be filial to their fathers. Confucius also attached great importance to music, which he thought would edify people. In this way he proposed "formalities" for the external attainment and "music" for the "internal accomplishment".

Confucius thought highly of man and valued the power of knowledge. He upheld "erudition" and thought those who are well-read with will, modest with meditation will be endowed with "benevolence". Though Confucius held that "as life and death are preordained by fate, so wealth and rank are decreed by heaven", he also attached importance to efforts made by man, which he thought would lead to the carrying forward of morality and justice. Confucius stressed "golden mean", pursuing a stable and harmonious state. But he was not conservative. He said, as the Yin stuck to Xia's formalities, the losses it suffered was conceivable and the Zhou stuck to Yin's formalities so that it also suffered understandable losses. And he adopted a positive attitude towards the social development and progress. Confucius was not superstitious. He did not believe in the existence of ghosts and spirits and protesting the idea of "ghost" or "spirit", saying that "Being unable to serve the people, how can you serve the ghosts?"

Confucius maintained that in education there should be no distinction of social status, that is, education should be open to everyone, no matter what social status they belonged to. So he started private schools which broke the monopoly of officials and nobles on education. It is said that Confucius had 3000 students, including both nobles

Confucius meeting Lao Zi, Han, brick carving, unearthed at Suide county, Shaanxi province

and peasants. As Confucius advocated the application of knowledge, what he taught was far-ranging, including the so-called six "arts": rite, music, archery, riding, writing and arithmetic. As to learning methodology, Confucius put forward the ideas "Gain new insights through reviewing old materials" and "Never pretend to be knowledgeable, be honest with what you know". He held that people should not feel ashamed to seek advice from one's subordinates.

The classical works combined by Confucius include *Book of Odes, Book of History, Book of Rites, Book of Changes, Book of Music* and *The Spring and Autumn Annals*, which are also called "Six Classics", among which *Book of Music* has been lost. Confucius' own statements were compiled into a book entitled *the Analects* by his disciples. Confucius Thought set up the basis for Confucianism, which has become the mainstream of Chinese culture since Han Dynasty with its influence felt throughout the east as well as the whole world.

Confucius (551 B.C.-479 B.C.), whose personal name was Qiu and courtesy name Zhongni, was born in Zouyi, Lu (to the southeast of today's Qufu, Shandong Province). His ancestors used to be slave-owners of Song. But his father died while he was a child and his noble family gradually declined. He was, for a time, master of ceremonies, and later was appointed as a low-ranking official managing warehouses, tending domestic animals and so on. He also used to take charge of judicature of Lu. However, as he dissented with those in-power-nobles in politics, he resigned and traveled from state to state with his disciples to advocate his political beliefs, but failed to get accepted. Therefore, when he returned to Lu, he took in lots of disciples, undertaking the work of education and devoted his life to the collation and editing of literary work as well.

Confucius was a great thinker and educationist. He yearned for the formalities of Zhou Dynasty and was worried about the decadency of formalities and social vogue of Zhou. So he advocated the establishment of proper rites for a harmonious and ideal society.

"Benevolence" was the central point of Confucianism.

Main hall of a Confucian temple, Qufu, Shangdong province

4. Contention of a Hundred Schools of Thought

The Warring States Period was a time full of great social changes, at which time the seven states contended for hegemony and all the states made great efforts to strengthen themselves. These social changes enabled the culture to be spread among the people. Those ambitious took the salvation of the world as their responsibilities and offered their political propositions one after another. Some of them went canvassing among different states to offer advice to the rulers; some opened private schools and wrote books; some were unconventional and unrestrained and showed their concern for the worldly life in the form of criticism; some assisted the rulers to govern the states. In this way, the scene of " contention of a hundred schools of thought " emerged. Besides Confucianism, there were Mohism, Taoism, Legalism, Yin-yang School, the Schools of Logicians, strategists, agronomists as well as eclectics. The Spring and Autumn-Warring States Period was a time of great liberation of mind and people of talents emerged in succession.

Mohism and Confucianism are both famous schools. The founder Mo Di (478 B. C.?-392 B.C.?), a native of either Lu or Song, used to be a senior official of Song. His ideas were written into the book Mo Zi. Mo Zi advocated "universal love" and "non-aggressiveness"; he proposed the idea of "love each other and you will benefit each other" as an effective way to save the world; he also held that the sovereign should appoint talents disregard of their origins and asked people to live a simple life with frugalities on funerals and other occasions.

The founders of Taoism School are Lao Zi and Zhuang Zi. Lao Zi, whose surname was Li and personal name Boyang, was also known as Lao Dan. It's said he was born in Lixiangqurenli, Ku County, Chu State (today's Guide, Henan Province) during the Spring and Autumn, Warring States Period. He used to be in charge of state libraries, which made him quite knowledgeable. It was said Confucius once asked him about "rites", and was told lots of profound principles. He devoted all his life to the cultivation of virtuous life and wrote the book Lao Zi (also called Daodejing) during his latter years. In this book, Lao Zi founded his philological system centering around the Way-an

Lao Zi, Li'er

Zhuang Zi, Zhuangzhou

Meng Zi, Mengke

Mo Zi, Modi (468-376 BC)

absolute, overriding spirit transcending time and space and encompassing the whole universe. He advocated "inaction"- letting things take their own course and suggested defeating the strong with weakness, conquering the firm with gentleness.

Zhuang Zi (369 B.C.?-286 B.C), whose personal name was Zhou, hailed from Meng, in the state of Song (to the northeast of today's Shangqiu, Henan Province). He avoided facing reality with detached attitude and regarded everything as relative so that he denied the validity of the concepts of right and wrong. Thus, he took the optimistic attitude of "living a peaceful life at any time". The book Zhuang Zi was one of the classics of Taoism, the thoughts expressed through which was close to Lao Zi's. Lots of philosophical ideas were put forward in the form of allegories so that many beautiful and moving stories were created, making it an excellent literary work.

Mencius (390 B.C.?-305 B.C.), whose personal name was

Ke, was a native of Zou (modern Zou County, Shandong Province). It's said that he used to learn from Confucius' grandson Zisi. He admired Confucius, claiming himself as a disciple of the sage. His book Mencius was one of the classics of Confucianism. Mencius thought that man was born with goodness and attached importance to the influence of environment. He advocated the molding of a person's temperament and maintained that so long as we were willing , every one could be a sage like the old emperors Yao and Shun. He proposed that "the people are the most important, the god of the land and the god of grain come after, the sovereign comes last", considering the sovereigns should care about the people. He was against tyranny and advocated benevolent government, which he thought was the only way to rule the world.

Xun Zi, also known as Xun Kuang or Xun Qing, hailed from the state of Zhao in the late Warring States Period. He inherited and developed Confucianism. He both criticized and learned from the other schools. He held, in opposition with Mencius, that Man was born evil. Therefore, he emphasized rites and law. Also, he carried forward Confucianism's view that the rulers must be virtuous and benevolent and maintained that to govern a country, it was important to love the people. He compared the sovereign to ships, the common people to water, thinking that "water can both hold the ships and overturn the ships as well." The book *Xun Zi* contains his works.

Legalism School, together with Confucianism and Mencius School made up three famous schools, whose representative was Han Fei, who lived in Han in the late years of the Warring States Period. Han Fei used to be the student of Xun Kuang. He wrote the book *Han Feizi*, in which he synthesized and balanced various schools of thoughts, enabling him a great success in Legalism. Shang Yang's law, Shen Buhai's strategies, Shendao's power were combined together; Lao Zi's inaction, Xun Kuang's emphasis on rites and law, Mo Zi's pursuing for universality, as well as the idea of "referring to substance in other names" in the Confucianism were all absorbed by him selectively. He didn't think that virtue, benevolence and justice alone could govern the country; instead, law, strategies and power must be employed. This idea greatly influenced the coming generations.

The famous representatives of the school of strategists were Sun Wu in Qi, in the late Spring and Autumn Period and Sun Bin of Qi, in the middle of the Warring States Period. The thirteen articles on the art of warfare written by Sun Zi was one of the classics among the books concerning the strategies of war. The book *Sunzi's Art of Warfare* represented the highest level of the art of warfare in the Warring States Period. The representative of the

Sun Zi, Sunwu

Xun Zi, Xunkuang

Dragon-shaped pendant, Warring States Period (475-221 BC), 19.5cm long, 0.5cm thick, unearthed from Qin Tomb at Weichengwan in Xianyang, Shaanxi province

school of Logician was Sun Long of the state Zhao in the Warring States Period, whose book *Gongsunlongzi* reflected his art of eloquence. The representative of eclectics was Lu Buwei, whose book *Spring and Autumn of Lu* adopted the strong points of Confucianism, Mohism, Legalism, strategists and other schools, and summarized historical experience, making great contributions to historical theories and materials.

Hanfei Zi

Lao Zi, silk book, unearthed from Han Tomb at Mawangdui, Changsha

5. Historiography and Literature

Qu Yuan (340-278 BC)

The Tomb of Qu Yuan, Miluo, Hunan province

Bronze dragon-shaped pendant, Spring and Autumn Period (770-476 BC), 19.5cm long

It's said *the Spring and Autumn Annals* which recorded the history of Lu was written by Confucius. The historical official Zuo Qiuming of Lu wrote commentaries on *the Spring and Autumn Annals*, which offered concrete explanations with historical facts to the book. Zuo Qiuming's work was entitled *the Spring and Autumn Annals of Zuo*, or *Zuozhuan* for short. This book recorded the history of 268 years from 722 B.C. to 454 B.C. Zuozhuan was adept at the description of wars as well as the presentation of characters through language in a vivid and succinct way so that many of its chapters were well-read through generations.

The other works of historiography of this period also includes *Speeches of Different States*, which recorded the characters, stories, speech of different states like Zhou, Lu, Qi, Jin, Zheng, Chu, Wu and Yue. This book was also named *Unofficial Biography of the Spring and Autumn Period*. *Strategies of the Warring States*, combined in the late years of the Warring States, Qin and Han Dynasty, is a historical book, recording the speeches and stories of orators. The style of writing sometimes is flowery; sometimes imposing, sometimes exquisite, all of which is of great literary value. Besides, there are other works such as the *Annals Written on the Bamboo, Shiben* and so on.

The Book of Songs is the first comprehensive anthology of poems in China, which is said to be edited by Confucius. This book contains 305 poems, including folk songs, ceremonial songs and sacrificial songs. Its rich content and polished language has nurtured generations of poets, scholars and writers. During the Warring States Period, the first great poet of China, Qu Yuan (340 B.C-278 B.C) came forth. He was famous for the Elegies of Chu. Qu Yuan, whose personal name was Ping, was a native of today's Quping, Zigui County, Hubei Province. Though being faithful to Chu as a knowledgeable and ambitious scholar, he was pushed aside by crafty sycophants and finally gave up his life in the Miluo River on the way of his banishment.

Qu Yuan's magnum opus was a long lyric poem *The Lament (Li Sao)*, which was imbued with romanticism and full of indignation for the suffering of the state. In the poem *Questioning the Heaven*, with great momentum and rich imagination, he put forward 172 questions, inquiring the origin of the universe, the journey of the sun, the naissance of human being and the merits of history, demonstrating his profound mind in the pursuit of truth. *Lamenting Yin* and *Huaisha* were two articles written to express his patriotism. *Nine Songs* were created according to the folk songs sung at the time of offering sacrifice to Heaven, reflecting the Chu people's love for their country, pursuit of happiness and admiration for the heroes who died for their country. Qu Yuan's works were imbued with passion as well as beautiful language, exerting great influences on the later generations.

The senior officer meets an old fishman

The picture of Boya playing the zither, Yuan, by Wang Zhenpeng

逐鹿中原

6. Science and Technology

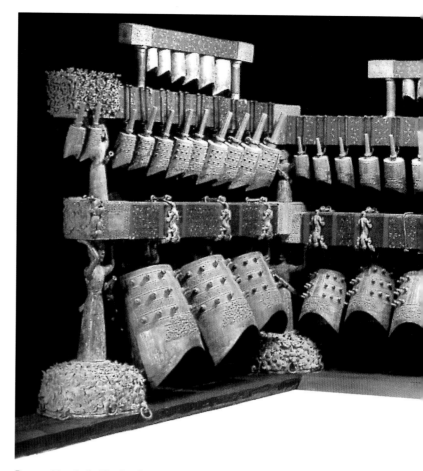

During the Spring and Autumn Period, great progress has been made in astronomy. It's said in *the Spring and Autumn Annals* that there were 37 records of solar eclipse in a period of 242 years, among which 30 records were proved reliable. The record of comet in *the Spring and Autumn Annals* is the earliest in the world, more than 670 years earlier than that in Europe; the record of the fall of aerolites is more than 2000 years earlier. During the late Spring and Autumn Period, Quarter Calendar, the most accurate calendar of that time, was invented, prescribing that a year was made up of 365 days and 6 hours. During the Warring States Period, Xia Calendar was widely adopted among all the states, which included 24 solar terms.

The Qi native Gan De wrote eight volumes of *Chronometer and Horoscopy* which consisted of eight volumes, and the Wei native Shi Shen wrote eight volumes of *Chronometer*, which were combined to make the book *Gan Shi Horoscopy*. It kept a record of the appearance and disappearance of five big planets, the law of their movement,

Bronze chime bells, Warring States Period (475-221 BC), the height of frame 265-273cm, unearthed from Zenghouyi Tomb, Suizhou, Hubei province

and measured the orientation of 121 stars. Besides, it recorded the names of 800 stars, forming the first table of stars, about 200 years earlier than the first European table of stars.

A lacquer-box cover was once unearthed in the Zenghouyi Tomb in Suixian County, Hubei Province, in the middle of which was a big Chinese Character "*Dou*" with 28 names of stars like "Green Dragon", "White Tiger" around, which demonstrated a basic frame of Chinese ancient astronomy system.

Pharmacology also got rid of the fetters of primal witchcraft and became an independent discipline. Bian Que was a famous doctor during the Warring States Period, who initiated the methods of "feeling the pulse", acupuncture and massage to treat the patients. Besides, the book *The Yellow Emperor's Canon of Internal Medicine*, written in the middle of the Warring States Period sets up the theoretical basis for Chinese traditional medicine and remains a classic of it till now.

The inventions of iron and steel are important signs of scientific and technological development. In the middle of the Spring and Autumn Period, Qi had made full use of iron utensils. During the late Spring and Autumn Period, Jin had begun to use iron cooking vessels, ploughs and the three states Chu, Wu, Yue became the center of iron production. Iron utensils of various types were widely employed during the Warring States Period. Besides farming devices, axes, saws, wimbles, hammers and knives as well as weapons like armours, staves, swords, halberds, spears and daggers, and other daily utensils were in existence. The block steel sword unearthed in Yanxiadou, Yi County, Hebei Province, is 100.4 cm long and used to be the most advanced weapon in the world at that time.

During the Spring and Autumn, the Warring States Period, more exquisite bronze vessels were made and new technologies like carving and filagree were invented. Among the serial bells excavated in Zenghouyi Tomb in Hubei Province, a set of bells weighed more than 2500 kilograms, with exact tune and high forging technology.

Also, Qin's Dujiang Dam, Zhengguo Channel fully demonstrated the development of irrigation technology in the Warring States Period.

Chuwang Xiongzhang Bell, Warring States Period (475-221 BC), 92.5cm high, unearthed from Zenghouyi Tomb, Suizhou, Hubei province

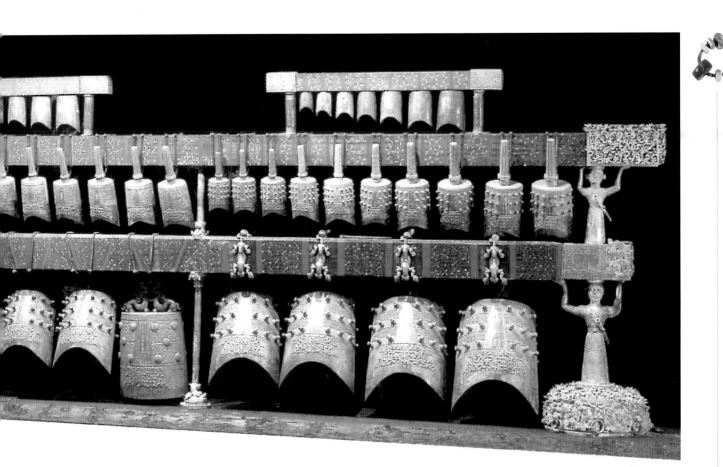

Dujiangyan, Sichuan Province

第三篇

逐鹿中原

48

Chapter 4
Great Unification of the Whole Country
--The Qin and the Han Dynasties

The Qin established the first centralized sovereignty, set up the basic political structure of Chinese history which lasted for more than 2000 years. But it ended up very soon as the result of its tyranny. The Han inherited the Qin's system and made great efforts to build it into a powerful empire. The Chinese nation has come to stand firm in the world since then.

Taishan Mountain, Tai'an, Shandong province

1. The First Emperor -- Qin Shi Huang

Qin Shi Huang, Ying Zheng (259-210 BC)

Emperors of Qin Dynasty

- 1. The First Emperor, Yingzheng (221-210BC)
- 2. Huhai (209-207BC)
- 3. Ziying (207BC)

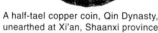

A half-tael copper coin, Qin Dynasty, unearthed at Xi'an, Shaanxi province

Qin Shi Huang, which means the first emperor of the Qin Dynasty, named Ying Zheng, was the son of King Zhuangxiang of state Qin. He ascended the throne at 13, and became the emperor at 19. His rule over the Qin lasted for 37 years.

At the time of King Zhaoxiang, state Qin had been so powerful that it was about to take charge of the whole world. In 238 B.C., King Ying Zheng began to take order with state affairs himself. After the pacification of the rebels and elimination of the party led by Lu Buwei, he appointed Li Si as prime minister and started wars of annexing six states.

Qin eliminated Han, Wei, Chu, Yan, Zhao and Qi one after another and accomplished the unification in 221 B.C. Then, he drove away Xiongnu (an ancient ethnic minority in the north also known as the Huns), expanded further to the south and set up an empire of huge territories. The great unification of six states was the fruit of downright reforms. As Qin appointed people according to their capacity, all the talents of six states were at its service. Shang Yang, Zhang Yi, Fan Wei, Lu Buwei, Li Si and Wei Liao all made contributions to the strengthening of the Qin.

After the unification, King Ying Zheng thought that he was even greater than the three 'sage kings' (Fuxi, Suiren and Shennong) and five virtuous emperors (Huang Di, Zhuanxu, Di Ku, Tang

Han Zhao Wei   Yan Qi Chu   Qin

The unification of currencies in Qin Dynasty

Qi   Chu   Yan   Han   Zhao   Wei

↓ Qin ←

馬 (馬)
宑 (安)

The unification of the written languages in Qin Dynasty

The Territory of Qin Dynasty

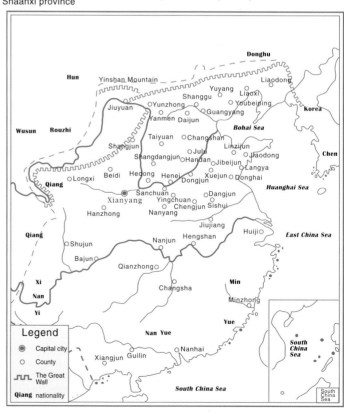

Epang Palace, part of the drawing, Qin
Dynasty, by Yuan Yao (18th century)

Bronze figurine with
umbrella, 50cm high

A gilded-copper dancer, Qin
Dynasty, 11cm high

Yao and Yu Shun),
thus giving himself a
more distinguished
title, the First
Emperor (Qin Shi
Huang), and decreed
that his successors be
titled the Second
Emperor, the Third
Emperor and so on,
so that his dynasty
and empire would
never collapse. He set
up a complete
autocratic system of
state administration

The relics of Epang Palace, Xianyang, Shaanxi province

with emperor as the center and "Three *Gong* and nine *Qing* (Gong and Qing both refer to
the highest ranking officials)" as the frame. Besides, he abolished the system of enfeoffment
and set up the prefecture-county system.

Qin Shi Huang ordered the written language, weights, measures and currency be
standardized. He also stipulated universal law, removed all the fortresses that
obstructed the transportation, built roads stretching every direction with Xianyang
as the center and Canal Lingqu connecting the south with the north. In order to stop
the northern Xiongnu (an nomadic people) going southward, he ordered the walls
of the original six states be linked to form the Great Wall extending from Lintao in
the west to the Liaodong Peninsula in the east, which created a wonder of human
civilization.

Besides, Qin Shi Huang went in for large-scale construction. He built six palaces
modeled on those of the six states and got all the beauties to fill them; and had the Epang

Palace and Lishan Tomb constructed. He went on five large-scale tours, carving characters and observing his achievements on every famous mountain that he had visited so as to display his power. In pursuit of an elixir that could keep him from dying, he sent thousands of men and women to the East Sea to seek help from the immortal, which cost so much national strength and manpower that people have neither enough to eat though men never ceased farming nor enough to clothe themselves though women never ceased weaving. Meanwhile, he governed the country by exhorting heavy punishment and harsh control of people's mind. He once burned books and buried confucian scholars alive, which snuffed out the contention of a hundred schools of thoughts that flowered during the Warring States Period.

Yangling copper tiger tally issued to a general as imperial authorization for troop movement in Qin Dynasty, unearthed at Lincheng, Shandong province

Eaves tile, Qin Dynasty, unearthed at Xi'an, Shaanxi province

A kneeling archer figurine, Qin Dynasty, 120cm high, unearthed from the terror cotta warriors and horses pit in Qinshihuang Mausoleum, Lintong, Shaanxi province

Bronze Carriage and horses, Qin Dynasty, 225cm long, unearthed from the terror cotta warriors and horses pit in Qinshihuang Mausoleum, Lintong, Shaanxi province

Unearthed from the terracotta warriors and horses pit in Qinshihuang Mausoleum, Lintong, Shaanxi provinc

第四篇

一统天下

2. The Downfall of Qin and Rise of the Han

Chen Sheng

Wu Guang

The relics of the front hall of Weiyang Palace in Chang'an in the Western Han, nowadays the northwestern outskirts of Xi'an, Shaanxi province

Bronze ornament with figures of two dancers, Western Han (206 BC-6 AD), 12cm high, unearthed at the tomb of the King of Dian in Ningjin county, Yunan province

In 210 B.C., the First Emperor (or: Qin Shi Huang) died in Shaqiu (today's Guangzong County, Hebei Province) while on an inspection tour. The eunuch Zhao Gao and Prime Minister Li Si conspired to place Hu Hai-the second son of the emperor on the throne and poisoned the eldest son Fu Su. The Second Emperor was very cruel and aroused great anger among the people and the country was in turmoil.

In July, 209 B.C., 900 poor conscripted peasants were delayed at Dazexiang (to the southeast of today's Su County, Anhui Province) by heavy rain while heading for the frontier, and they could not arrive on time. According to Qin's law, those who failed to arrive on time should be executed. At that time, the peasants had to risk danger in desperation. They made Chen Sheng and Wu Guang as the leaders and cut sticks as weapons, rising in rebellion. Chen Sheng claimed King in Chen County (today's Huaiyang, Henan Province), naming his reigning dynasty as Zhangchu. Shortly after that, Wu Guang was killed by the military officials under his command and Chen Sheng was also killed by the rebels, which led to the failure of their uprising. However, the anti-Qin's wave was stirred and the Qin's rule was constantly challenged.

After the outbreak of Chen Sheng and Wu Guang's uprising, the descendants of a Chu noble Xiang Liang and Xiang Yu killed the head of Huiji County (today's Suzhou, Jiangsu Province) and staged an uprising against the Qin, leading 8000 men northwards across the Changjiang River. Meanwhile, Liu Bang, a native of Pei County (today's Jiangsu) also gathered rebels to rise against Qin. With the help of Xiao He and Cao Can, he claimed himself as Duke Pei. Before long, he went to Xiang Liang for shelter. Then, Liu and Xiang went north to fight Qin from two directions. They made an agreement that the one who entered the central Shaanxi Plain first would be the king. In Julu (today's Henan Province), Xiang Yu defeated 200,000 soldiers of Qin's army, making him renowned enough to be elected as the great above all the vassals. Liu Bang's armies also took advantage of the weak point of

Hegemonic King of Western Chu, Xiang Yu (232-202 BC)

Gilded figure with "Eternal Fidelity" palace lamp, Western Han (206-24 BC), 48cm high, unearthed at the tomb of Dou Wan, Mancheng County, Hebei province

Bronze pot with nail pattern, Western Han (206-24 BC), 45cm high, unearthed at the tomb of Liu Sheng, Mancheng County, Hebei province

像 祖 高 漢

Emperor Gaozu of Western Han Dynasty, Liu Bang (256-195 BC)

the enemy and captured Wuguang, entering the central Shaanxi plain and approaching Xianyang.

At that time, Zhao Gao, a eunuch of the Qin murdered the Second Emperor and placed the emperor's nephew Zi Ying on the throne, who assumed the title "King of Qin" instead of the Third Emperor. Zi Ying had Zhao Gao killed and surrendered to Liu Bang. In 207 B.C., the Qin regime came to an end.

After the entry into the central Shaanxi Plain, Liu Bang abolished Qin's cruel laws, closed Qin's palaces, and promised the people that those who killed the others would be killed, who wounded others as well as those who committed stealing would be paid back, which enabled him to gain support from the Qin people. When Xiang Yu heard about Liu Bang's entry into Xianyang, he led his army into Hangu Pass and Hongmen, attempting to destroy Liu Bang. Knowing that he would not be able to resist, Liu Bang went to Xiang Yu's station in person, where he made apologies humbly so as to get away and he luckily did. This was the famous "Hongmen banquet". After "Hongmen banquet", Xiang Yu brought his armies into Xianyang, where he had King Ziying killed and Qin's palaces burned, causing lots of robbing and killing. Soon after, He claimed himself as "Hegemonic King of Western Chu" and made Pengcheng (now Xuzhou, Jiangsu) the capital of his dominion. Also, he named 18 generals as dukes and granted territories to them. Liu Bang was accorded the title "Duke of Han", with a diminished fief covering Hanzhong, Ba and Shu. Xiang Yu's allocations aggravated abruption and caused the breaking up of wars among the vassals.

Liu Bang, with a limited territory in the corner, appointed Han Xin as the Great General and marched eastward, entering Hanzhong (the central Shaanxi Plains) again. Then, he attacked Pengcheng eastward. However, he was defeated by Xiang's 30,000 men and his father and wife were taken as hostages. While escaping, Liu Bang kept fighting with Xiang Yu along Xingyang and Chenggao. Suffering lots of failures, Liu Bang made an agreement with Xiang Yu that he would share the world with him with Honggou as the border. Xiang Yu agreed and released the hostages, gave up barracks and the enclosing walls and brought his armies eastward.

However, Liu Bang, adopting Zhang Liang and Chen Ping's advice, broke the promise and chased Xiang Yu's armies. Finally, he joined hands with Han Xin and Peng Yue and surrounded Xiang Yu in Gaixa (today's Lingbi, Anhui Province), where Xiang Yu was besieged on all sides. While he was fighting his way to Wujiang (today's He County, Anhui Province), he committed suicide.

In 202 B.C., Liu Bang ascended the throne and chose "Chang'an" (today's Xi'an, Shaanxi Province), naming his dynasty as "Han".

3. The Magnificent Han Dynasty

Han Dynasty saw a powerful and unified great empire. As it's capital was in Chang'an, it was called Western Han to distinguish itself from East Han, which was established later and took Luoyang as the capital.

Han followed Qin's system, with "three Gong and Nine Qing" Duke and ministers as the frame of its central administrative system. At the beginning of its regime, it ordained the heroes who made contributions to the founding of Han as Chief minister. The regional administrative system of Western Han consisted of prefectures and counties as well as principalities and marquisates. Marquisates were those bearing the royal surnames, while principalities belonged to the heroes. At that time, the princes of the principalities included King of Chu-Han Xin, King of Liang-Peng Yue, King of Huainan-Ying Bu, King of Han-Xin, King of Zhao-Zhang Ao, King of Yan-Zang Tu and King of Chang Sha-Wu Bing. They each had armed forces of their own and monopolized power, which imposed great threat to Liu's rule so Liu Bang found excuses to kill Han Xin and others one by one. He gathered all the princes and ministers to make an agreement that "Anyone who is not from the Liu family cannot be the king or prince and anyone who is not a hero cannot be a duke. Let anyone who is not from the Liu family and who dares proclaim himself king or prince suffer universal attack."

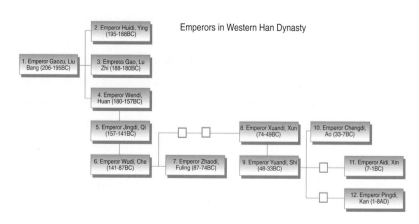

Emperors in Western Han Dynasty

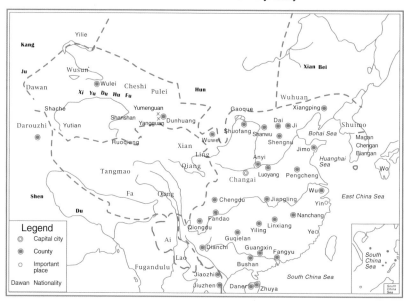

The Situation of Western Han Dynasty

The marquisates of the early Han appointed their own officials, levied their own taxes, issued their own money, adopted their own system of counting the years, and therefore controlled their fiefdoms, posing a formidable threat to the central government. Later, Emperor Jing Di adopted Chao Cuo's proposal to reduce the territories of the various fiefdoms. However, Prince of Wu, in alliance with the other kingdoms staged a revolt in the name of putting Chao Cuo to death and purged the emperor's court, which was pacified by Marshal Zhou Yafu. After that, Emperor Jing Di ordered that the officials of all the marquisates be appointed by the emperor so as to limit the power of the princes. Later on, Emperor Wu Di decreed that when a prince died, his sons were to succeed him, and the territory of his marquisates was therefore divided among his sons. Besides, he also abolished lots of principalities. As a result, the princes of the marquisates lost their power, being simply rich royal families.

As the economy was stagnant during the early years of Western Han Dynasty, Emperor Gaozu (Liu Bang) practiced the policy "Relaxing the common people's burden", looking up to the school of Huanglao's inaction. The school of Huanglao was a branch of Taoism, which was said to be

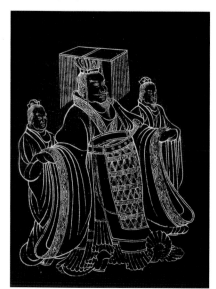

Emperor Wudi of Western Han Dynasty, Liu Che (156-87 BC)

Jade mask, Western Han (206 BC-8 AD)

Bronze running horse, Western Han (206 BC-8 AD), unearthed Leitai, Wuwei, Gansu province

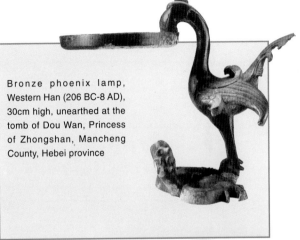

Bronze phoenix lamp, Western Han (206 BC-8 AD), 30cm high, unearthed at the tomb of Dou Wan, Princess of Zhongshan, Mancheng County, Hebei province

created by the Yellow Emperor (Huang Di) and Laozi. During the reign of Emperor Wen Di and Jing Di (202 B.C.-141 B.C.), "inaction" was further advocated with light taxes and mild punishment so that social economy was recovered and developed, forming the famous period of "Peace and prosperity during the reign of Emperors Wen and Jing".

At the time of Emperor Wu Di (156 B.C.-87 B.C.), the policy of inaction couldn't meet the requirements of the situation any more so Emperor Wu Di accepted Dong Zhongshu's (179 B.C.-104 B.C.) advice "belittling a hundred schools of thought and showing respect for Confucianism alone", ensuring the supremacy of Confucianism and set up an educational system of training the future officials with Confucian classics. Therefore, the highest seat of learning was founded in the court and learned men of the five classics were retained to strengthen the cultural and ideological dominance.

At the beginning of Western Han, Xiongnu (Hun), the nomadic people in the north, posed a great threat to the Han Dynasty. Though placatory policies were adopted, the Han Dynasty failed to stop Xiongnu's invasion. During the reign of Emperor Wu Di, Generals Wei Qing and Huo Qubing went on lots of large-scale expeditions against Xiongnu. However, all the expeditions were defeated. Decades later, Xiongnu lost its power due to their internal split. Part of it was brought to the rule of Han Dynasty by Hun Chieftain Huhanxie, moving to the area around Mount Yinshan. In the year 33 B.C., Emperor Wu Di, Emperor Yuan Di arranged a marriage between Wang Qiang (Zhaojun) and Chieftain Huhanxie, bringing 40 years' amicable settlement.

When Emperor Wu Di sent troops to fight Xiongnu, he also got Zhang Qian to the western regions as envoy, which opened up the road to central Asia and facilitated the economical and cultural communication between the central plains

Warming vessel, Han Dynasty (206-220 BC), 14.8cm long, 12.9cm high, unearthed at Jingyang County, Shaanxi province

The Routes of Zhang Qian's Journey to the Western Regions

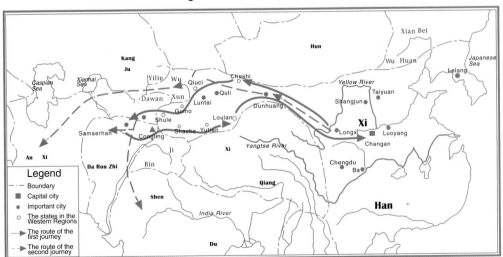

Jade leopard, Western Han (206 BC-8 AD), 23.5cm long, unearthed at Shizishan, Xuzhou, Jiangsu province

第四篇

一统天下

and Western regions. Besides, Emperor Wu Di also pacified South Yue (today's Guangdong Province), set up nine counties there, defeated southwest Yi, Yelang and other ethnic minorities, which consolidated the empire and facilitated the communications and amalgamation among different nationalities.

After Emperor Wu Di died, Emperor Zhao Di (Liu Fuling) and Emperor Xuan Di's period came, who brought a stable and prosperous scene, renowned as "Peace and prosperity of Zhao and Xuan". Relying on its powerful military strength and brilliant culture, the empire of Han stood erect in the east of the world, shining in contrast with the Roman Empire which dominated the west.

In the late years of Western Han, the government of Han Dynasty declined. The trend of annexing land was getting out of hand. Among those peasants who lost their land, some were reduced to servants; some formed insurgent groups in the mountainous woods. Harsh conflicts for the

Jade clothes sewn with gold thread, Western Han (206 BC-8 AD), 188cm long, unearthed from the tomb of Liu Sheng, Mancheng county, Hebei province

possession of servants took place among the nobles, bureaucrats and rich merchants. Since Dong Zhongshu, "restraining land and power" was constantly proposed, but the opposition it encountered prevented it from being carried out. People lost confidence on Han Dynasty's rule. After the death of Emperor Yuan Di, Emperor Cheng Di ascended the throne. His nephew Wang Mang was appointed Minister of Defence and began to interfere in state affairs. In the year 8 A.D., he disthroned the little

The picture of Mingfei (Zhaojun) goes beyond the Great Wall, Ming Dynasty, by Qiu Ying

Emperor Ziying, proclaimed himself emperor proper and named his regime the Xin Dynasty. Western Han thus met its end.

Wang Mang attempted to "Change the Old System in the Name of Old Traditions" so as to solve complicated social problems. He decreed that farm land be called "royal field" and maidservants be called "private dependents". Selling and buying farm land and servants were forbidden. And he issued imperial edict to carry out *Wujun* (namely, officials of *Wujun* were set up to even prices,

Silk embroidery with Kui-phoenix design, Han Dynastyy (206 BC-220 AD), 105cm long, 45cm wide, unearthed at Suide county, Shaanxi province

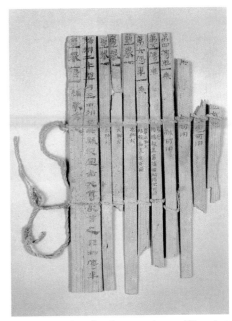

Inscribed wooden slips, the second year of Yangshuo Period, Western Han (23 BC)

Infantryman, Western Han Dynasty (206 BC-8 AD), 48cm high, unearthed from the accompany tomb of Changling Mausoleum, Shaanxi province

collect taxes, undertake credit sale and so on), credit sale, *Liuguan* (namely, the government took charge of salt, iron, wine, money-making, and so on). In this way, he hoped to control business deals, prices and taxes as well. He also reformed the currency system and forbade private money-making for several times. Meanwhile, he constantly changed the local and central official systems and titles, the names of the prefectures and counties as well as the division of administrative areas. He also launched wars against the Xiongnu twice on large scales and forced the heads of the surrounding tribes to hand in the royal seal of Han Dynasty and accept the debased titles conferred by the emperor of Xin Dynasty. The tyranny executed by Wang Mang aroused widespread dissatisfaction, caused social and economic chaos and finally led to the downfall of Wang Mang's reign.

Bronze Ding supported by bears, Western Han (206 BC-8 AD), 8.1cm high, unearthed from the tomb of Liu Sheng, Mancheng County, Hebei province

第四篇

一统天下

The Sketch of Silk Road

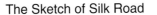

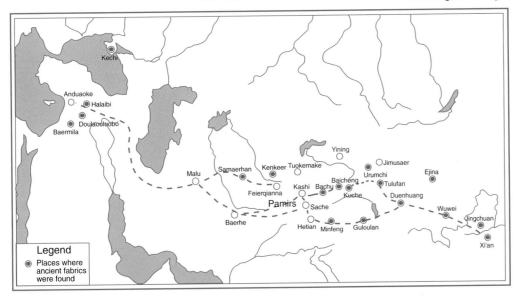

Legend
● Places where ancient fabrics were found

4. Resurgence of Emperor Guang Wu

Emperor Guangwu of Han Dynasty (6 BC-57 AD)

Emperors in Eastern Han Dynasty

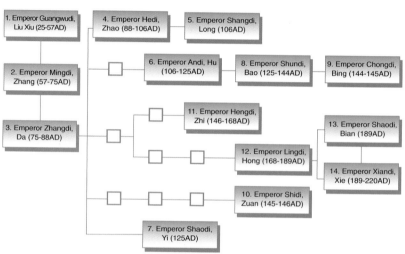

Jade Zun with mythological animals design, Eastern Han (25-220 AD), 10.5cm high, unearthed at Anxiang County, Hunan province

The failure of Wang Mang's systematical reforms brought more disasters to the common people, resulting in constant peasant uprisings, most of which were in the name of combating Mang and resuming Han. The Greenwood Army led by Wang Kuang, Wang Feng and the army of the Red Eyebrows led by Fan Chong were the most powerful. In the year 24 A.D., the Green Army thrust into Chang'an and killed Wang Mang, marking the end of Xin Dynasty. Meanwhile, Liu Yan and Liu Xiu on the north of the Yellow River gained power in the struggle against the new armed forces. In June, A.D., 25, Liu Xiu proclaimed himself emperor in Haonan (modern Baixiang County, Hebei) and is known in history as Emperor Guangwu. He moved the capital to Luoyang so that it is named Eastern Han Dynasty in history. As he restored the Han house, his reign is also renown as "Resurgence of Guang Wu".

Liu Xiu was very magnanimous and good at employing talents. Learning the lesson from Wang Mang, he limited the power of the relatives of his mother or wife in interfering in state affairs, and prevented the heroes who made contributions to the country from taking control of the armed forces. The three chancellors -- the Chancellor of Civil Administration, the Chancellor of Military Affairs and the Great Censor -- no longer had any real power, which was instead in the hand of the Cabinet Minister. Locally, Liu Xiu dismantled and annexed more than 400 counties, impaired the local military strength so that the emperor was more powerful. Besides, he abolished Wang Mang's severe decrees and issued nine orders which prohibited the mistreat or cruel slaughter of servants and freed the slaves. And he ordered a country-wide check-up on land reclamation and census so as to strike the landlords. And he changed the tithe into one thirtieth so that the society became more stable.

The improvement of iron-smelting techniques led to mass production of steel and advancement of iron farming tools. Also, due to the spreading of ox-ploughing and the extensive construction of irrigation works, agricultural productive force was greatly enhanced. Besides, technology of handicraft industry was improved as well. Delicate bronzeware, lacquerware and silk reflected high technology of handicraft. Trade business was flourishing in Eastern Han Dynasty with the merchants' footprint reaching as far as Western Regions and foreign countries. With more than ten years' hard work, Eastern Han Dynasty saw economic prosperity.

Eastern Han developed certain relationship with the minorities in the bordering areas. In the early stages of Eastern Han, Xiongnu grew strong, posed a threat to Han again and once even intruded Fufeng, Shangdang, Tianshui and other counties. But soon after, Xiongnu was divided into two parts-south and north. Southern Xiongnu King Rizhu followed his grandfather Huhanchanyu's title, leeched on to Han. On the other hand, Northern Xiongnu controlled Western Regions and often invaded the south. Eastern Han Dynasty, taking advantage of Northern Xiongnu's suffering of converging attack and its dispersed forces, sent troops to attack it so as to protect the four counties west of the Yellow River and sought chances to recover transportation with Western Regions. Under the attack of Han Dynasty time and again, Xiongnu was forced to move further towards the west.

When Xiongnu entered Western Regions, King Shache, having united other states to fight with Xiongnu, formed friendly relations with Han. However, at the time of Emperor Guangwu, limited national strength

Beacon tower of Han Dynasty, Yangguan, Gansu province

failed to enable Han to control Western Regions so that Cheshi, Shanshan, Qiuci and Yutian were controlled by Xiongnu. In A.D. 73, after the reoccupation of Yiwu, Eastern Han set up Western Region Official Residence (a local government). Meanwhile, he sent Sima Banchao on a diplomatic mission to the Western regions, who got rid of the guarding messengers of Xiongnu in Shanshan, Yutian and Sule, got through the southern road of the Western regions and had troops stationed there. The troops of Eastern Han defeated Xiongnu for many times and drove off the invasion of Darouzhi so that Beidao, Qiuci and other states also surrendered to Banchao. Han Dynasty appointed Banchao as the highest administrative commanding officer of the Western regions, quartering at Qiuci. Shortly after, Yanqi and other states turned to Han for shelter, enabling the opening of the passage of Beidao and resulted in the submitting of more than fifty states in the Western regions to the authority of Han. Banchao was therefore appointed as Duke Dingyuan. In A.D.97, Banchao sent Ganying on a mission to Daqin (Roman Empire), who was blocked at the Persian Gulf and therefore returned. Eastern Han also pacified south of the Five Ridges (the area covering Guangdong and Guangxi provinces) and installed barrack officers in Wuhuan, enabling direct communication with the minorities in the south, southwest and northeast.

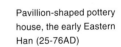

Pavillion-shaped pottery house, the early Eastern Han (25-76AD)

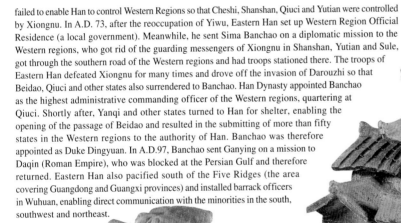

Stone chimera, Eastern Han (25-220AD), 168cm long, unearthed at Luoyang, Henan province

第四篇

一统天下

The picture of people's life in Han Dynasty on the brick and stone relieves unearthed around China

Sowing seeds, 38 x 24cm, Deyang

Husking rice, 39 x 25cm, Pengshan

Carriage crossing a bridge, 45 x 40cm, Yangzishan, Chengdu

Yangzun's wineshop, 42 x 25cm, Pengzhou

Shooting an arrow and harvesting, 49 x 40cm, Yangzishan, Chengdu

Brewing, spinning and weaving, 275 x 135cm, Chengdu

Enjoying drinking together at a banquet, 48 x 40cm, outskirts of Chengdu

In the kitchen, 46 x 42cm, outskirts of Chengdu

Delivering lectures and passing on one's valuable experience, 45 x 40cm, Qingganpo, Chengdu

Playing games, 46 x 37cm, Baozishan, Xinjin

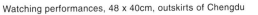

Watching performances, 48 x 40cm, outskirts of Chengdu

第四篇　一统天下

5. End of Eastern Han

Ploughing with cattle, Eastern Han (25-220 AD), 139cm high, 61cm wide, unearthed at Mizhi, Shaanxi province

Queen mother of the west and king father of the east, Eastern Han (25-220 AD), 168cm long, 38cm wide, unearthed at Suide county, Shaanxi province

Procession of people by chariot and horses, Eastern Han (25-220 AD), 181cm long, 36cm wide, unearthed at Mizhi, Shaanxi province

At the time of Emperor He Di, the social situation was more turbulent. More than 60 years' war between Xiqiang and Han Dynasty greatly weakened Eastern Han's reign. Eunuchs and relatives of the emperor on the side of his mother or wife conflicted with each other, causing more chaos in the political situation. In the late years of Han Dynasty, "Just Comment" was promoted, which helped to drive out evil and usher in good. Students of the highest seat of learning and righteous officials attempted to control political situation by resorting public opinions. However, they were stricken by the force of eunuchs, ended in the 'disaster of one-party dictatorship'. In A.D.166 (the ninth year of Yanxi period), seduced by eunuchs, Emperor Huan Di arrested more than 200 "party members". Even the righteous officials were involved. In the second year of Jianning period during Emperor Ling Di's reign, as many as six to seven hundred people were embroiled in the disaster of 'one-party dictatorship', who were either killed, removed, disabled or prisoned. More than 1000 of the students of the highest seat of learning were arrested, and the relatives and pupils of the party as well as the officials were all removed from their place and got confined.

In the late years of Eastern Han, the corruption of the ruling class and visitation of Providence such as floods, droughts, locusts, storms, hail, earthquakes and plague forced the peasants to move from one place to another, leading to uprisings of those who had been deprived of home.

Zhang Jiao was leader of a branch of Taoism-"*Taiping Tao*" (Doctrine of Justice). He made full use of this doctrine, for equality and sympathy for the common people were advocated in it. Besides, he claimed himself to be "Virtuous Master", dispensed 'Taoist Magic Water' as free treatment to the sick, and sent his followers to preach everywhere. Over ten years, his followers spread to Qing, Xu, You, Ji, Jing, Yang, Chong, Yu (today's Shangdong, Hebei, Henan, Jiangsu, Anhui, Hubei and so on), with a number of several hundred thousand. He spread the idea that "Blue Heaven" (referring to the Eastern Han government) had already "passed away" and it was time for the "Yellow Heaven" (referring to the ideal leader of Taiping Tao) to take over; the whole country would be blessed in the cyclical year of Jia Zi (i.e., the year 184), which was an obvious call for an uprising against the Eastern Han. And they decided to stage an uprising. However, in the year 184, a turncoat informed against the Yellow Turbans so 7 states and 28 counties had to rise ahead of time in February simultaneously. Zhangjiao called himself "Heavenly General", his brother Zhang Bao, "General of the Earth" and Zhang Liang "General of Men". Since all the risers wore yellow turbans, they were called Yellow Turban Army.

The uprisings of the Yellow Turban spread all over the country and had many officials killed, which caused a great stir in the capital. However, as they were not well organized, they couldn't

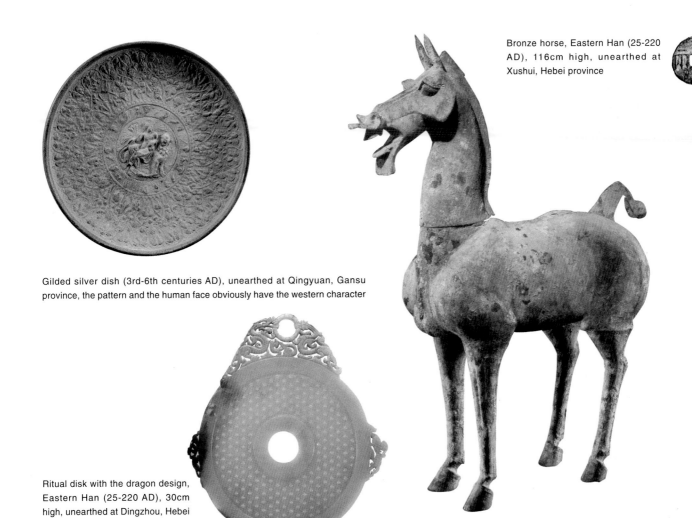

Bronze horse, Eastern Han (25-220 AD), 116cm high, unearthed at Xushui, Hebei province

Gilded silver dish (3rd-6th centuries AD), unearthed at Qingyuan, Gansu province, the pattern and the human face obviously have the western character

Ritual disk with the dragon design, Eastern Han (25-220 AD), 30cm high, unearthed at Dingzhou, Hebei province

cooperate with each other. So the Han army was able to guard the passes and suppress them easily. Various military forces including Yuan Shao, Yuan Shu, Gongsun Zan, Sun Jian, Liu Bei and Cao Cao, took the advantage to develop their forces and defeated the Yellow Turban for many times. Shortly afterwards, Zhang Jiao died of an illness, while Zhang Liang and Zhang Bao died in the battles. The main force of the Yellow Turban was therefore suppressed.

Though the Yellow Turban was defeated, the foundations of Eastern Han Dynasty were shaken and separate regimes were set up by different military forces, leading to mix-up everywhere.

第四篇

一统天下

6. Science, Technology and Culture

Dong Zhongshu (179-104 BC)

Sima Qian (145-86? BC)

The act of burning books and burying Confucian scholars alive by the First Emperor brought great disaster to the ancient classics. In the early stages of Western Han, Qin Dynasty's law was observed so Confucianism was despised and the thought of "inaction" advocated by Lao Zi took control. The classics produced before Qin Dynasty didn't come out until the time of Emperor Hui Di, which used to be hidden among the people. At the time of Emperor Wu Di, the name of Lao Zi was excluded from the official learning and Confucianism won legitimacy. However, the ideas of great unity, combination of virtue and punishment, and three main-stays of kingcraft that "*Chen* (officials in the court) should obey their sovereign, wives should obey their husbands, children should obey their father" expressed in Dong Zhongshu' *Grand Dew of Spring and Autumn* became ideological foundation of monarchy over two thousand years.

In Han Dynasty, the teaching of Confucianism also experienced different divisions such as modern Confucian classics and ancient Confucian classics. Modern studies of Confucian classics did not only differ from ancient Confucian classics in words, chapters, but also differ in lots of explanations. Zheng Xuan, born in the late Han Dynasty, was a learned Confucian, who adopted both studies, learned from the prime and became the mainstream of Han Dynasty's studies of Confucian classics.

In the late Western Han, a study of divination combined with mystical Confucian belief emerged (study of *Chen and Wei*), which explained history in the name of spirits. Since Emperor Guangwu believed in Chen, the study of Chen and Wei became vigorous. However, the theory of Chen and Wei only gave a farfetched interpretation, making the content of Confucian classics absurd and empty. Scholars like Huan Tan and Zhang Heng tried their best to repute the study of *Chen and Wei*, and Wang Chong wrote *Lun Heng (On Balance)*, including 85 articles, which shines with reason.

Buddhism was spread to the inland by way of mid-Asia in the late Western Han. At the time of Emperor Huan Di and Ling Di, Monk An Sigao, native of Anxi, and Monk Zhi Chen, native of Darouzhi came to China one by one and translated lots of classics of Buddhism so that the common people had Buddhist tenet to follow. Taoism came into being in the late Eastern Han, with Book of Taipingqingling as the main classic, combining witchcraft popular among the common people and theories of Yellow Emperor and Lao Zi together. At that time, there was "Tao of Five-Dou-Rice" advocated by Zhang Ling and his descendants besides "Taiping Tao" spread by Zhang Jiao.

The tradition of recording the history of their dynasty by the official was inherited. Sima Qian (145 B.C.-86 B.C.), whose personal name was Ziyang, was a native of Xiayang (today's Han city, Shaanxi Province). While he was young, he toured a lot along the middle and lower reaches of the Changjiang River and on the Central Plains. Besides, he went on four tours of inspection accompanying Emperor Wu Di. In 108, he followed his father to take charge of history-compiling and was determined to improve the writing of history.

In 99 B.C., he suffered the punishment of castration because of his exculpation for Li Ling who surrendered to Xiongnu after his troops were defeated. Despite all the hardship, he struggled to write *The Historical Memoirs (Shiji)*, in the hope of "discovering the law governing the relationship between the universe and human being, gaining a thorough understanding of the changes since antiquity and forming his own concept". This book consists of 130 essays and covered the 3000-year history of China starting from the time of Yellow Emperor to the reign of Emperor Wu Di. Being able to summarize the experience of the past and form his own ideas, this book was the first historical work with complete content and precise structure. Sima Qian thus initiated the genre of chronology, being regarded as a model to be followed by generations of historians.

Gilded bronze leopard, Han Dynasty (206-220 BC), 17cm high

Ban Gu (32-92 BC)

Another famous historical work following *The Historical Memoirs* was *The History of the Han Dynasty* written by Ban Gu. Ban Gu (92 B.C.-32 B.C.), a native of Anling (northeast of today's Xianyang, Shaanxi Province), spent more than 20 years writing most of the book, based on the Later Historical Memoirs written by his father Ban Biao. He died in prison as the result of embroilment. His sister Ban Zhao and Ma Xu finished it. The History of the Han Dynasty, following and developing the stylistic rules of The Historical Memoirs, was the first complete historical of a whole dynasty in China.

The Historical Memoirs and *The History of the Han Dynasty* represent the highest level of essay in the two Hans. The former is even regarded as "the Lament (Li Sao) in unrhymed form". Alongside of them are Jia Yi and Chao Cuo. Ban Gu was good at Ci and classical poetry conforming to a definite pattern and poems, and was renowned for the poem "*the Song of Two Capitals*" and others. Endowed with the same talents were Mei Cheng, Sima Xiangru, Yang Xong and others of Western Han, Zhang Heng of Eastern Han. Another literary achievement of Han is the "folk songs of official conservatory (Yuefu)" or "folksongs in the Han style ". The court set up an official conservatory as a special institution to manage music affairs, which both compiled court music and folk music. Many famous songs were existent in the Yuefu Songs, such as "*Joining the army at fifteen*", "*Walking at Moshang*", "*Going to the Gate Eastward*" and so on.

Astronomy and calendar gained further development in Qin and Han Dynasties. A "star table" was unearthed from the tomb of Mawangdui in Changsha, which kept a record of the movement of five big planets and comets within 70 years from Qin to early Han. At the time of Emperor Wu Di of Han, Sima Qian was sent to establish a new calendar-*Taichu Calendar* (also *Santong Calendar*) with other astronomic experts like Sheshi, Dengping, Tangdu, Luo Xiahong and others, which made the calendar more accurate than ever before.

During the time of Emperor Wu Di of Han, the first mathematical book *The Mathematical Classic of Zhoubi* came out, which recorded ways of getting the height of sun with a bamboo pole measuring the shade of sun so that Pythagorean proposition was understood. The accomplishment of *The Mathematics in Nine Sections* demonstrated mathematics in ancient China had developed into a complete system. The book *Zhouyi Participation Contract* written by Wei Boyang of Eastern Han summarized the experience of alchemists on the making of pills of immortality, and recorded the phenomena of matter-transformation as well as the knowledge of chemical reaction.

Hua Tuo and Zhang Zhongjing, two famous doctors at the end of Eastern Han Dynasty, completed the book *A Treatise on Fevers*, which was later arranged into two books *On Typhoid Fever* and *Gold Chest Dissertations*, which are the two most influential ancient classics on clinical science of Chinese medicine. Hua Tuo was good at internal medicine, surgery, pediatrics, gynecology, and acupuncture, and excellent at surgery. He initiated abdominal operation, honored as Father of Surgery. He also invented anesthetic named "*Mafusan*" and was the first doctor who adopted general anesthesia.

The invention of paper is a brilliant flower of the civilization in Han Dynasty. At the time of Emperor An Di of Eastern Han, Cai Lun summarized the experience of Western Han when the fiber of hemp was employed to make paper, and made use of tree bark, rags and old fishing nets to produce paper. Later, Cai Lun was honored as Marquis of Longting. Therefore, the paper he invented was also called Marquis Cai's paper. The technique of paper-making made great contributions to the accumulation and spreading of human culture.

Zhang Heng in Eastern Han Dynasty was a versatile Scholar. Being a writer, painter and thinker, he invented Houfengyi (an instrument used to predict the orientation of wind), drew a topographic map, wrote an astronomic book *Ling Xian* (Law of the Universe) and improved the planetarium (an instrument used to observe astronomical phenomena). The seismograph that he invented could forecast orientations of earthquakes thousands of kilometers away. Therefore, he was regarded as father in the studies of earthquake.

The arts in the Qin-Han Dynasties was magnificent and in plain, simple style. The great pit containing pottery figures to the east of the First Emperor's mausoleum in Xi'an, Shaanxi Province is referred to as the Eighth Wonder of the World. This massive underground battle array vividly displayed the prowess of Qin's troops annexing the territory of other states. The martial soldiers, high-spirited horse pottery and delicate bronze carriages represent the charms of the arts of Qin. Han Dynasty inherited and developed Qin's plastic arts. The stone carving in front of Huo Qubing's tomb was a representation of Han's plastic arts, which was also the oldest and most intact among ancient Chinese stone carvings. The bronze Tianma (Holy

第四篇

一统天下

Jade dancing figure, Western Han, the early South Yue Country Period (219-122 BC)

Bronze cowrie-container, Western Han (206 BC-8 AD)

Painting on silk, Western Han (206 BC-8 AD), 205cm long, unearthed at Mawangdui, Changsha, Hunan province

Embroidery, Western Han (206 BC-8 AD), unearthed at Mawangdui, Changsha, Hunan province

Yi vessel, lacquer, Western Han (206 BC-8 AD), unearthed at Mawangdui, Changsha, Hunan province

Lacquer Ding, lacquer, Western Han (206 BC-8 AD), 28cm high, unearthed at Mawangdui, Changsha, Hunan province

Zhong vessel, lacquer, Western Han (206 BC-8 AD), 51.5cm high, unearthed at Mawangdui, Changsha, Hunan province

Table with cups and plates, lacquer, Western Han (206 BC-8 AD), unearthed at Mawangdui, Changsha, Hunan province

Horse) unearthed in Wuwei, Gansu Province in Eastern Han Dynasty reached the height of perfection and was embodiment of strength and beauty. Drawings of Qin and Han also formed the style of rusticity and gravity. The fresco of Qin was in the form of patterns, which were colorful and brilliant. Court painters were in existence in Han Dynasty, whose duty was to praise the achievements and virtue of the court. The painting-stones and painting-bricks were artistic curiosities particularly in two Hans, which represented plentiful tales, historical stories and real life. The silk-paintings unearthed from Mawang Tomb in Changsha were of fresh color and fluid lines, despite the passing of two thousand years. Music in Qin-Han Dynasty was remarkably improved and different styles from different districts mingled with each other, making Chinese music more vigorous. The Qin Dynasty set up a music institution-official conservatory for the first time and Han Dynasty followed suit with Emperor Wu Di further developing it. Thanks to the intercourse with the Western regions, music and musical instruments also spread to the inland from the Western regions, bringing new vigor to the development of music and dance.

Jade ring in fretwork, Western Han (206 BC-24 AD), the outer diameter 7.9cm, unearthed at a tomb of Western Han in Xuzhou, Jiangsu province

Gauze Buddhist clothes, Western Han (206 BC-8 AD), 128cm long, unearthed at Mawangdui, Changsha, Hunan province

Green dragon, 134 x 60cm, engraving on a stone coffin

White tiger, 26 x 6cm, Jintang

Rosefinch, 70 x 79cm, engraving on a stone coffin in Xingjing

Turtle, 44 x 40cm, engraving on a stone coffin

一统天下

70

Chapter 5

Progressing in Turbulence

--The Wei, the Jin, the Southern and Northern Dynasties

Minorities were constantly rising from the north, joining in the contention on the Central Plains, entertaining a high ambition to seize sovereignty, challenging the traditional culture of the Central Plains. However, the Central Plains finally absorbed fresh blood from various minorities, becoming more vigorous. Not only were the northern tribes blending with the Han people, but also the Han people were blending with the northern tribes. In fact, they mingled with each other.

Huanglong, Songpan, Sichuan province

1. Tripartite Confrontation of Three Kingdoms

Emperor Wu Di of Wei, Cao Cao (155-220 AD)

Emperor Zhao Lie of Shu, Liu Bei (161-223 AD)

Emperor Tai Zu of Wu, Sun Quan (182-252 AD)

In late Eastern Han Dynasty, the vast area along the Yellow River and the Changjiang River had become a stage for the contention among all the powers, the most famous of which was the great tripartite confrontation of Cao Cao, Liu Bei and Sun Quan.

Cao Cao (155-220), whose original surname was Xiahou, and personal name Mende, was from Peiguoxiao (today's Hao County, Anhui Province). He was born in an official's family and later adopted by the eunuch Cao Teng. Therefore, he changed his surname into Cao accordingly. He enjoyed reading books about strategies and was good at poems. He demonstrated his talents for the first time during the suppression of the Yellow Turban. He led all the counties in the crusade against Dong Zhuo in the name of "Raise a righteous army to quell rebellion." In 196, he forced Emperor Xian Di to move his capital to Xuchang, and had the Emperor under his thumb and ordered the vassals about in his name. Later, he eliminated the forces of Yuan Shu, Lu Bu and others one by one. In 200, Cao Cao and Yuan Shao fought a decisive battle at Guandu (north of today's Zhongmou, Henan Province). Cao Cao sent five thousand soldiers to secretly attack Wuchao (northeast of today's Yanjin, Henan Province), and destroyed Yuan's impedimenta and provisions, killed over 70,000 Yuan's soldiers. Later, he occupied four states-Qing, Ji, You and Bing so that the Central Plains got unified.

Liu Bei (161-223), whose personal name was Xuande, was a native of Zhuo Jun (today's Zhuozhou, Hebei Province) and offspring of Liu Sheng-King Zhongshan Jing (son of Emperor Jing Di). He also anticipated in the battle against Dong Zhuo, but was not powerful enough. He tried every means to win the support of all the talents. It was said that he had paid three visits to Zhuge Liang (181-234) so as to seek strategies from him. Thereafter, Zhuge Liang became a major strategist for Liu Bei. Famous generals like Guan Yu, Zhang Fei and Zhao Yun were also at Liu Bei's service.

The Situation of the Three Kingdoms

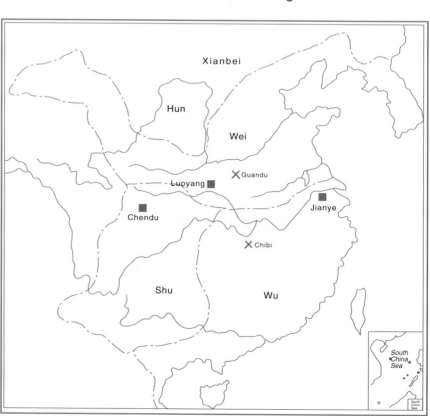

Emperors of Wei Dynasty

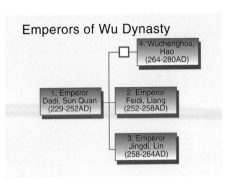

```
Cao Cao ──┐           ┌─ 3. Emperor
          │           │   Chenliuwang, Huan
          │           │   (260-266AD)
1. Emperor ──┐ ┌──── 4. Emperor
Wendi, Cao Pi │ │      Gaoguixianggong,
(220-226AD)   │ │      Mao (254-260AD)
              │
2. Emperor
Mingdi, Rui
(226-239AD)
```

Emperors of Shu Dynasty

```
1. Emperor ──── 2. Houzhu, Chan
Zhaoliedi, Liu Bei   (223-263AD)
(221-223AD)
```

Emperors of Wu Dynasty

```
                    ┌─ 4. Wuchenghou,
                    │   Hao
                    │   (264-280AD)
1. Emperor ──── 2. Emperor
Dadi, Sun Quan   Feidi, Liang
(229-252AD)      (252-258AD)
                 │
                 3. Emperor
                 Jingdi, Lin
                 (258-264AD)
```

In 208, Cao Cao brought his troops southward, aiming at the seizure of Jingzhou (today's Xiangyang, Hubei Province) and further occupation of east of the Changjiang River so as to unify the whole country. Threatened by Cao' troops, Liu Bei escaped to Jingzhou and was defeated at Xiangyang by Cao's troops. Zhuge Liang persuaded Sun Quan, who ruled east of the Changjiang River to unite their troops against Cao Cao. The allied troops of Sun and Liu encountered Cao's troops at Chibi (south of the Changjiang River or today's northwest of Puqi County, Hubei Province), where they confronted each other with the Changjiang River lying between. Though Cao's troops included 200,000 soldiers, claimed to be more than 800,000, Sun and Liu united to defeat Cao with 50,000 soldiers by means of fire. As a result, Cao was forced to move back to the north. The battle at Chibi helped Sun Quan consolidate his

Relics of the battlefield at Guandu, Guandu village, Zhongmou County, Henan province

occupation in the east of the Changjiang River, enabled Liu Bei to win part of Jingzhou and further gain Yizhou. In this way, a situation arose in which the country was divided and ruled by the three feudal lords Cao, Sun and Liu.

In 216, Cao Cao was titled as King Wei and died in 220. His son Cao Pi proclaimed himself Emperor of Wei, with Luoyang as his capital, with the title of his dynasty "Wei" and of his reign "Huangchu". So Eastern Han came to an end. The following year, Liu Bei declared himself Emperor of Han in Chengdu, historically known as the Kingdom of Shu, with "Zhangwu" as the title of his reign. Sun Quan accepted the title "King Wu" conferred by Cao Pi and called himself Emperor of Wu in 229 at Jianye (today's Nanjing), whose title of reign was "Huanglong". In 263, Wei eliminated Shu. Two years later, Sima Yan-the son of Sima Zhao, King of Jin in Wei, dethroned the Wei emperor and named himself Emperor Wu Di and established Jin Dynasty (historically known as Western Jin), with the capital remaining at Luoyang. In 280, Western Jin defeated Wu and ended the turbulence caused by the wars that had lasted for more than ninety years among the three kingdoms and the division of separate regimes by armed forces.

第五篇

动乱融合进步

Zhuge Liang (181-223 AD)

Bronze tortoise, Wei Jin (220-420 AD)

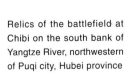

Relics of the battlefield at Chibi on the south bank of Yangtze River, northwestern of Puqi city, Hubei province

2. Five Ethnic Minorities and Western Jin

Sima Yi (179-251 AD)

Emperor Wu Di of Jin, Sima Yan (236-290 AD)

At the beginning of Western Jin's reign, Emperor Wu Di conferred titles on more than 20 relatives in the Sima family in the hope of building up the influence of the royal family. However, after the death of Emperor Wu Di, "Disturbances caused by the Eight Princes" took place, which lasted 16 years. The wars among the eight princes dislocated the social economy and shook Western Jin's rule.

In 308 (the second year of Yongjia Period), Liu Yuan, a noble of Xiongnu (Hun) proclaimed himself Emperor of Han at Pingyang (today's Linfen City, Shanxi Province), historically known as "Chenghan". In 311 (the fifth year of Yongjia Period), the Hun people led by Liu Cong captured Luoyang and took Emperor Huai Di of Jin prisoner. The troops of Jin then made Min Di as emperor in the bleak and desolate city, Chang'an, which

The States of Eight Kings in Western Jin Dynasty

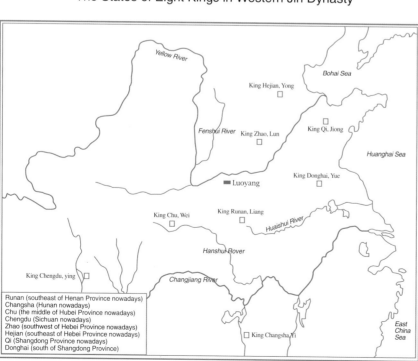

Runan (southeast of Henan Province nowadays)
Changsha (Hunan nowadays)
Chu (the middle of Hubei Province nowadays)
Chengdu (Sichuan nowadays)
Zhao (southwest of Hebei Province nowadays)
Hejian (southeast of Hebei Province nowadays)
Qi (Shangdong Province nowadays)
Donghai (south of Shangdong Province)

Terra-cotta soldier holding a knife, Jin Dynasty, unearthed at Changsha, Hunan province

Emperors in Western Jin Dynasty

| 1. Emperor Wudi, Sima Yan (266-290AD) | 2. Emperor Huidi, Zhong (290-306AD) | 3. Emperor Huaidi, Chi (306-313AD) | □ | 4. Emperor Mindi, Ye (313-316AD) |

Tree-shaped ornament, Northern and Southern Dynasties, 28cm high, unearthed at Sanyan Mausoleum

was historically known as the "Turmoil of Yongjia". In 316 (the fourth year of Jianxing), the Hun people Liu Yao seized Chang'an and therefore brought an end to Western Jin.

During this period, more than 20 regimes were set up by seven minorities on the Central Plains, which was known later as "Period of Five Ethnic Minorities and Sixteen States". The five ethnic minorities referred to the Hun, Xianbei, Jie, Di and Qiang people and the sixteen states included Xia, Chenghan, Two Zhaos (Former and Latter Zhaos), Three Qins (Former, Latter and Western Qins), Four Yans (Former, Latter, Southern and Northern Yans), Five Liangs (Former, Latter, Southern, Northern and Western Liangs).

This period was also called Period of "Five Ethnic Minorities Rising Against Western Jin", for all the peoples were fighting with each other on the Central Plains. After decades of disturbance, amalgamation of the Han people and minorities was realized during the contention, which made an important phase for the unification of the Chinese nation.

Pottery stable, Yongjia Period of Jin (307-312 AD)

Pottery irrigated fields, Yongjia Period of Jin (307-312 AD)

Celadon Zun with the design of mythological animals, Western Jin Dynasty (216-336 AD), 27.9cm high, unearthed at Zhouchu family's tomb in Yixing, Jiangsu province

The Situation of 16 States and 5 States of the Western Regions

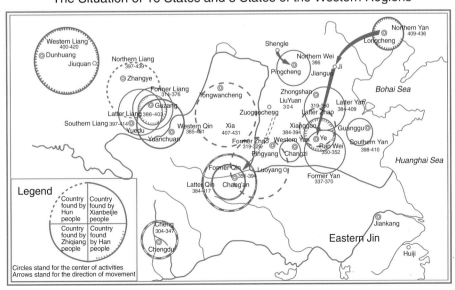

第五篇

动乱融合进步

3. Eastern Jin Retaining Sovereignty Over a Part of the Country

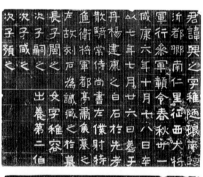

Sima Rui, Emperor Yuan of Jin (276-322 AD)

Inscription on the memorial tablet in Wang Xianzhi's tomb, rubbing, Eastern Jin Dynasty (317-420 AD), 37.3cm wide, unearthed at Nanjing, Jiangsu province

Emperors in Eastern Jin Dynasty

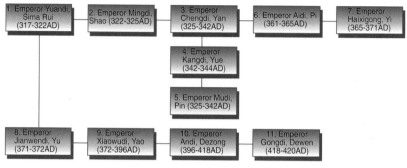

In the second year following Western Jin's end, Sima Rui, a member of Jin's family, proclaimed himself emperor of Eastern Jin (known in history as Emperor Yuan Di) at Jiankang (today's Nanjing). Depending on the support of northern and southern landlords, he was able to prop up the Eastern Jin regime in southern China. Among those landlords, the Wangs of Langya led by the brothers Wang Dao and Wang Dun contributed most, known as "Wangs and Simas share the world".

The Eastern Jin was full of internal conflicts. The immigrant northern landlords and southern landlords ostracized each other. And the turn-taking rule by northern landlords Wang, Yu, Huan and Xie conflicted with the royal power. However, as the rulers of Eastern Jin stayed in the

The Confrontation between Former Qin and Eastern Jin

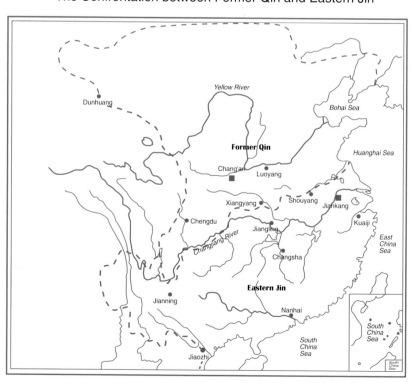

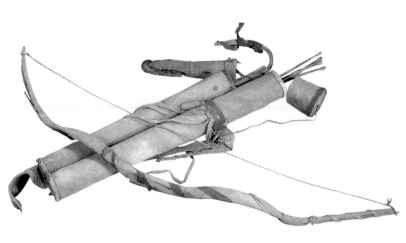

Bow, arrow, arrow quiver, bow case and scabbard, Han and Jin (206 BC-420 AD)

troops were half-way across. However, Eastern Jin troops took the advantage to launch a full-scale attack so that the Qin troops panicked and ran as quickly as possible. Their general Fu Rong was therefore killed. So Xie Xuan, jumping at the opportunity, scattered the enemy and eventually defeated Qin. During the battle, the dead bodies of Qin were everywhere, many of which were caused by the trampling on each other. And those who were fleeing for their lives thought the Jin troops were closely behind and apprehended danger in every sound. Fu Jian suffered an arrow shooted in his body and ran northward. The victory of Feishui Battle consolidated Eastern Jin' reign. The Jin Troops recovered Shouyang, stabilized southern economy, and avoided the devastation of culture so the society gained further development.

After Feishui Battle, the Former Qin declined quickly. In 385, Fu Jian was killed shortly after he was back to Chang'an. Therefore, the Former Qin collapsed and the landlords broke away from Qin's control one by one. The turmoil in the north lasted as long as 40 years.

south, they were not enthusiastic to recover the Central Plains. In 313, Zu Ti went on a northern expedition, which recovered some of the lost land. However, he was not supported by the court. After the death of Zu Ti, the northern expedition was over accordingly. Though Huan Wen led another three northern expeditions in 354,356 and 369 respectively, he suffered setbacks all the time and the regained land got lost again. When Huan Wen died, Xie An became chief minister, who brought peace to the situation of Eastern Jin. He broke rules to choose talents and recruited a powerful troop, called "Northern Camp Soldiers". In this way, he accumulated certain military force.

At that time, the Former Qin with the capital at Chang'an, became more and more powerful. It annihilated Former Yan, Former Liang and Dai successively and the north was united. In 383, King Fu Jian of Former Qin, led an army of 800,000 in a march on the Eastern Jin attempting to destroy Eastern Jin. Xie An of Eastern Jin, leading his troops, fought back.

Qin and Jin met at Feishui (today's Feihe, Anhui Province), where they were separated by a river. Xie Xuan asked the Qin troops to move back a little so that Jin could cross the river for a decisive battle. Fu Jian complied, hoping to strike his blow home when the Jin

Xie An (320-385 AD)

Wang Dao (276-339 AD)

Painted stone figurine of a standing Buddha, Northern Qi Dynasty, 97cm high

Woven shoes in silk and flax with Chinese characters, Eastern Jin (317-420 AD)

第五篇

动乱融合进步

4. The Rising and Declining of the Southern Dynasties

After Feishui Battle, Eastern Jin didn't take the advantage to go on a northern expedition so that the internal conflicts sharpened and Jin's power declined. Between the year 399 and 411, a large-scale peasant rebellion led by Sun En and Lu Xun broke out. Liu Yu, a subordination of Liu Lao-general of "Northern Camp Soldiers" suppressed Sun En, Lu Xun, annihilated separate regimes, and further eliminated Southern Yan and Later Qin. Gaining more and more power, Liu Yu dethroned Emperor Gong Di in 420, and proclaimed himself as emperor with the national title "Song", and the title of his reign "Yongchu". Therefore, he was later known as Emperor Wu Di of Song. This marked the beginning of Southern Dynasties as well as the beginning of confrontation between the Southern and Northern Dynasties.

Liu Yu had undertaken some reforms and constituted laws to strike cruel landlords and rectified the administration of officials so that a prosperous scene emerged during the reign of his son Liu Yilong, historically known as "Peace and Prosperity of Yuanjia". When Liu established his reign, Tuoba clan of the Xianbei tribe, rose from the north and advanced southward. They set up Northern Wei and unified the north in 439. In 450, Tuoba Shou launched an attack on Song with an infantry of 100,000 soldiers consisting of an infantry and a cavalry unit.

The war between Song and Northern Wei devastated the power of Song greatly. Soon, Emperor Wen Di of Song (Liu Yilong) was murdured and the following years were full of scrabbling for the kingship by his offsprings, who constantly killed people of their own blood in order to gain power. In 479, Xiao Daocheng, Commander of the Imperial Guards, usurped the power of the Song and changed its name to Qi, or the Southern Qi as historians call it. In the late Southern Qi, imperial clans slaughtered each other and caused lots of internal strives. In 502, Xiao Yan, governor of Yongzhou Prefecture marched to Jiankang, usurped imperial power and renamed the national title as "Liang".

Emperor Wu Di (Xiao Yan) lived a simple life and worked hard to conciliate various

The Situation in the Northern and Southern Dynasties

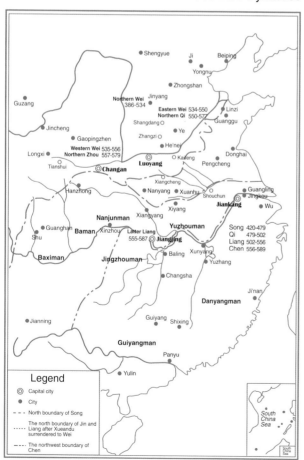

Stone Carving of the Southern Dynasties, outskirts of Nanjing city

conflicts so as to avoid wars during his 48 years' reign. Besides, he advocated Buddhism and built lots of temples, bringing prosperity to Buddhism in the south. But he was cruel to the common people so that he aroused lots of revolts. In late years of Emperor Wu Di of Liang, "Disturbance of Hou Jing" broke out. In 557, Chen Baxian, who demonstrated his talents in the pacification of "Disturbance of Hou Jing", deposed the emperor and established the Chen family. During the whole Southern Dynasties, Chen Dynasty was the smallest in its territory and made little achievements in economy. The last emperor Chen Shubao was a noted incontinent emperor who never attended state affairs. In 589, his reign was destroyed by Sui Dynasty so that the Southern Dynasties came to an end.

像祖高齊

像帝武梁

像帝武陳

Emperor Wu Di of Song, LiuYu (363-422 AD)

Emperor Gao Zu of Qi, Xiao Daocheng (427-482)

Emperor Wu Di of Liang, Xiao Yan (464-549 AD)

Emperor Wu Di of Chen, Chen Baxian (503-559 AD)

Emperors in Song Dynasty

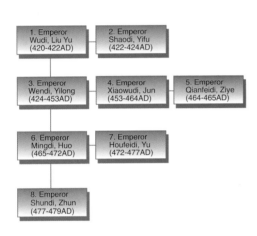

1. Emperor Wudi, Liu Yu (420-422AD)
2. Emperor Shaodi, Yifu (422-424AD)
3. Emperor Wendi, Yilong (424-453AD)
4. Emperor Xiaowudi, Jun (453-464AD)
5. Emperor Qianfeidi, Ziye (464-465AD)
6. Emperor Mingdi, Huo (465-472AD)
7. Emperor Houfeidi, Yu (472-477AD)
8. Emperor Shundi, Zhun (477-479AD)

Emperors in Qi Dynasty

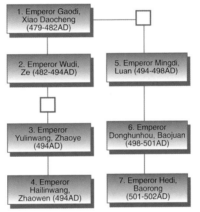

1. Emperor Gaodi, Xiao Daocheng (479-482AD)
2. Emperor Wudi, Ze (482-494AD)
3. Emperor Yulinwang, Zhaoye (494AD)
4. Emperor Hailinwang, Zhaowen (494AD)
5. Emperor Mingdi, Luan (494-498AD)
6. Emperor Donghunhou, Baojuan (498-501AD)
7. Emperor Hedi, Baorong (501-502AD)

Emperors in Liang Dynasty

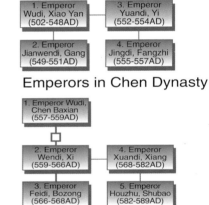

1. Emperor Wudi, Xiao Yan (502-548AD)
2. Emperor Jianwendi, Gang (549-551AD)
3. Emperor Yuandi, Yi (552-554AD)
4. Emperor Jingdi, Fangzhi (555-557AD)

Emperors in Chen Dynasty

1. Emperor Wudi, Chen Baxian (557-559AD)
2. Emperor Wendi, Xi (559-566AD)
3. Emperor Feidi, Bozong (566-568AD)
4. Emperor Xuandi, Xiang (568-582AD)
5. Emperor Houzhu, Shubao (582-589AD)

Lacquer screen painted with the story of virtuous women and wise men, Northern Wei (386-543 AD), unearthed from the Sima Jinlong's tomb in Datong, Shanxi province

Wudang Mountain, Danjiangkou, Hubei province

第五篇

动乱融合进步

5. The Rising and Declining of Northern Dynasties

Emperors in Northern Wei Dynasty

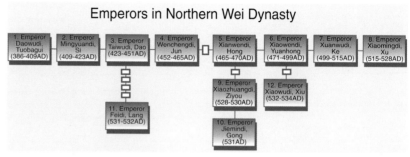

| 1. Emperor Daowudi, Tuobagui (386-409AD) | 2. Emperor Mingyuandi, Si (409-423AD) | 3. Emperor Taiwudi, Dao (423-451AD) | 4. Emperor Wenchengdi, Jun (452-465AD) | 5. Emperor Xianwendi, Hong (465-470AD) | 6. Emperor Xiaowendi, Yuanhong (471-499AD) | 7. Emperor Xuanwudi, Ke (499-515AD) | 8. Emperor Xiaomingdi, Xu (515-528AD) |

| 11. Emperor Feidi, Lang (531-532AD) |
| 9. Emperor Xiaozhuangdi, Ziyou (528-530AD) | 12. Emperor Xiaowudi, Xiu (532-534AD) |
| 10. Emperor Jiemindi, Gong (531AD) |

Gilded silver pot, Northern Zhou (557-581), 37.5cm high, unearthed at Guyuan, Ningxia, with the relief of men and women of northern tribes

The establishment of Northern Wei and unification of the north accelerated the amalgamation of different minorities. Reforms centered on assimilating the minorities advocated by Empress Feng of Northern Wei and Emperor Xiaowen Di (Tuoba Hong) conformed to the trend of history. They neatened the administration of officials, strengthened the local rule and facilitated the stability of the country. In 494, Northern Wei moved its capital to Luoyang, where Emperor Xiaowen Di ordered all the people to wear the same clothes as the Han people, the Han language to be used in the court and encouraged intermarriage between the Xianbei and Han people, persuaded the Xianbei people to use the Han people' surnames and stipulated different statuses for Xianbei nobilities. The removal of capital and reforms of administrative system facilitated the development of Northern Wei's economy, strengthened its reign, facilitated the amalgamation between the Xianbei and Han people, leading Northern Wei to great prosperity.

As the rulers of Northern Wei enjoyed a life more luxurious than all the antecedents, exploited the peasants and soldiers cruelly, and spent a lot of money and labor on Buddhism, which aroused the revolt of

The Situation in the late Northern and Southern Dynasties

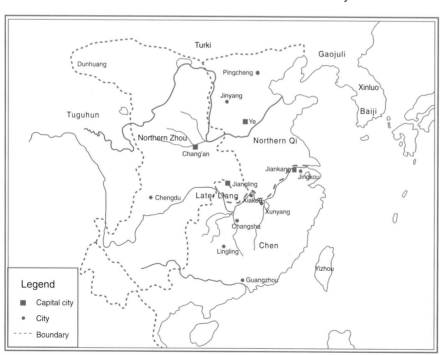

Legend
- ■ Capital city
- • City
- --- Boundary

Guardian animal, Northern Qi (570), 50.2cm high, unearthed at Taiyuan, Shanxi province

Relics of Niya, Han and Jin (206 BC-420 AD), north of Mingfeng County, Hetian, Xinjiang

Brocade brassard with Chinese characters, Han and Jin (206 BC-420 AD), unearthed at Niya, Xinjiang

common people and soldiers in six towns of northwest and north. In 528, Er Zhurong, prince of Taiyuan, launched a revolt in He'nei (today's Qinyang, Henan Province) so that the reign of Northern Wei collapsed. In 534, Gao Huan, subordination of general Erzhu Rong made Yuanshanjian as emperor and moved the capital to Ye, historically known as Eastern Wei. In 550, Gao Yang, son of Gao Huan, abolished Eastern Wei and set up Northern Qi. In 535, Yuwen Tai, a clan of the Xianbei people murdered Emperor Xiao Wu Di and established Emperor Wen Di, historically known as Western Wei. Yuwen Tai renovated official administration, reformed official systems and carried out Northern Wei's policy of assimilation, enabling its strength to exceed that of Eastern Wei. In 557, Yuwen Yue, son of Yuwen Tai, dethroned Wei and established Northern Zhou. Emperor Wu Di of Zhou (Yuwen Yi) continued reforms, advocated Confucianism, abolished Buddhism and Taoism and freed slaves, which made it more powerful than Northern Qi. In 577, Emperor Wu Di annihilated Northern Qi and unified the north of China.

The exterior of Yungang Grottoes and open-air big Buddha, Northern Wei

Traveling, Northern Qi (479-502 AD), the fresco in the tomb of General Lou Rui, Taiyuan, Shanxi province

第五篇

动乱融合进步

6. Glory in a Disturbed Period
--Culture and Science

Tao Yuanming (376-427 AD)

It's said that the country Fusang where he arrived might be in today's Mexico. However, as Emperor Taiwu Di of Northern Wei believed inTaoism and Emperor Wu Di of Northern Zhou held Confucianism in high esteem, they ordered all the Buddhist temples to be destroyed during their reign. Nevertheless, Buddhism grew flourishing through lots of ups and downs. In Later Northern Wei, the number of temples reached as many as 30,000, monks and nuns 2,000,000; in Northern Qi, the number of temples was 40,000, monks and nuns 3,000,000. The flourishment of Buddhism was fully displayed in this way.

While Buddhism and Taoism were all the rage, famous atheists also appeared. For example, Fan Ye, at the time of Song of Southern Dynasties, thought the soul of a person also would die together with his body. And Fan Zhen wrote *the Destructibility of the Soul.* Buddhism exerted great influence on Chinese ideology, culture and arts.

Being good at drawing huge figures as well as Buddhist portraits, Cao Buxing was regarded as Father of Buddhist portraits in the Three Kingdom Period. Gu Kaizhi of Eastern Jin, Lu Tanwei of Qiliang and Zhang Sengyou together were renowned as "Three Outstanding Persons of Six Dynasties", among whom Gu Kaizhi' pictures *Eminent Woman* and *Goddess Luo* were

The chaos since Wei, Jin, Southern and Northern Dynasties provided social conditions for the spreading of Buddhism. As Buddhism advocated abstention from killing, believed in comeuppance and the possibility to enjoy happiness in the other world through hard work in this life, it touched the suffering people and soon got widely spread. At that time, *Xuan Xue* (metaphysics) and Buddhism pervaded into each other. Under the influence of *Xun Xue*, many monks did a lot of reading on classic books, speeches of hundreds of schools, studied Lao-Zhuang and joined in metaphysical discussions.

Many monks came from Western Regions at that time to preach and many Chinese also went west to pursue Buddhism. At the reign of Later Zhao, Futuchen, monks from Western Region, were regarded highly by Shi Le and Shi Hu and took in nearly 10,000 disciples. In Later Qin, Jiumoluoshi, a monk from Western Region, was invited to Chang'an to translate sutras. He translated 74 sutras and 380 volumes successively. In 399 (the third year of Longan), Fa Xian of Eastern Jin went to Buddhism's homeland in search of sutras. He spent fourteen years traveling, which covered thirty countries all the way, including *Mojietuo* (east of today's India) and the *Lion Country* (today's Sri Lanka). Through long-standing transformation, Buddhism took on Chinese flavor. In Southern Dynasties, an intelligent Chinese monk Huishen also traveled abroad to preach.

Wulingyuan in Zhangjiajie, Hunan province

the most famous. In later Eastern Han, calligraphy became an art. Du Du, Zhang Zhi and Zhong You were all calligraphists. As Zhang Zhi was good at the grass style, he was called as "Sage of the Grass Style". Wang Xizhi of Eastern Jin and his son Wang Xianzhi held important position in calligraphy. Wang Xizhi initiated a new style in calligraphy and was regarded as "Sage of Calligraphy" with his masterpiece *Preface for Lanting*.

During this period, Buddhist grottoes were of great value among ancient Chinese civilization. As Xinjiang came into contact with Buddhism much earlier, there were lots of grottoes along the "silk road", such as Kuchemutula Grotto, Shenmusaimu Grotto and Baizikelike Groto, Tuyugou Grotto along Turpan.

Mogao Grottoes, built on lower levels of the Mingsha Mountain is forty miles away from the southeast Dunhuan County of Gansu Province. It is one of the three largest grottoes in China and was first built in 366 (the first year of Taihe, Eastern Jin). Between Former Qin and Northern Wei, more than 20 grottoes were dug. Besides, Yulin Grotto in Anxi, Maiji Mountain, in Tianshui, Bingling

Wang Xizhi (321-379 AD)

The Preface of Lanting, Wang Xizhi (part of the reproduction of Tang Dynasty)

Wang Xizhi and the Geese, Qing Dynasty, by Ren Yi (1840-1896), paper scroll, water painting, fill in colors, 65.9cm wide, 133.4cm high

The Goddess of the Luo River, partial, Jin Dynasty, Gu Kaizhi(c.345-406AD), silk scroll, fill in colors, 27cm high, 572cm wide

Temple in Yongjing, Tianti Mountain in Wuwei and Mati Temple in Zhangye are all among the famous grottoes and temples.

Yungang Grottoes, in Datong City, Shanxi Province, west of Wuzhou Mountain, came to be dug between 460 and 465, in Northern Wei, which is the earliest grotto temple on the Central Plains. With more than a hundred small grottoes, it makes a massive sight. Among them, five were dug at the reign of Emperor Wencheng Di of Northern Wei. The statues in Yungang Grottoes are extremely huge with some of the Buddhist images higher than ten meters.

Longmen Grottoes lies on the cliffs west of the Yi River, in Luoyang, Henan Province, being dug around the time of Emperor Xiaowen Di's removal of capital to Luoyang in Northern Wei. The representative grottoes dug in Northern Wei include Guyang Grotto, Bingyang Grotto and Lotus Grotto. Besides, there are other grottoes like those in Gong County of He'nan Province and Xiangtangshan Grotto in Handan City of Hebei Province on the Central Plains. The art of grotto temple is a brilliant record of cultural communication between the east and west.

Due to great amalgamation, various musical instruments appeared, such as *Quxiang Pipa* (Crooked-neck *Pipa*), Five-stringed *Pipa, Bo, Jiegu* (an ancient drum) and so on. And music from both the east and west was very popular in inland, including musics of Qiuci, Xiliang, Gaochang, Kuangguo, Sule, Tainzhu, Anguo, Gaoli and so on. Famous musican Ji Kang was excellent at playing "*Guanglingsan*-a piece of famous music" and wrote theoretical works such as *on the Absence of Lament in Music* and *on Musical Instruments*.

The achievements of literature in the Three Kingdoms Period were represented by Jian'an Literature. Jian'an was the title of Emperor Xian Di of Han's reign (196-219). Among the famous writers were Cao Cao, his son Cao Pi and "Seven Talents of Jian'an"-Kong Rong, Chen Lin, Wang Can, Liu Zhen, Ying Chang and Xu Gan. As their works were noted for their bleakness and strength, they were called "Style of Jianan". Cai Yan wrote wuyan poems (poems with five characters to a line) like *Poem of Grief* and I*ndignation and Eighteen Beats of Hu Jia* (Hu Jia refers to a reed instrument), which were full of vigorous and unrestrained feelings. The then renown "Seven Talents of Bamboo Woods"-Ji Kang, Ruan Ji, Shan Tao, Xiang Xiu, Ruan Xian, Liu Ling and Wang Rong were all representatives of "Literature of Zhengshi (240-249)". They admired

Zhaoming prince, Xiao Tong (501-531 AD)

Yellow Emperor (Huangdi) and Lao Zi, talked about metaphysics and behaved in an unbridled way. Their poems and essays were imbued with the thought of Lao Zhuang and full of cynicism.

In Eastern Jin, Tao Yuanming's poems and essays were the most outstanding. He glorified rural life and demonstrated his lofty dignity against the corrupted court. He expressed his political thought in Poem of *the Peach Garden* and his preface *Something About Peach Garden* and visualized a world free of tyranny and oppression with every one enjoying a pleasant life. The literary style of Northern Dynasties was noted for its simplicity, freshness and powerfulness, such as the folk songs "*Song of Chile*" and "*Song of Mulan*", which were all of great value with their brightness and optimism. Lu Ji's *Ode of Essay*, Liu Xie's *Wen Xin Diao Long* and Zhong Rong's *Critique of Poetry* are all great literary critical works. *Selected Works of Essays* compiled by Liang crown prince Xiao Tong was the earliest collection of essays.

Private history-compiling was very popular at that time. The most famous works include *History of Later Han Dynasty* by Fan Ye of Liu-Song Period and *History of the Three Kingdoms* by Chen Shou, which together with *the Historical Memoirs* and *History of Han Dynasty*, were called "Former Four Historical Works". And Li Daoyuan's *Commentary on the Waterway Classic* and Yang Xuanzhi's *Temples and Monasteries* in Luoyang are of great literary value as well as of important

The Seven Sages of the Bamboo Grove, Wanli reign bingchen year of Ming Dynasty (1616), Li Shida, 25.4cm wide, 157.2cm long

literature of geography and Buddhism. The eighteen maps of *Relief Map of Gongyu* drawn by Pei Xiu of Western Jin enjoys a certain status in world history of cartology and geography.

Taoism in Wei, Jin, Southern and Eastern Dynasties, having absorbed thoughts of Buddhism and Confucianism, became more colorful. During the Two Jins, Ge Hong wrote *Bao Pu Zi*, in which he suggested integrating the principles of Confucianism with the theory of Taoism. Famous Taoists Lu Xiujing and Tao Hongjing in Southern Dynasty assimilated the ideology of Confucianism and Buddhism so that Taoism was greatly enhanced. Tao Hongjing wrote *Annotations to "Emperor Shennong's Materia Medica"*, in which he included 356 kinds of medicine that he had collected. Besides, he wrote *Supplement to "Prescriptions for Emergencies"* and other pharmacology books.

Court doctor Wang Shuhe of Western Jin wrote ten volumes of *Treatise on Pulse*, which summarized experience of pulse studies and was the earliest extant treatise of its kind in China. Moreover, he carefully neatened Zhang Zhongjing's book A Treatise on Fevers into two books *On Typhoid Fever* and *Gold Chest Dissertations*.

During Wei and Jin periods, Liu Hei's notes on *The Mathematics in Nine Sections* wrote that the ratio of circumference to diameter was 3.1416. Zu Chongzhi of Southern Dynasties worked out the ratio to seven decimal places, which made it somewhere between 3.1415926 and 3.1415927, which was 1000 years earlier than European's discovery. Zu Chongzhi's son Zuhen was the first to invent the way to compute the volume of sphere, which was also 1000 years ahead of European's. With respect to astronomy and calendar, Yu Xi of Eastern Jin discovered "precession" and applied it into Daming Calendar, stipulating the length of a year as 365.24281481, which has no more than 50 seconds' gap with the result measured by modern science. On mechanism, Ma Jun improved looms and got it five times more efficient than the original in the Three Kingdom Period; the keel waterwheel used for irrigation was a hundred times more

Gilded bronze figurines of Buddha, the late Northern Wei to Eastern Wei (386-550 AD), 35cm high, unearthed at Xi'an, Shaanxi province

Zhu Chongzhi (429-500 AD)

exquisite. Ma Jun also invented Guiding Wagon employing the law of differential gear mechanics. On agriculture, Jia Sixie wrote ten volumes of *The Manual of Important Arts for the People*, which summarized the farming experience along the middle and lower reaches of the Yellow River concerning agriculture and animal husbandry and was the first extant complete agricultural work.

Bull, Northern Qi (570 AD), 35cm high, unearthed at Taiyuan, Shanxi province

Crouching Lion, Northern Zhou (557-581 AD), 25.3cm high, Xi'an, Shaanxi province

Pottery figure, Northern Qi, 19cm high, unearthed at Taiyuan, Shanxi province

Tao Qian Returns to the Village, Yuan, by He Cheng

第五篇

动乱融合进步

Chapter 6

A Flourishing Age

--The Sui, the Tang, the Five Dynasties The grandeur of the Chinese nation

Lies in its capability to absorb various excellent civilizations with broad mind. The amalgamation of ethnic minorities beams the light of civilization, Magnificent and dazzling. Glory of Tang was a piece of history worth being proud of by the Chinese nation.

Dunhuang Mogao Caves, Gansu province

86

1. Grandeur of Kaihuang in the Sui Dynasty

Emperor Wen Di of Sui, Yang Jian (541-604 AD)

Emperor Xuan Di of Northern Zhou died of an illness in 580 with Emperor Jing Di ascending the throne at the age of eight. Yang Jian, left prime minister, dominated the court, naming himself "King of Sui". In 581, Yang Jian forced Emperor Jing Di to give up the kingship to him and proclaimed himself emperor, later known as Emperor Wen Di of Sui, with the title of his reign

Emperors in Sui Dynasty

"Kaihuang", keeping Chang'an as the capital. In 587 (the seventh year of Kaihuang Period), Sui eliminated Later Liang and conquered Chen two years later, which brought the confrontation between the north and south to an end and got the whole country unified.

In the early years of Kaihuang Period, Emperor Wen Di of the Sui spared no efforts to make the country prosperous. He resumed the system of Han-Wei Dynasties and established an administrative system centering on three ministries and six departments. Among the three ministries, the Secretariat was in charge of decision-making, the Grand Council examined and approved the decrees, and the Chancery was responsible for the administration of daily affairs. Under the Chancery, six departments were set up, including Ministry of Official Personal Affairs, Ministry of Rites, Department of War, Board of Revenue and Population, Ministry of Punishments and Ministry of Engineering. These six departments took charge of different affairs respectively. This system laid basis for the fundamental framework of central institutions for later dynasties over a thousand years. Locally, a two- system was set up-prefectures and counties. Local officials from the ninth grade up were appointed or removed by the court and other local officials were transferred every three years without being granted any important tasks. In this way, the control on prefectures and counties were strengthened. In the system of armed forces, the domicile of soldiers was included in the prefectures and counties together with that of the people so that the source of soldiers was broadened and the cost of maintaining an army was saved. Concerning laws and punishment, Emperor Wen Di of Sui ordered Pei Zheng to stipulate a new penal code *Law of Kaihuang*, which abolished former harsh punishment and retained five kinds of punishment-death, exile, imprisonment, heavy flogging and light flogging and five hundred articles such as those called "Ten Evils" and "Eight Proposals".

This penal code was commonly observed by the Tang, Song and other dynasties. Emperor Wen Di also abolished the system of nine ranks with wealthy families holding power, set up institutions of learning in prefectures and counties and selected officials through examinations. During the reign of Yang Di, ten subjects were set up to recruit scholars, which launched imperial examinations, making great reforms on the selective system and exerting important influences on later generations. With respect to economy, Emperor Wen Di of Sui carried out the Law of Equal Division of Fields and system of renting to deal out land to peasants. Besides, taxes were reduced, domiciliary register was cleared up, and currency system as well as the system of weights and measures was reformed so that the national economy was greatly enhanced. Furthermore, Emperor

The Territory of Sui Dynasty

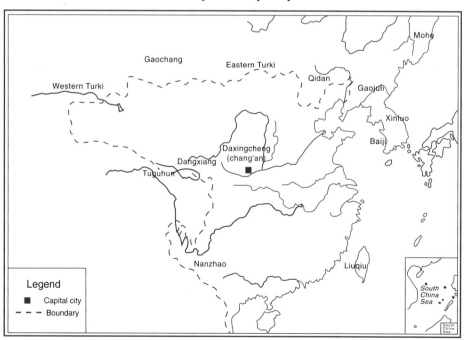

Zhaozhou Bridge, Sui, Hebei province

Wen Di lived a simple life. In this way, the clothes and food that the court stored could satisfy the expenses of the court for five years. Meanwhile, the population at that time reached from around five million to about seven million and handicraft industry as well as commerce also developed so that the fame "Peace and Prosperity of Kaihuang" came into existence.

However, the reign of Emperor Yang Di was noted for his dissipated life and cruality. While he was on the throne, he started to build the capital Luoyang and dig the Great Canal from Zhuojun (now Beijing) to Yuhang (now Hangzhou City). Luoyang became a political, military and transportational center, and the construction of the Great Canal strengthened the economic relationship between the north and south. Nevertheless, they took a heavy toll among the builders and imposed a heavy strain on the nations' manpower and material resources. Moreover, Emperor Yang Di launched three successive wars against Korea, which involved millions of soldiers. During his second expedition to Korea, the noble Yang Xuangan took the advantage to rebel against Sui and people on the Central Plains rushed to him for shelter. Thus peasant uprisings spread all over the country. Among the famous uprising were also Wagang Army led by Zhai Rang and Li Mi in Henan Province, and other uprising forces led by Dou Jiande in Hebei, Du Fuwei and Fu Gongyou along the Changjiang River and Huaihe River. Meanwhile, many aristocrats also led army revolts against Sui. In the spring of 618, Yu Wenhua, Ji general of the government troops got his troops to assassinate Emperor Yang Di and brought Sui Dynasty to an end. In the same year, Li Yuan declared himself emperor in Chang'an, initiating a new dynasty of unprecedented prosperity-Tang.

Pottery camel, Sui (581-618 AD), unearthed at Hulucheng Tomb at Taiyuan, Shanxi province

Emperor Yang Di of Sui, Yang Guang (569-618 AD)

The scenery of the Great Canal, Yangzhou, Jiangsu province

The Distribution of Canals Built in Sui Dynasty

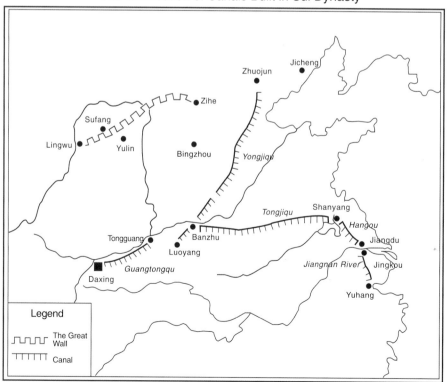

Legend

⊓⊔⊓⊔ The Great Wall

⊤⊤⊤⊤⊤ Canal

Pottery figurine of a woman with a dustpan, Sui (581-618 AD), 15cm high

Head of a Bodhisattva, Sui (581-618 AD), 12cm high, unearthed at Xi'an, Shaanxi province

Glazed pottery carriage and cattle, Sui (581-618 AD), 41.5cm high

Donors and carriage, Sui (581-618 AD), fresco in Dunhuang Mogao Grottoes

第六篇

雍容盛世

2. Emperor Taizong of the Tang

Emperor Gao Zu of Tang, Li Yuan (566-635 AD)

Grand Council and the Chancery in the early stage of Tang were all called prime ministers and there were many prime ministers in Zhenguan Period. Fang Xuanling and Du Ruhui were appointed as Left Pushe of the Secretariats simultaneously. Fang Xuanling was good at tactics while Du Ruhui was good at decision-making, both of whom were major assistants of Emperor Taizong of Tang and were named "Fang's Brain and Du's Decision".

Emperor Taizong of Tang was always ready to hear various opinions from officials. Many righteous officials turned up in Zhenguan Period, among whom Wei Zheng was the most famous. He offered lots of advices for Emperor Taizong to consolidate his rule and was determined to do so even at the risk of angering Emperor Taizong. He once said to Emperor Taizong, "The masses are like water, which can both hold the ship and overturn it". In this way, he managed to remind Emperor Taizong to be prepared for danger in times of peace and be as prudent as ever. At that time, the emperor was clear-minded and officials upright, which supplemented each other and formed a much-told history.

Emperor Taizong was expert in using those talented people, without regarding whether he was from royal family or from common people or of humble origin, or whether he was once a political enemy. In order to foster officials, Emperor Taizong enlisted famous scholars into his service and set up lots of schools both in the capital and local areas. The imperial civil examination initiated under the Sui was also extended with special attention to Jing Shi (advanced Scholar). After Zhenguan Period, most of the prime ministers were selected from Jing Shi.

Emperor Taizong also advocated shorter and lighter punishments and worked out a new penal code in Zhenguan Period. During the reign of Emperor Gaozong, *Exposition of the Tang Penal Code* was stipulated, which was the earliest extant statute in Chinese history and had lighter punishment and conviction than the laws of the Sui. Emperor Taizong emphasized that statutes should be obeyed by all the people and could never be changed according to personal likes or dislikes.

Besides, Emperor Taizong combined many counties and prefectures, and reduced the number of various levels of officials from 2000

After the establishment of the Tang, the second son of Li Yuan-Li Shimin was made Prince Qin. In 626, he defeated Prince Li Jiancheng and other princes during the "Turmoil of Xuanwumen" in Chang'an's court, gained the kingship and changed the title of his reign to "Zhenguan", historically known as Emperor Taizong of Tang.

After his ascension, Emperor Taizong absorbed some talented though not experienced officials to participate in the state affairs. The Secretariat, the

The Territory of the Prime of Tang Dynasty

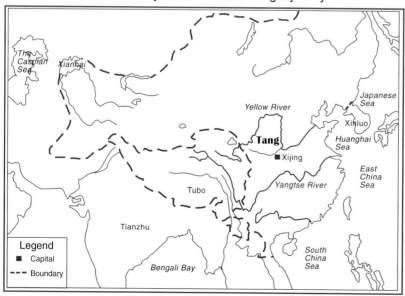

Legend
- ■ Capital
- --- Boundary

Emperor Tai Zong of Tang, Li Shiming (599-649 AD)

Emperors in Tang Dynasty

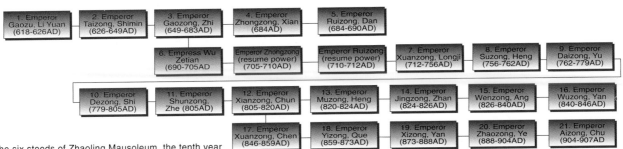

1. Emperor Gaozu, Li Yuan (618-626AD)	2. Emperor Taizong, Shimin (626-649AD)	3. Emperor Gaozong, Zhi (649-683AD)	4. Emperor Zhongzong, Xian (684AD)	5. Emperor Ruizong, Dan (684-690AD)

	6. Empress Wu Zetian (690-705AD	Emperor Zhongzong (resume power) (705-710AD)	Emperor Ruizong (resume power) (710-712AD)	7. Emperor Xuanzong, Longji (712-756AD)	8. Emperor Suzong, Heng (756-762AD)	9. Emperor Daizong, Yu (762-779AD)

10. Emperor Dezong, Shi (779-805AD)	11. Emperor Shunzong, Zhe (805AD)	12. Emperor Xianzong, Chun (805-820AD)	13. Emperor Muzong, Heng (820-824AD)	14. Emperor Jingzong, Zhan (824-826AD)	15. Emperor Wenzong, Ang (826-840AD)	16. Emperor Wuzong, Yan (840-846AD)
17. Emperor Xuanzong, Chen (846-859AD)	18. Emperor Yizong, Que (859-873AD)	19. Emperor Xizong, Yan (873-888AD)	20. Emperor Zhaozong, Ye (888-904AD)	21. Emperor Aizong, Chu (904-907AD)	

The six steeds of Zhaoling Mausoleum, the tenth year of Zhenguan in Tang Dynasty (636 AD), 171-175cm high

TEQINBIAO

SALUZI

QINGZHUI

QUANMAOGUA

SHIFACHI

BAITIWU

第六篇

雍容盛世

Wei Zheng (580-643 AD)

Lotus-leaf Lid, Tang (619-907 AD), 4cm high, 25.6cm long, unearthed at Dangtu, Jiangsu province

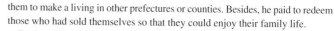

Gold-inlaid agate cup with a cattle head

to 600. He avoided any large-scale construction against farming season so as to benefit agricultural production. While Guandong and Guanzhong Districts suffered from floods, droughts, frosts and locusts during Zhenguan Period, Emperor Taizong ordered the barns to be open to the peasants so as to relieve them and allowed them to make a living in other prefectures or counties. Besides, he paid to redeem those who had sold themselves so that they could enjoy their family life.

During Zhenguan Period, Emperor Taizong firmly resisted against the infestation of Turks from the north and finally annihilated Eastern Turks and subdued Yiwu (today's Hami, Xinjiang Province), Tuguhun, defeated Gaochang and set up administrative government in Anxi as well as four towns such as Qiuci, Cuiye, Yutian and Sule. In 641, Emperor Taizong accepted the request of Songzanganbu, leader of Tubo to marry Princess Wencheng to him, which expanded the close relationship among different minorities.

At that time, the society was stable, and economy was recovered and developed rapidly, which was historically known as the period "Peace and Prosperity of Zhenguan". However, during the later years of Emperor Taizong, he was not able to accept criticisms and expostulations from others. And, due to years' wars against Korea and construction of Cuiwei Palace as well as Yuhua Palace, they exerted heavy taxes on the people so that complaints were heard everywhere. In 649, while looking for immortality, Emperor Taizong died from taking pills of immortality made of stones and metals, buried in Zhaoling.

The southern god, Dunhang, Dunhuang Yuli Grottoes

Embroidery, Tang (618-907 AD)

Gilded roller with design of swan and clouds, Tang (618-907 AD), unearthed Famen Temple, Fufeng, Shaanxi province

Silk shoes, Tang (618-907 AD), 29.7cm long, unearthed at Asitana Mausoleum, Tulufan, Xinjiang province

Gold bowl with design of mandarin ducks and lotus, Tang (618-907 AD), diameter of rim 13.7cm, unearthed at Hejiang village, Xi'an, Shaanxi province

Blue glazed plate with design of flowers and leaves, Tang (618-907 AD), unearthed from the underground palace of Famen Temple, Fufeng, Shaanxi province

Gold cup in octagonal shape with musicians, Tang (618-907 AD), unearthed at Hejiang village, Xi'an, Shaanxi province

Cup with design of running horse, Tang (618-907 AD), 18.5cm high, unearthed at Hejiang village, Xi'an, Shaanxi province

Openwork silver cage with flying geese design, Tang (618-907 AD), 17.8cm high

Donors, Dunhuang Yulin Grottoes

Silver lotus, Tang (618-907 AD), 39cm high, unearthed at Famen Temple, Fufeng, Shaanxi province

Enamelled guardian animal, Tang (618-907 AD), 44.3cm high

第六篇

雍容盛世

3. Empress Wu Zetian

Wu Zetian (624-705 AD)

"Zhao". Meanwhile, Wu Zetian changed Tang into Zhou, historically known as "Wuzhou". She became the only empress in Chinese history, whose rule lasted as long as fifty years.

In 684, Xu Jingye and Luo Binwang rose against Wu Zetian in Yangzhou in the name of supporting Li Xian. In 688, princes of Tang family also launched a revolt, but soon failed. In order to secure her power, Wu Zetian stroke harsh blows on the political enemies, put a premium on those who would tell on others, relied heavily on cruel punishment and murdered more than hundreds of Tang's relations, prime ministers, and numerous prefectural governors and officers.

In order to buy people's support and consolidate her rule, Wu Zetian tried her best to recruit talents and often urged officials to recommend talents. She set out a bronze box to encourage

Wu Zetian, a native of Wenshui, Bingzhou (today's Wenshui, Shanxi Province), was chosen by Emperor Taizong and went into the palace. After the death of Emperor Taizong, she went to a nunnery and became a nun. During the reign of Emperor Gaozong, she was recruited into the palace and became an imperial concubine. Later on, in order to become empress and prop up her own power, Wu Zetian even killed her infant daughter and shifted the responsibility to empress. In 655, Emperor Gaozong, reduced empress to a common person with the excuse that she had no son and entitled Wu Zetian empress.

Wu Zetian was a talented woman, who was knowledgeable about arts and history. Once she wrote *Twelve Pieces of Advice* to Emperor Gaozong, in which she suggested developing agriculture, reducing taxes, stopping wars and recruiting talented people. This book brought her great fame. Gradually, Wu Zetian took all the power in her hands and, together with Emperor Gaozong, enjoyed the title "Two Sages". Later, she poisoned her oldest son Li Hong, deposed the second son and made Li Xian prince. In 683, Emperor Gaozong died and succeeded by Emperor Zhongzong with Wu Zetian playing a great role in court affairs. The following year, Wu Zetian dethroned Emperor Zhongzong and set up the fourth son Li Dan as Emperor Ruizong. In 690, Wu Zetian herself ascended the throne, called herself Sheng Shen (a sage) and renamed herself

Longmen Grottoes, Luoyang, Henan province

Wu Zetian had hoped to pass her power to her nephew Wu Chengsi, but encountered rejection from various officials. In 698, she eventually gave up to Li Xian and made him prince again. In 705, while Wu Zetian was seriously ill, prime minister Zhang Jianzhi led all the officers and officials in the support of Emperor Zhongzong' restoration. Wu Zetian died in the same year at 83, buried together with Emperor Gaozong in Qianling.

Silver brazier with five legs, Tang (618-907 AD)

God, the peak period of Tang, north of the west niche in the 46th cave of Dunhuang Mogao Grottoes

officials and common people to submit remonstrance. Imperial examinations were constantly held to enable the common people to find way into the court.

Wu Zetian encouraged agriculture so that economy was constantly being developed and population was constantly increasing; she recovered the four important towns in Anxi, reestablished Anxi Official Government. Later on, she set up Beiting Official Government in Tingzhou (today's Jimusa'er, Xinjiang). But she appointed cruel officials, killed lots of innocent people, believed in Buddhism, went in for large-scale constructions and gave loose to her relations, which exerted unhealthy influence on politics and brought heavy burden on the people.

Qian Mausoleum, the joint tomb of Li Zhi (628-682 AD), Emperor Gao Zhong of Tang Dynasty and his Empress Wu Zetian (624-705 AD)

Buddha, the late of Tang, north of central Buddha altar in the 196th cave of Dunhuang Mogao Grottoes

第六篇

雍容盛世

Shaanxi History Museum

Painted pottery figure of a lady with her hair done in two coils

Tri-colored pottery figure of a lady at her toilet, Tang (618-907 AD)

Tri-colored pottery figure of a lady with her hands folded, Tang (618-907 AD)

Guardian animal, Tang (618-907 AD), 102.5cm high, unearthed at Luoyang, Henan province

Standing Buddha torso, Tang (618-907 AD), 112cm high, unearthed at Taigu, Shanxi province

Painted pottery figure of a hunter on horseback, Tang (618-907 AD), unearthed at Xi'an, Shaanxi province

Pottery figure of a dancing woman, Tang (618-907 AD), 46cm high

Pottery figure of a dancing man, Tang (618-907 AD), 46cm high

Pottery figure of a lady, Tang (618-907 AD), 50.5cm high

Pottery figure of an old man, Tang (618-907 AD), 47.4cm high

第六篇

雍容盛世

4. Emperor Xuanzong of the Tang
--Dissolute Son of Heaven

Emperor Xuanzong of Tang, Li Longji (685-762)

Emperor Zhongzong was still so weak and muddle-headed after reposition that Empress Wei and their daughter Princess Anle followed Wu Zetian's way to poison Zhong Zong. Later on, Li Longji, the third son of Li Dan launched the Imperial Attack against Empress Wei, Princess Anle as well as their followers and killed them all, which enabled Li Dan, Emperor Ruizong, to ascend the throne. In 712, Emperor Ruizong gave way to Li Longji, who was Emperor Xuanzong. In 713, Emperor Xuanzong changed the title of his reign into *Kaiyuan*.

In the very beginning, Emperor Xuanzong was bent on making the country prosperous and demonstrated great talent in doing so. He appointed Yao Chong and Song Jing as prime ministers and was able to accept criticism. Besides, he reduced taxes and loosened punishment. At that time, the country was rich and the population was growing year by year. As Du Fu wrote in his poems, "I remember those days of Kaiyuan quite well when Tang was in full bloom, every small county was full of tens of thousands of families. Grains were plentiful enough to flow and rice white enough to shine, both the public and private barns were abundant in grains", presented a portraiture of the prosperity of Kaiyuan.

However, since Kaiyuan Period, social crisis had been slowly growing. New landlords annexed lots of land so that many peasants were deprived of land and had to leave their home, running elsewhere. The registered permanent population was reducing year by year. In order to control and protect against the minorities on the borders, Emperor Xuanzong set up military towns to govern prefectures with provincial governors as chief officers. Besides administering military affairs, these

Singing and Dancing, the middle of Tang Dynasty, on the north wall of 112th cave of Dunhuang Mogao Grottoes

governors also took charge of civil administration and finance, which made them powerful.

In 723, Emperor Xuanzong changed the system of court forces into that of conscription and abolished the system of frontier garrison. Those recruited soldiers greatly increased the financial expenses and gradually became powerful, private forces of the provincial governors, being hard to control and get rid of. Emperor Xuanzong was fond of military attacks. He launched lots of attacks towards the borders but failed to defeat Qidan, Nanzhao and Dashi in Mid-Asia. Since Tianbao Period (742), Emperor Xuanzong gradually grew arrogant and took to a luxurious life. Therefore, he was rather slack in state affairs. Moreover, he believed in treacherous minister Li linfu, refused to listen to other's opinions and doted on Yang Yuhuan (an high-ranking imperial concubine), favored her brother Yang Guozhong, which eventually led to disasters. Thus, An Lushan, a provincial governor, took the advantage to bring his army in a revolt against Tang.

An Lushan, a native of Yingcheng, Liuzhou (today's Jiangzhou, Liaoning Province) was a Mongol. He was provincial governor of three towns-Pinglu (Today's Chaoyang, Liaoning Province), Fanyang (Today's Beijing), Hedong (today's Taiyuan) and owned a force of 150,000 soldiers. After a long preparation for insurgence, he rose in revolts in Fanyang in 755 in the name of killing Yang Guozhong. The prefectures and counties surrendered at the sight of his troops so that An Lushan went across the Yellow River and captured Luoyang as well as Tongguan. The next year An Lushan proclaimed himself emperor in Luoyang with the title of his reign "Yan".

Emperor Xuanzong fled westward in panic, with a number of officials and the Imperial Guards accompanied. When the royal party reached Maweipo west of modern Xingping County, Shaanxi Province, the soldiers in his retinue mutinied killing the Prime Minister Yang Guozhong and forcing the emperor to put Yang Yuhuan to death and abdicate his power. Then Prince Li Xiang moved northward to Lingwu and ascended the throne, becoming Emperor Suzong. After his ascension, he appointed Li Guangbi and Guo Ziyi as generals to suppress An Lushan's rebellion. Before long, the Tang troops seized Chang'an. In 762, a coup broke out in the court. Emperor Suzong was shocked to death with Emperor Daizong succeeding him. Around this time, faction came out of the rebel army. An Lushan was killed by his son An Qingxu, who was in turn killed by Shi Siming, who was later killed by his son Shi Chaoyi.

After the ascension, Emperor Daizong made his son Li Shi as marshal and recovered Luo Yang. In 763, Shi Chaoyi committed suicide when he was chased by the Tang troops. The Eight-year An Lushan-Shi Siming Rebellion resulted in grave losses of economy. Tang Dynasty had declined sharply ever since, closing the prosperous era of "Grandeur of Great Tang".

Painted wooden figure of god, Tang (618-907 AD), unearthed at the Asitana Mausoleum in Tulufan, Xinjiang

Zhang Guo visits Ming Huang, Yuan Dynasty, by Ren Renfa

Stone figure of Buddha, Tang (618-907 AD), 57cm high, unearthed at Taiyuan, Shanxi province

第六篇

雍容盛世

5. Chang'an -- Capital of the World

The national strength of Tang and prosperity of economy was unprecedented in Chinese history. The capital Chang'an was properly designed with magnificent palaces. The whole city covered 84 square kilometers, made up of the City of Palace, the City of Emperor and the Outer City. The City of Palace was an area full of palaces, while the City of Emperor was an administrative area, which was the core of Chang'an City. In the Outer City, there were 108 resident areas, made up of 11 streets running from the north to south, and 14 streets from east to west. The royal families and officials' residences were among them. There were also over 100 temples. The East City and West City were seated symmetrically to the southeast and southwest of the City of Emperor, the former of which mainly dealt with curiosities from everywhere, the latter was a trading ground for minorities and foreign merchants.

Chang'an was the biggest cosmopolis in the then world and a link between the western and eastern economy and culture. Chang'an lay in the east end of Silk Road, where Chinese silk and tea were constantly transported to areas in West Asia, mid-Asia and South Asia. Also, goods from the west swarmed into China. Starting from Chang'an or

Tri-colored pottery figure of musicians on camelback, 58.cm high, Tang (618-907 AD), unearthed at the tomb of Xianyu Tinghai

Tri-colored pottery figure of a man controlling horse, Tang (618-907 AD), 71cm high

Red brocade with Persian characters, Tang (618-907 AD)

Painted pottery figure of a standing woman with the costume of northern tribes, Tang (618-907 AD)

Luoyang, it was possible to get to the countries in the southeast including India by way of Guangzhou; and if they went eastward, they could get to Xinluo (Southeast of today's Korean Peninsula) and Japan; if they moved out of Yumen Pass, they could get to the countries in Mid-Asia, such as Eastern Romen, Persia and North India. There lived many foreign merchants, envoys, monks, scholars, and students from abroad and music officials in Chang'an, the number of which even exceeded 10,000 at one time.

Among the cultural communication with other countries, religion was the most active. Xuan Zang, a Tang monk (602-664) went southward to India by way of Yumen Pass and brought back more than 650 Buddhist classics between 627 and 645. Meanwhile, large numbers of Japanese monks also came to China to learn Buddhism. In 754, Jian Zhen, a Tang dignitary, went to Japan despite of all the difficulties and spread Buddhism there, becoming the founder of Japanese religion. Besides, Chinese architecture, sculpture and medicine were also spread to Japan. And western Zoroastrianism, Nestorianism, Manicheism were also brought to Chang'an as well as other places one by one.

As both Korea and Japan sent envoys and students to China, Chinese culture exerted great influence on these two countries. Pyongyang, capital of Korea, Kyoto and Nara of Japan were all designed and built following the style of Chang'an. When the envoys, students and scholastic monks returned to their countries, they took musical instruments, books, Buddhist classics and Buddhist scriptures and so on with them. Chinese literature, especially Chinese poems was also spread overseas. Poems of Bai Juyi, Yuan Zhen and Du Fu were very popular then. And, these countries' politics, laws, culture and arts were also influenced by Tang Dynasty. For example, both Chinese characters and calligraphy prevailed widely in their countries.

Among the flourishing music and dances, many were from various countries in the west and east. Huxuan, Huteng, Tuozhi Dances were all from the Western regions. In the fields of science and technology, Chinese and Indian learned from each other on calendar and math; *Dayan Calendar*, invented by Yi Hang, a Chinese monk was adopted by Japanese, *Linde Calendar* used in Emperor Gaozong's reign was employed by Koreans. Besides, Chinese mathematics and medicine also exerted fundamental influences on Japan and Korea.

Ruins of the ancient town of Jiaohe on the Silk Road, Xinjiang Uygur Autonomous Region

The Communication Lines between China and Other Nations in Tang Dynasty

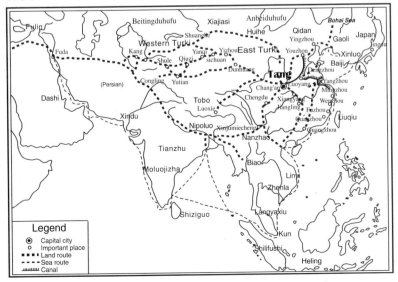

Eaves tile with design of a winged man, Tang (618-907 AD)

Parrot design silver pot with handle, Tang (618-907 AD)

Gilded silver Buddha, Tang (618-907 AD), 38.5cm high, unearthed at Famen Temple in Fufeng, Shaanxi province

Gilded silver plate with design of two foxes, Tang (618-907 AD), the longer diameter: 22.5cm, unearthed at Xi'an, Shaanxi province

第六篇

雍容盛世

6. Culture, Science and Technology

The Drunken Taibai (Li Bai), scroll, Qin Dynasty, by Su Liupeng (19th Century), ink and color on paper, 204.8cm, 93.9cm wide

Dayan Pagoda, Xi'an, Shaanxi province

Sedan Chair (partial), Tang, by Yan Liben (?-673 AD), silk scroll, 38.5cm high, 129.5cm long

From the late years of Southern and Northern Dynasties to Sui-Tang Dynasties, different sects appeared in Chinese Buddhism. Each sect not only had their own tenets but also their own temples. The main sects in Sui-Tang Dynasties included Tiantai Sect, Huayan Sect, Chan sect and Jingtu Sect. Taoism also prevailed in Tang. Many famous taoists were favored by emperors. And many litterateurs, including Li Bai and He Zhizhang also believed in Taoism. Meanwhile, some other litterateurs like Han Yu, Liu Yuxi and others attacked Buddhism and Taoism from different aspects.

Tang poems were a grand wonder in Chinese literature history, which made China of Tang a country of poems. During the early stages of Tang, though Parnassus hadn't got rid of the dispirited and raffish style of Southern Sui Dynasties, Wang Ji and the so-called Four Talents of Early Tang-Wang Bo, Yang Jong, Lu Zhaoling and Luo Binwang worked hard to make a rebound. In particular, Chen Zi'ang advocated that poems should be meaningful with simple and earthy language. A lot of distinguished poets came forth in the Golden Age of Tang. Among them, Meng Haoran and Wang Wei were expert in composing exquisite, and fresh poems with harmonious rhythm; Cen Shen, Wang Changling, Gao Shi's frontier poems contained both active ambitions and romantic ideals; Li Bai and Du Fu, known as "Poet-immortal" and "Sage Poet" respectively, pushed the poetic arts to the pinnacle and were outstanding representatives of Chinese classic poems. Li Bai's poems reflected the prosperity of the Golden Age of Tang with his ample imagination and touching vigor, while Du Fu's poems mirrored the Tang society more truthfully with religious narration and concise language, full of humaneness.

Since Mid-Tang, a new style of folk poems had been flourishing. Zhang Ji and Wang Jian were the initiators, while Yuan Zhen and Bai Juyi made the core, known as "Yuan and Bai". Bai Juyi's narrative poems were elegant and harmonious, among which *the Eternal Grief* and *A Singsong Girl* won universal praises. His poems were easy to understand so that they gained wide popularity. There were also other poets such as Liu Yuxi, Meng Jiao, Jia Dao, Li He, Li Shangying, Wen Tingjun, Du Mu and others. Famous poets of late Tang included Pi rixiu, Wei Zhuang and others, but their poetic style had declined.

In Tang Dynasty, Classical Prose Movement was initiated by Chen Zi'ang and led by Han Yu and Liu Zongyuan. They set up new style

Shang Yang Tai Tie, Tang, Li Bei (701-762 AD)
Cursive on paper, 28.5cm high, 38.1cm wide

of writing, which could rival the beauty of poems. As "Ancient Prose" was a kind of writing marked by substantiality and originality in content, the Movement of Ancient Prose advocated the recovery of these fine traditions and opposed the rhythmical prose style, marked by parallelism and ornateness. Insisting that prose should be substantial, Han Yu's prose was forceful, digressive and yet lucid, while Liu Zongyuan's works were colorful and plentiful, with his travelogues and essays standing out.

In Tang literature, legendaries were also contending in bizarreness and beauty. *Story of Pillows, Story of Liu Yi, Story of Li Wa,* and *Story of Huo Xiaoyu* were among the most mature and complete, exerting great influences on later literature.

During Tang Dynasty, under the influence of prevailing Buddhism, folk spoken literature adopted the form of sermons so that the lectures taking the common people as audience and the monks as audience appeared respectively. The original versions of these lectures were called "Changed Version", which had great influences on Tang legendary, later talking, singing, and colloquial novels.

Since Emperor Taizong, it had been a custom to compile history officially under the supervision of the prime ministers. The official history works included *History of Jin, History of Liang, History of Chen, History of Northern Qi, History of Zhou, History of Sui, History of Southern Dynasties, History of Northern Dynasties. Critique of Historical Works,* written by Liu Zhiji, was the first systematic theoretical historical work in China. In this book, Liu Zhiji pointed out that a historian should be well equipped with historical talent, knowledge and learning, which had great influences on the later generations. Prime Minister Li Jipu wrote *Pictorial Records of Prefectures and Counties in Yuanhe Period,* which was the oldest extant territorial map in China with great historical value.

Prosperity of economy and cultural communication among various nationalities and countries made the Tang arts colorful and magnificent. During Sui-Tang Period, Tartar Music was very popular. Among the ten kinds of music accepted by Emperor Taizong-Yan music, Qingshang Music, Western Liang Music, Indian Music, Korean Music, Qiuci Music, Sule Music, Kang State Music and Gaochang Music, except that Yan Music and Qingshang Music belonged to Han Music, the others were all Tartar Music. The famous dance music Nishang Yuyi Music was recreated by Emperor Xuanzong based on Music of Brahman contributed by Western Liang. The dances of Sui and Tang were made up of soft ones and strong ones. The former were characterized in the soft and elegant movements and postures of the dancers, while the latter presented the beauty of strength. The music of Sui and Tang Dynasties included "Daqu" (the longer music) and "Zaqu" (the shorter music). Puppet show was also very popular and called as "Kuleizi". Besides, acrobatics were quite developed and put on in court, cities as well as in the villages.

In early-Tang, many famous calligraphers, such as Yu Shinan, Ouyang Xun, Chu Suiliang, Xue Ji, admired the two Wangs (Xizhi, Xianzhi) of Sounthern Dynasties so much that they learned from their handwriting and made a lot of achievements respectively. In the Golden Age of Tang, Yan Zhenqing, Zhang Xu and Huai Su were representatives of new styles of handwriting. Zhang Xu and Huai Su were known for grass and highly cursive script respectively, while Yan Zhenqing and others won fame for their regular script, which demonstrated the great Tang's features from two aspects. Tang attached great importance to calligraphy, for example, calligraphy was one of the six subjects in the institutions of learning set up by the court; in the imperial examinations, calligraphy was one to be tested; when *Jinshi* (a successful candidate in the highest imperial examinations) was to be selected, calligraphy was a major part to be included.

Tang's paintings enjoyed a unique style. In early-Tang, Yan Lide and Yan Liben' portraits were most famous. For instance, the painting *Marching Chariot of Emperor Taizong* and others were vigorous and succinct in the style of drawing and presented the people in a vivid way. During the Golden Age of Tang, Wu Daozi was good at drawing Buddhist and Taoist images. With his portraits exceeding that of two Yan of early-Tang, Wu Daozi was respectfully called "Portrait Sage". Zhang Xuan and Zhou Fang were expert in portraying women. They portrayed

Buddhist scripture of wood block printing in Sanskrit, Tang Dynasty (618-907 AD), ink on paper, 30cm long, 31cm wide, unearthed at Xi'an, Shaanxi province

Fresco, Tang Dynasty (618-907 AD), unearthed from the tomb of Yongtai Princess in Xi'an, Shaanxi province

Tang women's daily life, such as spring-outing, snow-enjoying, tea-making and so on. Landscape paintings also attained new development in Sui-Tang period. The painting Sightseeing in Spring by Zhan Ziqian in Sui

The Poem of Zhang Haohao, partial, Tang Dynasty, Du Mu (803-852 AD), ink on paper, 28.1cm wide, 161cm long

第六篇

雍容盛世

Five Cattle, Tang Dynasty, Han Huang (723-787 AD), paper, 20.8cm wide, 139.8cm long

Dynasty depicted a warm spring full of sunshine, green trees and wavy water. Later on, Li Sixun of Tang Dynasty followed him to take landscape as his painting topic. Li Sixun's drawing was exquisite in lines, flowery in colors and true to nature, which created a touch of "riches", starting the kind of landscape painting full of gold and green colors.

Grotto arts were most representative of Tang's society. Tang's statuary was characterized in its distinctness, which made the statues more humanlike than those of Northern Wei Dynasty. The largest statue in Tang was the stone Buddha in Fengtian Temple cut during Wu Zetian's reign, which initiated a new artistic conception in Tang Buddhist arts. In Mogao Grottoes, works of Sui-Tang covered two-third. The Tang grottoes were magnificent in its scale. The four walls of Eastern Grotto were full of brilliant pictures of Buddhist and worldly stories. Among them, various social scenes were described, including hunting, competition in martial skills, plays, dances and music, dinners, farming, harvesting, animal-feeding, animal-butchering, medicine-practising, trading and wars. The providers in the fresco demonstrated Tang society more directly.

There were many masterpieces among Sui-Tang architecture, such as grand Chang'an City, Hanyuan Hall of Daming Palace, Nanchan Temple and Foguan Temple (both are wooden structure extant in Mount. Wutai). The ancient ingenious bridge built over the Xiaohe River, south of Zhao County, Hebei Province, was built more than 1300 years during the reign of Emperor Yang Di of Sui, by Li Chun, a craftsman. It displayed ingenuity in design and elegance in sculpts, carving both of its rails with breathing pictures of dragon and clouds, this bridge is really great treasure hard to come by.

Printing from engraved wood blocks appeard in the first years of the Tang Dynasty. Though this method was once employed by Xuan Zang of early-Tang to print Buddhist images, it was not widely applied. In late-Tang, this method had been popular in eastern and western Sichuan, south of the Huihe River, south of the Changjiang River, eastern Zhejiang, Jiangxi, Luoyang and other places. Chengdu was the then printing center. The earliest extant printed book is the Diamond Sutra of 868 by Wang Jie.

New advances were made in astronomy and calendar. In early-Tang, Wang Xiaotong wrote Collection of Mathematical Classics, in which he provided methods to work out cubic equation for the first time. Shuyan Calendar and Linde Calendar were used in Tang Dynasty successively and later Emperor Xuanzong ordered Monk Yi Xing to take charge of calendar improvement, who compiled Dayan Calendar, establishing patterns for later calendars. Yi Xing and Liang Lingzan together invented an Ecliptic Movement Instrument and discovered the movement of stars for the first time in the world, which was 1000 years earlier than Halley's discovery. Yi Xing also organized a survey of the length of meridian line. It was the world's first record to survey the length of meridian line. Besides, Yi Xing also made a waterborne armillary sphere, which employed water as power. It could display celestial phenomena such as the movement of the sun, the moon, the stars and so on, and was able to tell time, so that it was in fact the first astronomical clock in the world.

The medical achievement of Tang manifested in the development of pharmacological disciplines, such as internal medicine, external medicine, pediatrics, five sense organs (nose, ear, eye, mouth and tougue), diagnosis and massage, which had been in existence then. Famous medical works at that time included the Treatise on the Causes and Symptoms of Diseases by Cao Yuanfang and others in Sui Dynasty, the Precious Prescriptions and Supplement to "Precious Prescriptions" by Sun Simiao-"master of Pharmacology", Waitai Secrets by Wang Tao during Emperor Xuanzong's reign, and A New Compendium of Materia Medica by Su Jing on orders from Emperor Gaozong, some of which remain a must to be read among the list of traditional Chinese classics.

Autobiography in cursive, partial, Tang Dynasty (618-907 AD), Huai Su (737-799 AD)

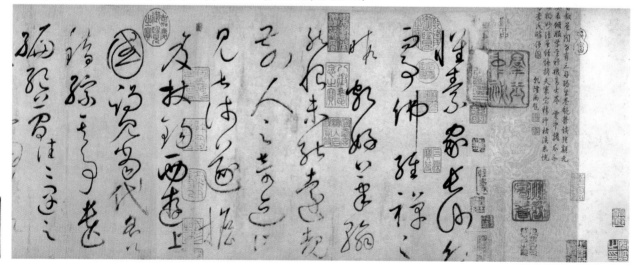

Liu Zongyuan (773-819 AD)

Du Fu (712-770 AD)

Thatched abode of Du Fu in
Chengdu, Sichuan province

Watching bird catch cicada

Wooden ox carriage, Tang Dynasty (618-907 AD)

第六篇

雍容盛世

7. Five Dynasties and Ten States

A shooter and horse, Five Dynasties, the late Tang Dynasty, Li Zanhua, silk scroll, 27.1cm wide, 49.5cm long

In 907, Zhu Wen, a senior general of Tang, dethroned Emperor Ai Di and ascended the throne himself, changing the title of his reign "Liang", historically known as Later Liang. From then to 979, when Emperor Taizong of Song annihilated Northern Han and got the whole country unified, fifteen reigns appeared in succession through the seventy years. Among them, five were on the Central Plains, including Later Liang, established by Zhu Wen, Later Tang by Li Cunxu, Later Jin by Shi Jingtang, Later Han by Liu Zhiyuan and Later Zhou by Guo Wei. Of the five dynasties, the longest one lasted not more than twenty years and the shortest one enjoyed a short history of three or four years. During the Five Dynasties, there were ten states in the south and north of China, including the state of Wu founded by Yang Xingmi, the state of Southern Tang by Li Sheng, the state of Wuyue by Qian Liu, the state of Chu by Ma Yin, the state of Min by Wang Shenzhi, the state of Southern Han by Liu Yin, the state of Former Shu by Wang Jian, the state of Later Shu by Meng Zhixiang, The state of Nanping by Gao Jixing and finally the state of Northern Han by Liu Min. These reigns had jurisdiction mainly over the southern

areas such as Jiangsu, Zhejiang, Fujian, Jiangxi, Hunan, Hubei, Guangdong, Guangxi and Sichuan, except that Northern Han set up its reign in the north with the capital in Taiyuan. Of these states, Wuyue had the longest history of over seventy years. This period thus was historically known as Five Dynasties and Ten States.

During the period of Five Dynasties and Ten States, as one dynasty followed another in quick succession and war raged on constantly, there were various disasters caused by the varied systems, numerous customs, uncountable injunctions, and extortionate taxes, not to mention the infertility of politics, economy and culture. Nevertheless, *Ci*, a poetic form, initiated in Tang, became flourishing, and calligraphy as well as painting enjoyed a certain status in history. The one worthy of being mentioned was Li Yu, the last Emperor of Nantang, who, though lost his kingdom and was kept prisoner, was excellent in poems, music, painting, and especially in *Ci*. His calligraphy was as vigorous as winter pines and frosted bamboo, known as "Golden Knife"; his *Ci*, offering a profound and moving description of deep love and sorrow of losing his homeland in the way of line drawing, enjoyed an important status in the history of *Ci's* development.

Another influential event happened to Emperor Shi Jingtang of Later Jin during this period. In 936, in order to gain the Qidan tribe's help in ascending the throne, Shi Jingtang, then

The Territory in Five Dynasties and Ten States

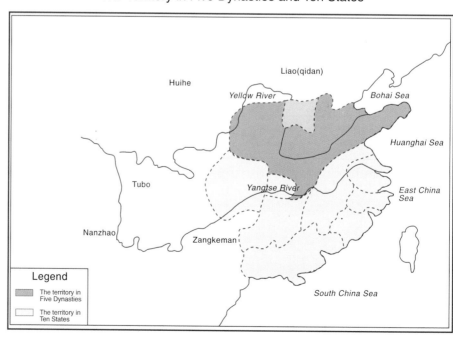

Relaxation, Five Dynasties, by Hu Gui, silk scroll, 33cm wide, 256cm long

A golden beast, Five Dynasties (907-960 AD), 8cm long

official governor of Hedong of Later Tang, didn't hesitate to honor emperor of Qidan as Father Emperor and called himself a "filial emperor", and promised to cede to the Qidan sixteen districts such as You, Yun and other districts. Besides, he provided Qidan with 300,000 *pi* (a Chinese measure of length) silk a tribute every year. However, his quislism couldn't meet Qidan rulers' greedy appetite. The Later Jin, established at the cost of deprivation of honor, was exterminated by the Qidan tribe ten years later. As a result, the Central Plains lost their northern barrier and the Qidan's cavalrymen were free to kill and rob the people southward, which brought severe disasters to the common people on the Central Plains. After that, the Song Dynasty had never succeeded in recovering the sixteen districts of Yan, Yue and others and a lot of trouble constantly arose in the north.

Buddha, Five Dynasties (907-960 AD), painting on silk, Dunhuang

第六篇

雍容盛世

Maids in imperial palace, painted relief, the third year of the late Liang Dynasty, (923 AD), 136cm long

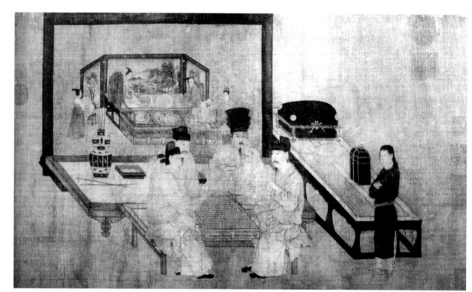

Playing chess, Five Dynasties, by Zhou Wenju, silk scroll, 403.cm wide, 70.5cm long

Han Xizai giving an evening banquet, Five Dynasty, by Gu Hongzhong, silk scroll, 28.7cm wide, 335.5cm long

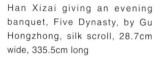

8. Incorporating things from diverse cultures --An open society

Owing to the unification from Sui through Tang Dynasties and the long-term merging of nationalities, the society boasted an unprecedented openness. The social customs took in many habits from neighboring nationalities and showed a "Hu" characteristic, thus became very charming and colorful.

In Sui and early Tang Dynasties, women's dress was greatly influenced by the clothes from the surrounding nationalities, especially from the Western regions. Women liked wearing men's clothing. The clothes usually worn by men since Northern Qi became very popular among women and this fashion started from the imperial palace. Women used to wear high hair buns, cone-shaped hats and long robes with turndown collar and narrow-sleeves. While riding horses or going out, they wore the hat with veil and drew a crescent-shaped beauty spot in the middle of the forehead. Since the middle Tang Dynasty, clothes were made larger and longer. Under the influence of Tufan, both of the hair-style and make-up changed. Women wore "Manhuanji" bun, the top of which looked like a wooden club, leaning to one side and decorated by hairpins. Some women even used several little wooden combs as adornments. They also applied red lip-cream and face powder. In the prime time of the Tang Dynasty, the shoes wore by the imperial maids were a kind of soft-sole embroidered boots, which were probably affected by the Western regions and Persia. After An Shi Zhi Luan, a new Hu clothing "Huihezhuang" came into fashion. From the fresco of Dunhuang, we can see noble women of Huihe nationality wear horn-shaped gold hat embellished with jewelry. This kind of clothing remained prevalent for a long time, until the Five Dynasties, imperial maids still wore them to ride with the emperor. In the trend of seeking unconventional and novel clothing, bizarre clothes often appeared in the late Tang Dynasty. The so-called "Tizhuang clothes" and "Leizhuang clothes" were fashions at that time.

In Chang'an and the east capital Luoyang, the culture acquired a foreign flavor. Envoys, merchants and pilgrims from mid-Asia, Japan, Korea and Tufan furthered people's understanding of the outside world. Things from afar, such as precious horses, jewelry, instruments and silk fabrics aroused boundless interests of the nobles. Foreign recreation, for example polo, became a favorite pastime of the wealthy. The trade caravans from mid-Asia were very much welcomed. Silverware were gradually attaining to perfection. Silver cups, plates, jars and other wares were in a Persian style. The new instruments and tunes coming from India, Iran and mid-Asia gave rise to great changes in the Chinese music. Though the habit of sitting on the ground or beds in Sui and Tang Dynasties still remained, people also accepted sitting on benches or chairs.

The food and drink of Sui, Tang and Five Dynasties were greatly affected by Hu nationalities. At that time, there were three Hu foods, namely Hu Cake, Biluo and sesame seed cake. One kind of Hu Cake is today's sesame seed cake. It was made from wheat powder, with two layers and covered by sesame seeds. Another was a cake like today's steamed bun; it came from the Western regions to Central Plains in Han Dynasty and became a common food in Tang Dynasty. There were many Hu cake shops in Chang'an. Biluo, the transliteration for Persian word "Pilan", was a kind of rice cooked with meat and dried fruits, like the rice eaten with hands in mid-Asia and Xinjiang nowadays. In Chang'an, Biluo with ginger was sold by Jin (500 grams) in some shops. People in Tang Dynasty were fond of drinking wine. There were many famous wines, such as the wine from Gangchang, Sanqin wine from Persia and Longgao wine. After the middle Tang Dynasty, wine from the Western regions became popular among the upper-class society. In Chang'an, people from the Western regions opened wine shops called "Hu Jia Jiu".

In Sui and Tang Dynasties, Buddhism became an inner component of Chinese people's life in the social atmosphere of opening to the world. The Buddhist stories were widely spread. In order to do missionary work, monks presented pictures and told Buddhist stories to illiterates. One of the most important festivals in China, the Ghost Festival on the 15th day of the 7th month of the Lunar Calendar, is derived from the story of Mu Lian saving his mother. According to the story, Mu Lian's mother was terribly tortured in the Hades. As a result, on the festival, Buddhists or pagans, learned monks or illiterates, all the people laid out the sacrifice for the hungry ghosts in the Hades.

Stone statue of Lao Jun, Kaiyuan and Tianbao Periods of Tang Dynasty (713-756 AD), 190cm high, in Chaoyuan Pavilion, Huaqing Palace of Tang Dynasty

Giant Stone Buddha in Leshan, Emei Mountain

Maids waving fans, Tang, by Zhou Fang, silk scroll, 33.7cm wide, 204.8cm long

第六篇

雍容盛世

God and Buddha, the peak period of Tang, south of the west niche of 194th cave in Dunhuang, Mogao Grottoes

Buddha, the peak period of Tang, north of the west niche of 45th cave in Dunhuang, Mogao Grottoes

Avalokitesvara and Bodhisattva, Tang (618-907 AD), Dunhuang, Mogao Grottoes

Princes in nirvana, the middle Tang Dynasty, north of 158th cave in Dunhuang, Mogao Grottoes

Musicians, the middle Tang Dynasty on the south wall of 159th cave in Dunhuang, Mogao Grottoes

Musicians, the middle Tang Dynasty on the south wall of 112nd cave in Dunhuang, Mogao Grottoes

Dancing and playing musical instruments, Tang Dynasty (618-907 AD), fresco in the tomb of Yongtai Princess

A Dancing Maid

第六篇

雍容盛世

Chapter 7

Competition and Unification

--The Song, the Liao, the Xia, the Jin, and the Yuan

On the Central Plains, historical institutions met once again the challenge from the north.

Land of China was just as a huge arena. Each rival of the Song regime was more valiant and powerful than the last. Without measures to cope with them, there would be no way but to step down from the stage of history. Under the Yuan regime, China's force reached its summit. A great empire was founded, under which the east and the west were linked together. And the Hans and barbarians merged into an organic whole. Not merely with armed forces did the young empire become powerful and prosperous. Such is an issue being worth thinking.

Huangshan Mountain, Anhui province

114

1. Founding of the Northern Song

Emperor Tai Zu of Song, Zhao Kuangyin (927-976AD)

Fresco, the second year of Yuanfu Period of Song Dynasty (1099), unearthed Baisha town, Yu County, Henan province

Fresco, the second year of Yuanfu Period of Song Dynasty (1099), unearthed Baisha town, Yu County, Henan province

Zhao Kuangyin, a native of Zhuojun (modern Zhuozhou, Hebei), had fought many battles for Chai Rong, Shi Zong of the Zhou Dynasty, and distinguished himself time and again on the battlefield, thus was promoted to the position *du dian jian* (a high official position in the Northern Song) in his Majesty's presence, commanding Zhou's imperial army that protected the capital city. In 959, Shi Zong died of illness and was succeeded by Gong Di, who was only seven then and was unable to administer the state affairs. In 960, Zhao Kuangyin led his troops northwards in the name of resisting the invading troops of Qidan tribe and Northern Han. After having marched to Chenqiao Post Station that was forty *li*, (a Chinese unit of length) northeast of Kaifeng, his troops staged a coup detat, known to historians as Chenqiao Mutiny. The supporters of Zhao Kuangyin draped him with the imperial yellow robe that had been prepared beforehand, escorted him to go back to Kaifeng and compelled Gong Di to abdicate. Zhao Kuangyin thereby ascended the throne, to be known later as Emperor Tai Zu of the Song. He titled his dynasty Song, historically known as the Northern Song, and the capital remained in Kaifeng.

The very next year after the Northern Song was established, Zhao Kuangyin plotted to deprive the generals, including Shi Shouxin, of their military powers. One night, he summoned Shi Shouxin, a veteran general in imperial army and others to wine and dine. When warmed with wine, he aired his private suffering of being the emperor and mildly enticed them to hand over their military power. Moreover, he persuaded them to accumulate more wealth and to purchase more real estate, more singing and dancing girls to spend their last years in peace. The following day, all the generals entreated to be dismissed from office one after another. This was the well-known highlight of Zhao Kuangyin, "to deprive the generals of their commands at a feast." Soon afterwards, he dismissed local officials who were in charge of military and administrative affairs of every feudatory in the same way. Thus both national and local military powers fell into the hands of Zhao Kuangyin

Emperors in Northern Song Dynasty

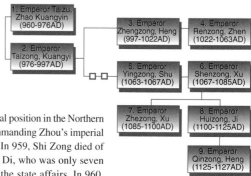

1. Emperor Taizu, Zhao Kuangyin (960-976AD)
2. Emperor Taizong, Kuangyi (976-997AD)
3. Emperor Zhengzong, Heng (997-1022AD)
4. Emperor Renzong, Zhen (1022-1063AD)
5. Emperor Yingzong, Shu (1063-1067AD)
6. Emperor Shenzong, Xu (1067-1085AD)
7. Emperor Zhezong, Xu (1085-1100AD)
8. Emperor Huizong, Ji (1100-1125AD)
9. Emperor Qinzong, Heng (1125-1127AD)

Fresco, the second year of Yuanfu Period of Song Dynasty (1099), unearthed Baisha town, Yu County, Henan province

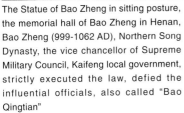

The Statue of Bao Zheng in sitting posture, the memorial hall of Bao Zheng in Henan, Bao Zheng (999-1062 AD), Northern Song Dynasty, the vice chancellor of Supreme Military Council, Kaifeng local government, strictly executed the law, defied the influential officials, also called "Bao Qingtian"

himself.

The civil service system of the northern Song followed that of Tang and the Five Dynasties. The political branch consisted of three key departments--the Secretariat, the Grand Council and the Chancery with the prime minister taking charge of national administrative affairs. There was the Supreme Military Council with its chancellor taking charge of military affairs. The chancellor of the treasury handled public finance. There was also a Censorate, with the duty of supervising all government officials. Local administrative divisions remained prefectures and counties. In the Northern Song Dynasty, the rulers

Shendao stone statues in the mausoleum of Song Dynasty, near the Xicun, Zhitian, Xiaoyi, Huiguo town in Gong county, Henan province

第七篇

竞争与统一

Armour of Song Dynasty

strengthened their control over prefectures (including government, military forces, and censorate). Civil officials were invested with the power of handling local affairs so that the power of military officers was weakened.In every prefecture a *Ton Pan* was established so that great events in both military affairs and civil administration could be instantly reported to the imperial government. Besides, special institutions were established in all of the prefectures so that the local finance and taxation could be controlled by the imperial government. Tax revenue of every prefecture, except that for prepaid expenses, should all be handed in to the central government. The best of local troops was incorporated into and absorbed by the Imperial Guards. By imperial edict, Garrison-relieving Law was passed, according to which, garrisons were

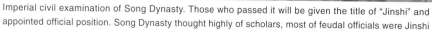

Imperial civil examination of Song Dynasty. Those who passed it will be given the title of "Jinshi" and appointed official position. Song Dynasty thought highly of scholars, most of feudal officials were Jinshi

Gilded silver mojie, Song (960-1279 AD)

Wooden statue of Avalokitesvara, Song (960-1279 AD), 127cm high

Celadon incense buner, the first year of Xianping, Northern Song Dynasty (998 AD)

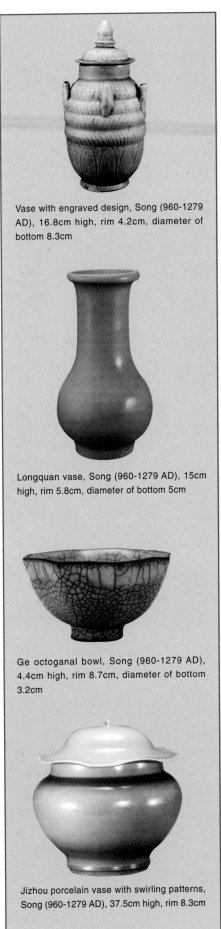

Vase with engraved design, Song (960-1279 AD), 16.8cm high, rim 4.2cm, diameter of bottom 8.3cm

Longquan vase, Song (960-1279 AD), 15cm high, rim 5.8cm, diameter of bottom 5cm

Ge octoganal bowl, Song (960-1279 AD), 4.4cm high, rim 8.7cm, diameter of bottom 3.2cm

Jizhou porcelain vase with swirling patterns, Song (960-1279 AD), 37.5cm high, rim 8.3cm

Longquan plum-blue glazed pot with lotus flower-shaped lid, Song (960-1279 AD)

divided into groups and guarded frontier towns in shift. Besides, commanders were transferred repeatedly so that they had no exclusive right on military forces. The death penalty had to be transferred to central government and be reexamined by the Board of Justice. All the power, including military, executive, financial and judicial powers, was centralized in the royal house and fell into the hands of the Emperor only. The feudal autocracy of the Northern Song was thereby increasingly strengthened.

Pearl statue of Ruiguang Temple, Northern Song (960-1279AD), 122.6cm high, at the southwestern of Suzhou

第七篇

竞争与统一

2. From the Qidans to the Liao

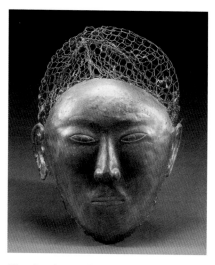

Silver head net and gold mask, Liao (916-1125 AD), 21.7cm high, unearthed from the tomb of princess of Chen State, in Zhelimumeng-naimanqi, Inner Mongolia

Gold mask, Liao (916-1125 AD), 20.5cm high, unearthed from the tomb of princess of Chen State, in Zhelimumengnaimanqi, Inner Mongolia

Silver boots with carved patterns, Liao (916-1125 AD), 20.5cm high, unearthed from the tomb of princess of Chen State, in Zhelimumeng-naimanqi, Inner Mongolia

Emperors in Liao Dynasty

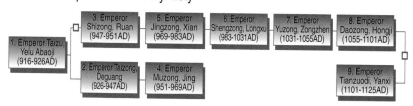

The Qidans, a nomadic tribe, inhabited for generations the valley of the Yellow River (modern Xar Moron River, Inner Mongolia) on the upper reaches of the Liaohe River. The Qidan people lived by fishing and hunting and also led a nomadic life. The Tang government once established Prefecture of Songmo and governors were appointed to administrate the area there. During the late-Tang period, the Qidans rose to become a powerful tribe, and its military commander *Yelu Abaoji* was later elected the Khan, a tribe leader. In 916, *Yelu Abaoji* claimed himself Emperor, to be known later as Emperor Tai Zu of the Liao, and titled his dynasty Qidan. On the bank of the Yellow River, the Qidans constructed a Western Tower City as its capital, which was called the official residence of the prefecture of Upper-jing Linhuang (now northeast of Bahrain Left Banner, Inner Mongolia) by later generations. The Qidans also created its own written language and legislation. In his later years, *Yelu Abaoji* brought an end to Bohai State, which was set up by Mohe people in the northeast China. During the reign of Tai Zong, *Yelu Deguang* (927-947), the Qidans got from the Later Jin sixteen prefectures in the northern part of modern Hebei and Shanxi provinces. The Qidans occupied a large territory, extending as far east as sea, as far west as Jin Mountains (modern the Altay Mountains), as far north as the Luju River (modern Kerulen River, Inner Mongolia) and as far south as Baigou River (to the north of modern Xiongxian County, Hebei). They even once took Kaifeng, capital of Later Jin. In 947, *Yelu Deguang* changed the title of his nation to Great Liao and the Liao government set up five jings (five administrative divisions) in its area of jurisdiction: namely, Prefecture of Upper-jing Linhuang, Prefecture of South-jing Xijin (southwest of present-day Beijing), Prefecture of Mid-jing Dading (southwest of Lingcheng County, Inner Mongolia), Prefecture of West-jing Datong (in present-day Shanxi province) and Prefecture of East-jing Liaoyang (in present-day Liaoling province.)

In Great Liao were people of different ethnic groups. The Han people and the people from former Bohai State lived by farming, while the Qidan people led a nomadic life and engaged in fishing and hunting. Therefore, the Liao adopted a dual system: the southern system, with its government office built to the south of Imperial Tent, for the Han Chinese and the people of former Bohai State; the northern system for the Qidans and ethnic groups other than the Han Chinese. The former employed a Han Chinese system and the latter employed a 'national system'. In addition to the above-mentioned prefectures and counties, local administrative divisions called the prefectures of Touxiajun were established to rule the population that were captured by and bestowed on the scions of the imperial family and tribal chiefs who had performed military exploits. Officials in these administrative divisions were appointed by the suzerains. Agricultural and commercial taxes were turned over to the suzerains, and liquor taxes to the emperor. Later these divisions were gradually controlled by the imperial government.

Silver hat with carved patterns, Liao (916-1125 AD), 20.5cm high, unearthed from the tomb of princess of Chen State, in Zhelimu-mengnaimanqi, Inner Mongolia

Infusing tea, fresco, Liao (916-1125 AD), unearthed at Xuanhua, Hebei province

The Sketch-map of Liao Dynasty

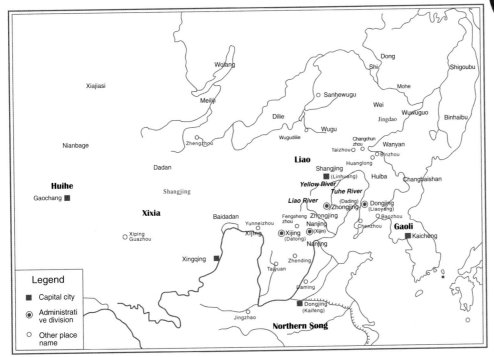

Tri-colored pot, Liao (916-1125 AD)

As it rose and expanded southwards, the Liao destroyed the economics and culture of the Central Plains and posed a great threat to the Northern Song. During the early years of the Northern Song, as Zhao Kuangyin devoted himself to the quelling of separatist rules within the state, the Northern Song was defensive in its relation with the Liao. Later, Zhao Guangyi, Emperor Tai Zong of the Song, wanted to seize the opportunity to recover the sixteen prefectures in the northern sections of modern Hebei and Shanxi Provinces

第七篇

竞争与统一

Fresco, Liao (916-1125 AD), unearthed at Chifeng, Inner Mongolia

after he had conquered the Northern Han. But he failed in his attempt as his army suffered disastrous defeats in their two northern expeditions. From then on, the Song was incapable of marching northward. In the autumn of 1004, Shen Zong of the Liao and Empress Dowager Chengtian personally directed a battle against the Song, with a troop that was claimed to be 200,000. Time and again, the situation in the northern prefectures and counties of Northern Song became critical. Shock reigned both at court and among the populace. Prime Minister Kou Zhun and

Gold pot with monkey design, Liao (916-1125 AD)

Fresco, Reading sutra, Liao (916-1125 AD), unearthed at Chifeng, Inner Mongolia

Miao Fa Lian Hua Sutra, the beginning of the forth chapter, Liao, 25cm high

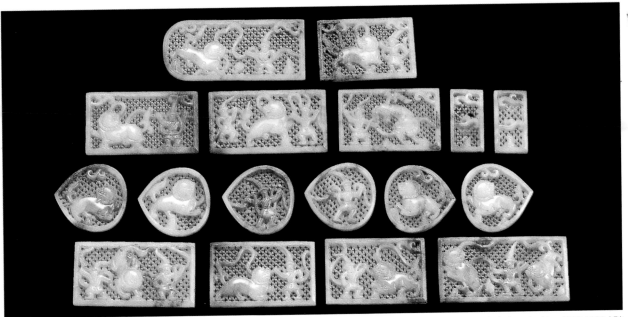

others were firm in their anti-Liao stand. Thus, Emperor Zhen Zong, Zhao Heng, pressed by Kou Zhun, directed the battle himself in November and crossed the Yellow River to Tanzhou (to the south of modern Puyang County, Henan), which greatly encouraged the Song force. Yet the Liao troops were severely discouraged for their chief commander was shot dead at the gate of Chanzhou. Thereby, the Liao had no choice but to conclude a peace pact with the Song and both sides ended their hostilities. The pact, known later in history as Treaty of Chan Yuan, stipulated that the Northern Song should deliver an annual amount of 100,000 taels of silver and 200,000 bolts of silk to Liao; both defend their own national borders and should not intrude on each other; the two states pledged to be fraternal nations. In 1042, Emperor Ren Zong of the Song was compelled to add another 100,000 taels of silver and an equal number of bolts of silk and a cession of 700 square *li*. During the next hundred of years, the Liao and the Song took charge of the northern region and the southern region respectively and no wars broke out again on their borders.

Fresco, Playing musical instruments, Liao (916-1125 AD), unearthed at Xuanhua, Hebei province

123

第七篇

竞争与统一

3. Dangxiang Qiang and the Western Xia

Emperors in Western Xia Dynasty

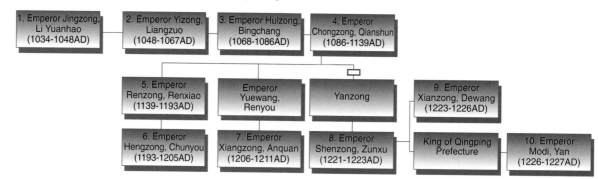

1. Emperor Jingzong, Li Yuanhao (1034-1048AD)	2. Emperor Yizong, Liangzuo (1048-1067AD)	3. Emperor Huizong, Bingchang (1068-1086AD)	4. Emperor Chongzong, Qianshun (1086-1139AD)

5. Emperor Renzong, Renxiao (1139-1193AD)	Emperor Yuewang, Renyou	Yanzong	9. Emperor Xianzong, Dewang (1223-1226AD)
6. Emperor Hengzong, Chunyou (1193-1205AD)	7. Emperor Xiangzong, Anquan (1206-1211AD)	8. Emperor Shenzong, Zunxu (1221-1223AD)	King of Qingping Prefecture / 10. Emperor Modi, Yan (1226-1227AD)

Bronze official seal in Western Xia script

Painted statue of arhat, Western Xia (1038-1227 AD), 50cm high, unearthed in Ningxia

Just when the Liao and the Northern Song confronted each other with neither side yielding, another regime dominated by an ethnic minority rose in the northwest. It was Xi Xia (also West Xia) established by a Tibetan tribe named Dangxiang, which formerly was a branch of Qiang and thus was called Dangxiang Qiang in *Old History of Tang*. During the Northern Zhou and the Sui period, the Dangxiangs roamed in the northwest. In the reign of Emperor Zhen Guan of the Tang, a Dangxiang chief named Tuoba Chici was conferred Military Governor of Xirong prefecture and was awarded the surname of the Chinese royal house, Li. In the end of the Tang Dynasty, the tribe chief Tuoba Sigong became Governor of Xiazhou (to the north of modern Shanxi and southwest of Inner Mongolia). After the Northern Song was established, Dangxiang sent emissaries and presented gifts to the Song. The year of 979 saw the Dangxiang assist the Song in conquering the Northern Han. In 982, Li Jipeng, a Dangxiang chief, had his kingdom under the Song's jurisdiction in addition to paying respects to Emperor of the Song and presenting him with land; while his younger brother Li Jiqian, unwilling to acknowledge allegiance to the Song, staged a rebellion. Relying on the Qidans, he was conferred the title of "King of the Xia" and made repeated intrusions on the Northern Song. In 1003, Li Jiqian was shot dead by a flying arrow when he marched westward to attack the Tufan. Three years later, Li Deming, son of Li Jiqian, pledged allegiance to the Song and was conferred the title of " King of Xi Ping". In return, the Dangxiang received from the Song an annual gift of tens of thousands of taels of silver, an equal number of bolts of silk, more than tens of thousands of strings of cash and 20,000 *jin* of tea. In addition, Song opened markets on its border for trade. Ever since then, the Song and the

The Sketch-map of Western Xia Dynasty

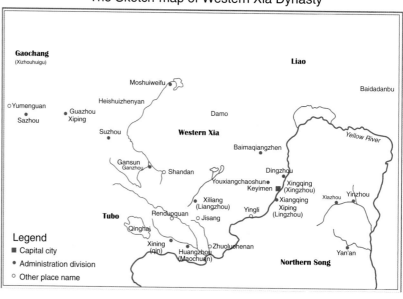

A bird's eye view of the imperial mausoleum of Western Xia, west of Yinchuan, Ningxia

Color glazed owl's tail, Western Xia (1038-1227 AD), 152cm high, unearthed at imperial mausoleum of the Western Xia, Yinchuan, Ningxia

The scenery of desert in Ningxia

Dangxiang got along in peace for nearly thirty years.

In the winter of 1031, Li Deming died and his son Yuanhao became the chief. He was adept in *kung fu* skills and knew Chinese well. Moreover, being an ambitious person, he had a good background of Buddhism, drawing. creation and military works. Once he became the ruler, Yuanhao promulgated laws and decrees, enforced strict discipline in the army and worked diligently on state affairs. He modeled his administrative organs after those of the Song, setting up four central agencies: Secretariat, Military Council, Treasury and Censorate. The local administrative divisions were prefectures and counties. Besides, he ordered his people to create their own written language by patterning on the Han Chinese and translate many ancient books and records written in Chinese. In 1038, Li Yuanhao assumed the imperial title and called his new regime *Da Xia* or Great Xia, known to historians as Xi Xia or West Xia. The capital was Xingqing (Yinchuan, capital city of modern Ningxia Autonomous Region).His Kingdom, more than ten thousand of square *li*, extended as far east as the Yellow River, as far west as Yumen (in modern Gansu), as far south as Xiaoguan (to the southeast of modern Guyuan County, Gansu), and as far north as the Gobi Desert.

After Xi Xia was established, it attacked the Song repeatedly and defeated the Song army time and again. In 1041, a Song force of more than ten thousand was all but close to total destruction in a battle fought at Liupan Mountain in Haoshuichuan (modern Tianshui River, originated from Ningxia), and more than half of the generals fell at the front.Both the court and the populace were greatly shocked. Therefore, the Northern Song took Fan Zhongyan's proposal, who was then a magistrate of Yanzhou County (989-1052), to defend tenaciously and develop production on the border in addition to drilling the commanders and fighters. Despite the military victories, the Xia had a heavy economic burden resulting from constant fighting. Both the annual gift from the Song and the bilateral trade came to a stop; shortages of grain and daily necessities were badly felt, complaints were heard everywhere. So Xi Xia was willing to negotiate peace. In 1044, the Song and Xia concluded a peace pact under which Yuanhao, removing his imperial title, was conferred the title of "King of the Xia". In return, the Xia received from the Song an annual gift of 70,000 taels of silver, 150,000 bolts of silk and 30, 000 *jin* of tea. Markets were reopened for trade and exchange. Thus the Northern Song, at the cost of huge wealth acquired temporary tranquility on its border. In 1066, Xi Xia attacked once again Qinfeng (now Tianshui, Gansu) and Jingyuan (now Pinglian, Gansu), breaking its amiable relation with the Song. From then on, the Song and the Xia were sometimes in peace, sometimes in wars. The northwest borders of Northern Song thereby were never free from disturbance.

Pottery Buddhist head (1038-1227 AD), unearthed in Ningxia

Stone statue, Western Xia (1038-1227 AD), 64cm high, unearthed from the imperial mausoleum of Western Xia, Yinchuan, Ningxia

Long scroll of Western Xia script, Western Xia (1038-1227 AD)

第七篇

竞争与统一

4. Reforms Initiated by Wang Anshi of the Song Dynasty

Emperor Ren Zong, Zhao Zhen (1010-1063 AD)

Over- concentration of power in the early years of the Song Dynasty had temporarily stabilized the Song regime but eventually had left behind countless hidden dangers. Such problems as redundant personnel and huge expenditure prevented the state power from proper running. By recruiting large numbers of soldiers, government made its military force increasingly unwieldy. In 967, there were 370,000 serving in the army, and the number went so far as to more than 1,250,000 in 1048. The military expenditure alone took up five sixths of the total budget. In order to curb the power of officers at various levels, the Northern Song separated officials from posts and errands, only "the one on errands" was on real mission. Thus the bureaucracy became more and more inflated and increased national expenses. In addition, the treasury became virtually empty largely because of the annual tribute presented to the Liao and the Xia, and the ever-increasing expenditures at the court. Ever since the early years of the Northern Song, large-scale annexation of land and excessive taxation made lots of peasants go bankrupt and be forced to leave their native land, and some others even made reckless moves in desperation. In the spring of 993, Wang Xiaobo and Li Shun staged an uprising in Qingchen (to the south of modern Dujiangyan City, Sichuan), raising the slogan of "We detest unequal distribution of wealth between the rich and the poor. Now we equalize it for you." After taking Chengdu and seizing control of the greater part of Sichuan, they founded a regime named the "Great Shu". From 1042 to 1048, peasants' uprisings erupted time and again.

From the middle era of the Northern Song Dynasty, the voice of literati demanding reform was constantly heard under the situation that declination and weakness came about over the years. In the third year (1043) of the reign of Qingli, Emperor Ren Zong of the Song, a magistrate named Fan Zhongyan, 'taking the destiny of his country as his own', devised ten proposals of reforms, which were adopted by Ren Zong and thus became the so-called "New Laws in the Reign of QingLi". Fan Zhongyan, however, soon being viciously slandered and banished, settled in remote and out-of-the way area. The failure of "New Laws" made social crisis from bad to worse. When Zhao Xu, Emperor Shen Zong, ascended the throne (1067), the fundamental way out for the Song was to reform. Hence, Shen Zong determined to carry out a reform, appointed Wang Anshi to initiate political reforms.

Wang Anshi (1021-1086), a man of Linchuan (modern Fuzhou, Jiangxi), known to later generations as Mr. Linchuan or Master Wangjing, drew a historical lesson from the failure of "New laws" and initiated reforms in 1069 under the auspices of Emperor Shen Zong. His reforms aimed at "managing money matters, training and consolidating the army, so as to make his country rich and build up its military might." A series of new laws were promulgated in succession, including Law of Irrigation and Water Conservancy, Law of Green Sprouts (namely, the government lent money or seeds to the peasants in the springtime), Law of *Baojia* (a Chinese village militia system), Law of *Mianyi* (namely, the peasants could exempt from serving in the army so long as they paid a certain amount of money and the officials must pay quitrent as well), Law of *Shiyi* (namely, the government bought those unmarketable goods and sold them when the people needed them at appropriate prices), Law of *Fangtian Junshui* (namely, the government levied

Wang Anshi (1021-1086 AD)

Emperor Shen Zong, Zhao Xu (1048-1085 AD)

Zong died of illness and was succeeded by the ten-year-old Zhe Zong named Zhao Xu. As then Sima Guang presided over the state affairs, the "New Laws" which had been carried out for more than ten years and which were proved to be very effective were abolished one after another. After Zhe Zong assumed the reins of government upon coming of age, the reformers won the upper hand for a time. However, they devoted most of their energies to retaliation and didn't think highly of the implementation of the "New Laws". As a result, many of the "New Laws" deteriorated and became pretexts for much crueler exploitation. After the death of Zhe Zong, Hui Zong (1082-1135) named Zhao Ji ascended the throne (1100). He went all out to rob and exploit the people, which aroused peasants uprisings. In 1120, Fang La staged an uprising in Muxi (modern Chun'an County, Zhejiang). He and his men rallied to pledge resolution to revolt against the government. Another peasant rebellion led by Song Jiang in the north swept across Shandong Province and He bei Province, thus shaking the foundation of the Northern Song.

Brick with Maidservants Design, Northern Song (960-1127 AD), side length 31.5cm

Gilded bronze flying dragon, Northern Song (960-1127 AD), 11.5cm high

graded taxes based on land survey), Law of *Jiangbing* (namely, more than 100 generals were dispatched everywhere within the country in charge of the training of army), Law of *Baoma* (namely, people were allowed to raise official horses with their taxes reduced). In addition, an ordnance office was set up and reforms of imperial civil examination system and that of the school system were also carried out.

The "New Laws", rich in content, touched some deep-seated social problems and thus were opposed by all sides. Not only the conservatives, including Sima Guang (1019-1086) and some others but once the firm reformers, such as Ouyang Xiu (1007-1072) and other persons, opposed to the "New Laws". In 1074 and 1076, Wang Anshi was dismissed twice from the post of Prime Minister, and thus became isolated from the central government. In 1085, Shen

You Guo Si Temple, Northern Song (1049 AD), octagonal, 13 floors, 54.6cm high, northeast of Kaifeng, Henan province

第七篇

竞争与统一

5. Rise of the Jin

Emperors in Jin Dynasty

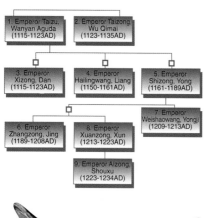

The Situation of Mongolia, Xia, Jin and Southern Song

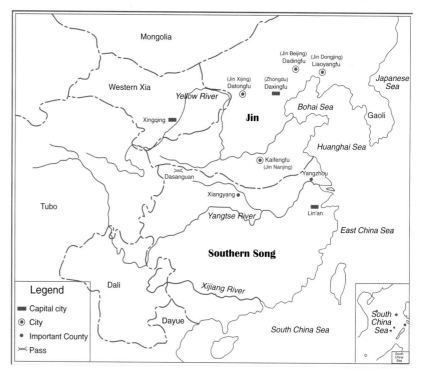

Pillow in shape of child holding lotus leaf, Ding ware, Jin (1115-1234 AD)

Seated bronze dragon, Jin (1115-1234 AD)

Just when the Northern Song dealt with its peasant army, the State Jin, established by the Nuzhens (the Manchu), rose rapidly. The ethnic group of Nuzhen was an old one, and its activities centered in the northeast regions of China. In ancient codes and records of the pre-Qin period, the relationships between their ancestors and the western Zhou Dynasty had been taken down and then the Nuzhen was called *"the sushen"* and the Tang *"the Mohe"*. During the Five Dynasties, the Mohe, a tribe then living in Heilongjiang River valley, changed its name to Nuzhen and were subjected to the rule of the Liao. Beginning with the early part of the eleventh century, the Wanyan tribe of the Nuzhen, rose speedily and thus became the core of all the tribes of the Nuzhen Union. In 1113, Aguda, from the Wanyan tribe, became the leader of the Nuzhen Union. In 1114, he brought his soldiers into a fight against the Liao and the Nuzhen forces grew quickly. In January 1115, Aguda assumed the imperial title, known later to historians as Tai Zu of the Jin, and titled his dynasty Jin. The capital was Huilingfu (to the south of modern Acheng County, Heilongjiang Province).

Aguda introduced *Meng'an-Mouke* system in the Jin, an administrative system organized on the basis of households, with each *Mouke* made up of 300 households and each *Meng'an* of ten *Moukes*. All the *Meng'ans* and *Moukes* went hunting in the peacetime and joined the services in wartime. He merged administration, military training and production into a single whole, which became a unique political system of the *Nuzhens*. In the same year, the Jin quickly took Huanglongfu (modern Nong'an County, Jilin),a place of strategic importance to Liao. The successive falls of the five *Jings* of the Liao indicated that the fate of defeat was as good as sealed. In 1125, the Jin captured Emperor Tian Zuo of the Liao when he tried to flee westward to Xi Xia. With his capture the Liao regime came to an end. While *Yelu Dashi*, a royal descendant of the Liao, led his men to march westward. In 1131, he declared himself emperor and reestablished the Liao (also known as Hala Qidan), historically known as West Liao.

During the time when the Jin marched southward to attack the Liao, the Song government once

A peasant woman, stone engraving, Dazu, Sichuan province

sent an emissary on a northward sea voyage to conclude an alliance with the Jin for a joint attack against the Liao. According to their agreement, the Jin forces would take Zhongjing (Mid-jing) and the Song troops would try to conquer Yanjing. Moreover, the Song would retrieve the prefectures in the northern area of modern Hebei and Shanxi and the Jin would receive from the Song an annual gift of a large amount of silver and cash which was once given to the Liao. This agreement between the Song and the Jin was known as "Treaty at Sea". Nevertheless, the Song troops proved incompetent for fighting. In 1125, the Jin attacked the Song on two southward fronts by imperial edict of Tai Zong of the Jin. The forces on the eastern route advanced straight to Kaifeng. At the beginning of 1126, Hui Zong of the Song named Zhao Ji, abdicated in favor of Zhao Heng,the Crown Prince, who was known as Emperor Qin Zong.

In 1126, the Jin forces crossed the Yellow River and pressed on towards Kaifeng, Song's capital. While Emperor Hui Zong fled in panic, Qin Zong appointed Li Gang (1083-1140) to the position of Right Prime Minister of the Chancery, who then stayed behind in Dong-jing (East-jing) to take care of things. Under his leading, the Song troops held fast to Kaifeng and armies coming to the rescue of the throne hurried in succession to the capital city from all parts of the country. Nevertheless, Qin Zong was busy with making peace with the Jin. He ceded territory and paid indemnities and granted hostages to beg the Jin to withdraw. In addition, he removed Li Gang from his position to please the Jin. As a result, headed by a student at the Imperial Academy named Chen Dong, soldiers and civilians, gathered in tens of thousands to protest against the capitulation of Emperor Qin Zong, who then yielded to the popular pressure by reinstating Li Gang. Seeing the Song forces intensify preparations for war, the Jin troops withdrew to the north.

In September of 1126, the Jin tore up the peace treaty and marched southward on two fronts. In December, the Jin captured Kaifeng and Emperor Qin Zong went twice to the Jin barracks to surrender himself to the Jin. As soon as the Jin forces entered, the thriving capital city had an unprecedented catastrophe. In May, 1127, more then two thousand people, including Emperor Hui Zong and Qin Zong, their wives and concubines, other members of the royal family and court ministers, were taken captive and carried off northward on two fronts to the Jin. Besides, men and valuables such as court dresses and carriages, musical instruments, sacrificial vessels, books,craftsmen, prostitutes and a large amount of treasures were captured. Thus the Northern Song was exterminated.

Because less than two years after Qin Zong declared himself Emperor he was carried off by the Jin and the title of his reign was Jingkang, this humiliation was known to historians as "Catastrophe of Jingkang".

Emperor Hui Zong, Zhao Ji (1082-1135 AD)

Bricks with Musician Design, Jin Dynasty (1115-1234 AD), square ones: 25.2-27.3cm long, 25.5cm wide, rectangular ones: 37.5-38.5cm long, 20cm wide

第七篇

竞争与统一

6. The Southern Song: Being Contented to Retain Control Over Part of the Country

Emperors in Southern Song Dynasty

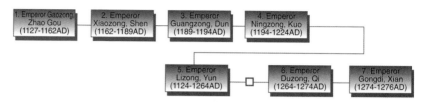

Emperor Gao Zong, Zhao Gou (1107-1187 AD)

In June,1127, one month after the downfall of the Northern Song, Prince of Kang named Zhao Gou, the ninth son of Hui Zong, was supported by former ministers of the Northern Song and thus was designated as emperor in Nanjing (modern Shangqiu County, Henan). Zhao Gou, also referred to as Emperor Gao Zong of the Song, reestablished the Song Dynasty,known to historians as the Southern Song, and changed the title of his reign to Jianyan.

Early during his reign, Emperor Gao Zong had no option but to reinstate Li Gang, Zong Ze (1059-1128) and other generals of the war faction. Nevertheless, power of the peace faction was strengthened day by day. The representatives of the peace faction opposed to return to Kaifeng and took a hostile attitude towards the fighting force of the populace against the Jin. Gao Zong thereby decided to abandon the Yellow River valley and fled first to Yangzhou (in modern Jiangsu), then Hangzhou (in modern Zhejiang) and then Wenzhou (in modern Zhejiang)under the pressure of the Jin forces. Not until the Jin forces were satisfied with the war booty they had required and withdrew to the north did Gao Zong come back to Hangzhou where he established the capital. Then Hangzhou was renamed Lin'an.

The Jin forces invaded the Central Plains, burning, killing and looting,and thus were resisted by righteous armies from all parts of the country and generals of the war faction, such as Li Gang, Han Shizhong and so forth. These generals organized soldiers and civilians to rise to resist, among whom General Yue Fei was an especially outstanding one.

Yue Fei (1103-1142), a native of Tangyin (in modern Henan), Xiangzhou County, joined the army at the age of thirty. Being strict in displine, valiant and skillful in battle, General Yue's Army, troops led by General Yue Fei, became so formidable that there was a saying among the Jin forces that "It is easier to move a mountain than to defeat General Yue's Army ". In 1134, Yue Fei led his force north and recovered Xiangyang and five other prefectures. Then he and his men marched into Xiangyang and approached the Yellow River. In 1140, Yue Fei recovered Caizhou, Zhengzhou and Luoyang and then won a decisive battle at Yancheng. While Yue Fei and other anti-Jin officers and men fought a bloody war, Gao Zong of the Song and Qin Hui ordered Yue Fei and his troops to withdraw from the front. In April, 1141,they relieved Yue Fei and Han Shizhong of their military power. On New year's Eve of 1141, Yue Fei was put to death on trumped-up charges.

By the end of 1141, the Southern Song and the Jin concluded a humiliating peace pact under which the Song, pledging allegiance to the Jin, declared itself a vassal state and Prince of Kang of the Song was conferred the title emperor by the Jin. Besides, the Song ceded large territories to the Jin, extending as far west as Dasanguan (present Dasanling, to the southwest of modern Baoji, Shaanxi), and as far east as the northern region of the middle stream of the Huaishui River. In addition, Song paid an annual tribute

The Territory of Southern Song Dynasty

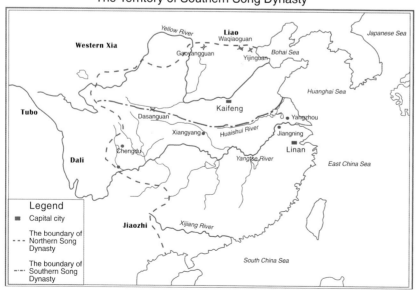

Legend
■ Capital city
- - - The boundary of Northern Song Dynasty
-·-·- The boundary of Southern Song Dynasty

of 250,000 taels of silver and 250,000 bolts of silk to the Jin. As it was concluded during the reign of Emperor Shaoxing, known as Gao Zong of the Song, historians named the pact as "Shaoxing Peace Treaty". From then on, China took the form of a long-term confrontation between the north and the south. Thereupon the royal court of the Southern Song, being contented to retain control over the southern part the country, could lead a depraved and

Memorial hall of Yue Wang Temple in Hangzhou, Zhejiang province

The ancient city of Lijiang, Yunnan province

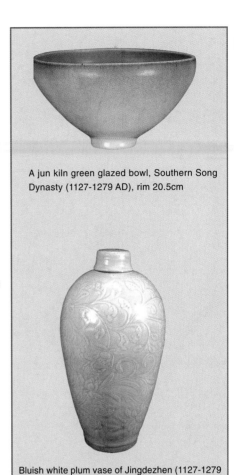
A jun kiln green glazed bowl, Southern Song Dynasty (1127-1279 AD), rim 20.5cm

Bluish white plum vase of Jingdezhen (1127-1279 AD)

befuddled life on the West Lake.

In 1162, Xiao Zong ascended the throne. He restored all the honors due to Yue Fei posthumously and put Zhang Jun, a general of war faction, in command to prepare for a northern expedition. For some time, both the government and the people took on an entirely new look.However, the Super - Emperor Gao Zong and members of the peace faction placed obstacles in the way and thus leading to the defeat of the northern expedition. In the second year of Longxing's reign (1164), Xiao Zong, submitting to the peace faction, concluded "Longxing Peace Treaty" with the Jin, under which emperor of the Song had to call emperor of the Jin his uncle for generations and the Song had to pay an annual cash instead of an annual tribute to the Jin. Besides promising to pay 200,000 taels of silver and 200,000 bolts of silk every year, the Song ceded Shang (modern Shangxian County, Shaanxi), Qin (modern Tianshui,Gansu)and other four prefectures to the Jin. Hereafter the Southern Song saw the reigns of four emperors, namely, Guang Zong, Ning Zong, Li Zong and Du Zong. All of them were fatuous and incompetent. Besides, influential senior court officials, such as Han Tuozhou, Shi Miyuan and Jia Sidao monopolized power one after another and thus inner struggles never came to stop.

After the conclusion of Shaoxing Peace Treaty, the Jin greatly reduced its foreign attacks. When he was on the throne, Xi Zong (1119-1149) carried out a series of reforms, such as establishing an administrative structure by following that of the Song and Liao and selecting officials through imperial examinations. In 1153, the Jin moved its capital to Yanjing (now Beijing), which was renamed Zhongdu, and further improved all the rules and regulations. During Shi Zong's reign, Jin came to its golden age. After Zhang Zong's reign, the Jin declined day by day. Meanwhile, the Yuan, a regime established by the Mongol nobility was rising in the north. With the Mongol troops marching southward., the Jin moved its capital for the second time to Bianjing. Emperor Ai Di of the Jin fled first to Guide (modern Shangqiu City, Henan) and then to Caizhou (modern Ru'nan County, Henan).In 1234, Emperor Ai Di abdicated in favor of Wanyan Chengling. At this moment, allied forces of the Song and the Mongols took Caizhou and Ai Di hanged himself. Wanyan Chengling, who was on the throne for less than one day, died in the scourge of war and thus the Jin came to an end.

After conquering the Jin, the Mongols attacked Song on a grand scale. In 1274, Emperor Gong Di of the Song ascended the throne. In the same year, the Mongol forces drove into Song territory over both land and river and routed the Song army time and again. In 1276, the Mongols took Lin'an and captured Gong Di, Empress Dowager Xie and Empress Dowager Jin. Then Prime Minister Chen Yizhong, Zhang Shijie (?-1279), Lu Xiufu (1238-1279) and other generals supported Prince of Yi, whose name was Zhao Shi, and designated him as emperor in Fuzhou, who was known later as Duan Zong. Driven by the Mongol forces, Duan Zong died in Gangzhou (in the sea to the south of Wuchuan County, Guangdong). Later, Wen Tianxiang and Lu Xiufu made Prince of Wei, Zhao Bing emperor. In 1278, Wen Tianxiang was defeated in Chaoyang and was taken captive. Zhang Shijie and others were also defeated by the Mongol troops on the sea. In 1279, seeing that the game was up, Lu Xiufu, carrying the nine-year-old emperor, Zhao Bing, threw himself into the sea from Mountain Ya and thus the Southern Song came to an end.

Shadowy blue porcelain statue, Southern Song Dynasty (1127-1279 AD)

7. Economics of the Song Dynasty

Silver handled pot with an elephant-shaped lid, Song (960-1279 AD)

The Festival of Pure Brightness on the River, partial, Song Dynasty, Zhang Zeduan, silk scroll, 527cm long, 24.8cm wide

The unification under the Northern Song Dynasty brought an end to the long-term chaos caused by wars that began with the Five Dynasties and thus social economics made evident headway. Water conservancy facilities had been repaired and rebuilt in the south as well as in the north. In South China, different fields such as *weitian, yutian, jiatian, hutian* were largely explored. Growing areas continuously increased. Tools of production were also improved. Tali, a laborsaving plough that could replace farm cattle, appeared. Besides, other farm implements, such as *yangma* by which people could transplant thousands of beds of rice seedlings each day, dragon bone water lifts, water-powered and cattle-driven waterwheels started to be widely used. Improved rice, called Zhancheng Rice, was popularized and thus its output was greatly increased.

In the Northern Song, there were nearly two or three hundred mines. With division of labor like panning, mining, boiling and refining, each miner had his own responsibility. As a result, the amount of iron then produced increased by a big margin. And *bai lian gang*, a kind of thoroughly tempered steel, was produced. Besides, the smelting of copper, iron, lead and tin was very popular in Min, Shu, Hu, Guang, Jiang, Huai and Zhe regions. In addition, the amount of coal produced was considerable and excavating techniques were much improved. Besides, great technological progress was also made in the mining of well salt in Sichuan, resulting in the increasing of output.

The silk weaving industry was very flourishing in the Northern Song Dynasty. Those that represented its developing standard were the world-famous Sichuan brocade, *Dingzhou kesi* weaving with an elegant design, the Shanzhou Weiwu fine silk as light as a mist and the Jingzhou *Fangshenghua* silk of which one bolt weighed only fourteen taels. Porcelains produced during the Northern Song were famous all over the world and were sold overseas. Among the famous kilns were *Guanyao* in Kaifeng, *Ruyao* in Ruzhou (modern Linru County, Henan), *Junyao* in Yuzhou (in modern Henan), *Dingyao* in Dingzhou (in modern Hebei) and *Yueyao* in Yuezhou (mordern Shaoxing County, Zhejiang), which were jointly known as "Five Famous Kilns". Porcelains produced in Changnanzhen gained fame for a time during Emperor Zhen Zong, Jingde's reign (1004-1007) and thus the town was renamed Jingdezhen. In addition, shipbuilding, papermaking, sugar refining and tea processing had all made evident progress compared with those in the period of Five Dynasties

and Ten States.

Flourishing commerce centers were found everywhere in the south as well as in the north. There were row upon row of shops and markets in Bianjing, the capital city of the Northern Song. A scroll of painting entitled *The Festival of Pure Brightness on the River* was the epitome of the thriving Bianjing city. With the commercial prosperity, the earliest paper currency called *jiaozi*, started to be issued in Sichuan. 'Quechang', opened on the northwest border of the Song, was a place where trading activities between the Song, the Liao, and the Xia were carried out. In addition, the Northern Song maintained frequent commercial contacts with the States in the western regions, with the Tufans on Qinghai Tibet Plateau, and other ethnic groups in the southwest. Overseas trading in the Northern Song was extraordinarily prosperous. A harbour administration, with its agency called *Shibosi*, took charge of foreign trade in such costal trading ports as Guangzhou, Hangzhou, Mingzhou (modern Ningbo, Zhejiang) and so forth. Thus the number of Korean, Japanese, Arabs and Persians who came to China to trade increased day after day.

Due to the fact that the Song government as well as large numbers of people moved to the south, the South China made a further development. Then the double-harvest rice had been planted in South China and thus there was the saying "When crops are good in Hunan and Hubei, the whole country will not be short of grain." which indicated the riches and prosperity in the southeast region in Southern Song dynasty. Both technology and output of the handicraft industry, including mining and smelting, shipbuilding, porcelain making and spinning and weaving has surpassed that of the Northern Song. A rapid improvement was then made in the technique of firearms making for the need of war.

Highly developed water transportation in the south served as favorable factors for the flourishing commerce. In the capital city Lin'an that was linked by canals, there were roads leading to the sea, wealthy merchants coming and going, shops and stores standing in great numbers along the streets and lanes. In the Southern Song Dynasty, quick development was also made in foreign trading. Chinese merchant ships sailed to the faraway *Dashi* (modern Arabian Peninsula) to do business. Meanwhile, merchants from *Dashi, Shepo* (modern Indonesia) and *Sanfuqi* (now Sumatra) came frequently to China as well. The Southern Song Dynasty thus established *Tiju Shibosi*, a harbour administration in charge of foreign trade and tariffs collection. Because of the frequent commercial activities, the Southern Song government set up an institution named Han zaihuizi wu, which specified in the issue and management of paper currencies. Besides, there were also many locally used paper currencies in all parts of the country.

Comparison of the ancient waterwheel and the modern one

Wuyi Mountain, Fujian province

During the Song Dynasty, a comparatively quick development of social economics could also be found in the north where the Liao, the Xi Xia, and the Jin established their regimes. Although animal husbandry and hunting dominated in Liao's economy, the proportion of agriculture was constantly increasing under the influence of advanced form of production and culture of the Han Chinese. Besides, the obvious progress in the handicraft industry could be found in mining and metallurgy. Advanced technique was employed in horse gear and carriage making. Porcelains and silk produced were quite elegant. "Quechang" linked the trade between the Liao and the Central Plains and the five Jings swarmed with wealthy merchants. In northwest Xi Xia, which had long been known as "a kingdom of the best animal husbandry in the world", handicraft industry, such as woolen spinning, weaponry making, salt industry, porcelain making and ironware processing, had developed to a certain degree. Commerce of Xi Xia was mainly trade between the Song, the Liao and the Jin, and currencies of the Jin and the Song could also be used in Liao. Agriculture in the Jin had made much progress and thus grain yield increased. In the field of handicraft industry, the amount of gold, silver, copper, iron and coal then produced was comparatively great. In addition, porcelain technology of some famous kilns in the north had gradually surpassed that of the Northern Song. Technical competence in silk spinning and weaving, papermaking, print and weaponry making was as good as that in the Southern Song. Quechangs were built for trade on the borders of the Song and the Jin, the Jin and the Xia, and the Jin and all the northern ethnic groups. Commerce in Kaifeng, of Nanjing, in Xiangzhou of Hebei and other places was also quite thriving. After having suffered destruction from wars, the social economy in the north started to revive and prosper with a comparative stability.

Yi Ze Bo Bell, the fourth year of Chongning Period in Northern Song Dynasty (1105), 28.2cm high, the handle 6.1cm high

第七篇

竞争与统一

8. A Thriving Culture

Zhou Dunyi (1011-1073 AD)

Shao Yong (1011-1077 AD)

of the Diagram of the Absolute (Taiji Tu Shuo) and *Almanac (Tong Shu)*, he put forward the idea that all the tangible material things came form the absolute substance, while "the Absolute" was just the intangible "Ultimate". Besides, there was a contemporary of Zhou Dunyi, Zhang Zai, whoes main works were *Zheng Meng, Dong Ming, Xi Ming* and so on.

In the Northern Song Dynasty, Cheng Hao and Cheng Yi, known to later generations as the "Cheng Brothers", contributed a lot to the development of Neo-Confucianism. Both studying under Zhou Dunyi, they advanced the idea of "reason" as the source of all material things and the essence of the universe, which had existed before anything else and would last forever. According to them, the broad masses must resign themselves to reality and place themselves at the disposal of the feudal order. Their opinions on public affairs were collected in *Complete Collection of Works of the Cheng Brothers*.

Zhu Xi (1130-1200) of the Southern Song Dynasty epitomized the thought of Neo-Confucianism. He believed that there existed reason and spirit in the universe, with the former the essence and the latter the implement of all material things. Things in the world came from reasons and reasons from heavenly principles, and heavenly principles were exactly the public orders under which the monarch was the heart. According to him, people must "eradicate human desires and maintain the heavenly principles". Delivering lectures in his whole life, ZhuXi was a great educationist as well. He wrote many books, the most important of which was *Collected Commentaries of the Four Books (i.e. the four major Confucian classics. The Great Learning, The Doctrine of the Mean, The Analects of Confucius and Mencius)*. In addition, many books such as *Classified Conversation of Master Zhu, Selected Writings of Master Zhu Xi* and *Posthumous Writings of Master Zhu* were compiled by later generations. Being trained in the school pioneered by the Cheng Brothers, Zhu Xi exerted great influence on later generations and thus Neo-Confucianism was also called Cheng-Zhu Confucianism. Lu Jiuyuan, another Confucian, advocated that "Mind is reason" and "The Universe lies in my mind", which was known as "Theory of the mind".

Xiao Yi Zhuan Lan Ting, Song Dynasty (960-1279 AD), artist unknown, silk scroll, 26.6cm wide, 44.3cm long

The Neo-Confucianism, especially the theory of Zhu Xi, enjoyed high prestige after the reign of Emperor Li Zong of the Song. The Cheng Brothers, Zhu Xi and other Confucians even won places in the Confucian temple and were offered sacrifices when people held a memorial ceremony for Confucius. In the following hundreds of years, Zhu Xi's explanation and analysis on Confucian classics was set up as an official one and thus became an orthodox learning.

In the Song Dynasty, a large number of historians were coming to the fore and thus many books of history were produced. The most influential one was *History as a Mirror* written by Sima Guang, which consisted of 294 chapters. Being written in an annalistic style, the book recorded the rises and falls of empires and political gains and losses during a period of 1362 years, from the beginning of the three powers in the Warring States to the end of the Five Dynasties and Later Zhou. During the Southern Song Dynasty, Yuan Shu, modeled after the *History as a Mirror,* compiled *Events in History as a Mirror*. He initiated a new way of writing history, i.e. to center on historical events, other than history presented in a series of biographies and annals known as history presented in separate accounts of important events. With *Compendium of Historical Events*, Zhu Xi broke a path for compendium writing.

Lixue, also known as *daoxue*, was a Confucian school formed by Buddhism and Taoism. Compared with traditional Confucianism, it was a great change. Zhou Dunyi (1017-1073) in the early period of the Northern Song Dynasty was the progenitor of this school. In the course of his denunciation of Buddhism and Taoism and his promotion of Confucianism, Zhou Dunyi established his own ideological system of Lixue, known as Neo-Confucianism. In *An Explanation*

Among books of history on institutions, *Historical Collections* compiled by Zheng Qiao of the

Southern Song Dynasty and *A Critical History of Institutions* written by Ma Duanlin of the late Song and early Yuan period were praiseworthy. In *Record of Ancient Writings* and *Record of Inscriptions on Ancient Bronze Objects(Jinshi Lu)* written by Ouyang Xiu and Zhao Mingcheng respectively, inscriptions on tablets and ancient bronze objects were collected, uncommon words and singular writings were observed and studied, as such a new branch of science called epigraphy was established. Other than the historical works described above, *New History of Tang* compiled by Ouyang Xiu, Song Qi and others, *Old History of Five Dynasties* by Xue Juzheng, *New History of Five Dynasties* by Ouyang Xiu, *A sequel to History as a Mirror* by Li Tao, *A Chronicle of the Most Important Events Since the Jianyan Reign Period* by Li Xinchuan *and A Chronicle of Three Song Emperors Dealing with the Northern Neighbour* by Xu Meng hua were all well-known historical works.

In the Song Dynasty, progress can also be found in the compiling and writing of local chronicles, including *A chronicle of the Reign of Taiping* written by Yue Shi, *A Record of Events in the Reign of Yuanfeng* by Wang Cun, *A Chronicle of Events on the Earth* by Ouyang Ming, *A chronicle of Events in Lin'an During the Reign of Qiandao* by Zhou Cong, *A Chronicle of Events in Lin'an During the Reign of Xianchun* by Qian Shuoyou, *History of Wujun* by Fan Chengda, *A Record of Events in Jiankang During the Jingding Reign of Jingding* by Zhou Yinghe and *A Record of Events in Huigui Prefecture During the Reign of Jiatai* by Shi Su, which were all famous annals of local history. *A Record of Flourishing Dongjing* written by Meng Yuanlao, *A Record of Thriving Lin'an* by Wu Zimu and *Old Events in Martial Arts Circles* by Zhou Mi, scenes of prosperity in the capital were vividly described.

Several full-length leishus, reference books with material extracted from various sources and arranged according to subjects, were compiled by a large number of people in the Northern Song Dynasty. In Tai Zong's reign, by imperial edict, Li Fang and others compiled *Imperial Works of the Taiping Era*, consisting of 1000 chapters, *The Selections from Records of the Taiping Era* , consisting of 500 chapters and *Choice Blossoms from the Garden of Literature*, consisting of 1000 chapters. In Zhen Zong's reign, also by decree of the emperor, Wang Qinruo, Yang Yi and other people compiled a 1000-chapter work, *Guide to Book*. All the four works mentioned above, which were jointly known to later generations as four great reference books in the Song Dynasty, were indeed a complete collection of the historical accounts of past events that survived at that time, as such many documents were preserved. Besides, these books created a precedent for the compilation of leishu, which was patterned on by later generations.

Ci poetry of the Song Dynasty enjoyed a high prestige in the area of Chinese literature. It originated from the Tang Dynasty and matured in the Five Dynasties. Works of Li Yu, known also as Li the Last Monarch of the Later Tang Dynasty, made great progress in the ability of depicting life and expressing feelings. By the Song Dynasty, *ci* poetry creation reached its summit. Su Shi, Lu You and Xin Qiji were famous *ci* poets then. Writing about a wide range of subjects and expressing bold and unrestrained feelings, Su Shi thus was all along regarded as founder of the powerful and free style. His works such as *Charm of a Maiden singer Memories of the Past at Red Cliff* and *Prelude to the Melody of Water. How Long Will Be the Bright Moon appear?* were full of heroic spirit and thus created a lofty artistic

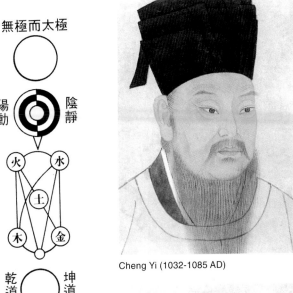

無極而太極

陽動　陰靜

火　水

土

木　金

乾道成男　坤道成女

萬物化生

Diagram of cosmological scheme

Cheng Yi (1032-1085 AD)

Cheng Hao (1033-110 AD)

Zhu Xi (1130-1200 AD)

Street Vendor, Song Dynasty (960-1279 AD), by Li Song, 25.5ocm wide, 70.4cm long

第七篇

竞争与统一

Landscape painting, Song Dynasty, Liu Songnian, silk scroll, each part 41cm wide, 69cm long

ambience. Works by Lu You were the most, nearly 10,000, all full of patriotic enthusiasm. Works of Xin Qiji eliminated the showy and subtle style of writing that was popular then in the circles of ci writers, and were filled with bold and unrestrained passions. Thus Xin Qiji and Su Shi were jointly called "Su-Xin" in the circles of ci writers. In addition, Li Qingzhao, a poetress of the Southern Song Dynasty, who's works had a fresh artistic conception, was a representative of subtle and restrained writing style.

Vernacular tales of the Song Dynasty, known as hua ben, originated from the master copies of thoes who engaged in storytelling and ballad singing. It dealt with such topics as classic, history and town life and thus exerted great influence on the novels of the Ming and Qing dynasties. Drama in the Song Dynasty, consisted of storytelling and ballad singing, puppet show, shadow show and *zaju*. Praiseworthy works in the literature of the Liao and the Jin were Yuan Haowen's poetry and Dong Xieyuan's *The West Chamber-zhugongdiao* (a ballad form of the Song).

Meng Chang of the later Shu in the Five Dynasties, first established the imperial art academy and that was the beginning of art academy in China. During the reign of Emperor Hui Zong of the Song Dynasty, art academy came to a time of great prosperity. The famous landscape painters were Jin Hao, Guan Tong of Later Liang, Dong Yuan, Ju Ran of later Tang, Li Cheng, Fan Kuan, Guo Xi,

Sima Guang (1019-1086 AD)

Su Shi (1037-1101 AD)

Li Qingzhao (1084-1151 AD)

Zi Zhi Tong Jian, manuscript

Cai Wei, Song Dynasty, by Li Tang, silk scroll, 27cm wide, 90cm long

Lushan Mountain, north of Jiangxi province

The Poem of Summer, Song, by Zhao Ji, ink on paper, thin and sturdy style, 33.7cm wide, 44.2cm long

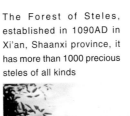

The Forest of Steles, established in 1090AD in Xi'an, Shaanxi province, it has more than 1000 precious steles of all kinds

Mi Fu and his son Mi Youren of the Northern Song. Besides, Li Tang, Liu Songnian, Ma Yuan and Xia Gui of the Southern Song Dynasty, all had their own distinctive achievements. Among painters of flowers and birds, Huang Quan of Later Shu, Xu Xi of Later Tang and Zhao Ji, known as Hui Zong of the Northern Song Dynasty, were famous ones. In the field of figure painting and genre painting, the most representative work was *The Festival of Pure Brightness on the River* by Zhang Zeduan of the Northern Song Dynasty. Besides, painters Hu Gui and Yelu Bei (Li Zanhua) were adept at figure painting. Painter Wang Tingjun of the Jin was good at landscape painting. A scroll of painting entitled *Wenji returning to the Han* by Zhang Yu of the Jin was a fine piece of figure painting.

Famous calligraphers emerged in large numbers in the Song Dynasty. Most of the monarchs of the Northern Song Dynasty were fond of the penmanship, among them was Tai Zong, who once ordered to print the imperial collections of books of successive dynasties to be used as books of models of calligraphy. Moreover, Hui Zong had a style of his own in calligraphy, known as shoujin style, featuring thin and sturdy strokes. Su Shi, Huang Tingjian, Mi Fu and Cai Xiang, jointly known as the "Four Calligraphers of the Song Dynasty" also enjoyed a high prestige in calligraphers' circles of the Song Dynasty.

第七篇

竞争与统一

9. The Four Great Inventions That Rock the World

Shen Kuo (1031-1095 AD)

The four great inventions of ancient China, the compass, gunpowder, papermaking and printing, are significant contributions of the Chinese nation to world civilization. By the time of the Song Dynasty, further progress was made in gunpowder, printing and compass.

The composition of gunpowder, also known as charcoal gunpowder, was nitre, sulphur and charcoal. A Taoist alchemist in the Tang Dynasty named Sun Simiao was the first one that discovered the explosive power of the materials of gunpowder. Towards the end of the Tang Dynasty, gunpowder had been widely used in hunting, blasting the mountains, quarrying and firearms making. During the reign of Ren Zong of the Northern Song Dynasty, by imperial edict, Zeng Gongliang compiled a book entitled *The Outline of Military Science* in which he described in detail the names, usages and formulae of many gunpowder weapons. Firearms at that time, including canons, rockets, fireballs, caltrops and firelocks, were used to attack a city, defend against enemy, launch an attack and to break through an encirclement, thus displaying great destructive power. Gunpowder was introduced into Arab via the Song, Jin and Mongolia, and then on a round about trip into Europe, which promoted the development of world civilization.

Movable-type printing which was based on block printing of the Tang Dynasty, was invented by a civilian named Bi Sheng during the reign of Qing Li (1004-1048) of the Northern Song Dynasty. He used moistened clay as material to carve out the movable characters and designed a set of devices for the arrangement of characters. Thus, he became the first person that used the movable type to print books. Movable-type printing was introduced eastward to Japan via Korea and westward to Europe via Arab, and thus encouraged the development of world culture. However, movable-type printing made its first appearance in Europe in the mid-fifteenth century.

It is said that Huang Di invented the compass, also known as box compass. During the Warring States Period, Han Fei recorded a southward-pointing instrument called "*si nan*". In the Northern and Southern dynasties, Zu Chongzhi and others once created a compass vehicle, a compass fish and so on. In the Northern Song dynasty, compass was employed in navigation. Captains of ships "use stars at night, the sun during the day", and compasses during rainy days for guidance in directions. In the thirteenth century, compass was introduced to West Europe, which contributed greatly to the discovery of the New Sea Route. Thus, this invention of China finally led to the improvement of world appearance.

Shen Kuo was a scientist of great learning in the Northern song dynasty. His great work, *Sketchbook of Dream Brook*, recorded inventions by the laboring people and his own research results. There were more than 200 records of natural science in his book, relating to various subjects, such as calendar making, mathematics, meteorology, geology, geography, physics, chemistry, biology, agriculture, water conservancy, architecture, medicine and pharmacology, which represented the advanced science and technology in the world at that time. Besides, he initiated the theory of elliptic orbit of the sun, which was 550 years earlier than the West. The British scholar, Jose Li called him "coordinate of science" in the 11th century.

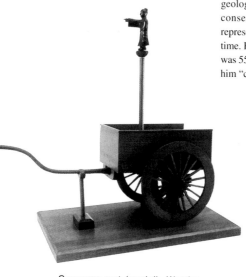

Compass cart (model), Warring States Period, Wei State

Compass, Han Dynasty, the earliest of magnetic compass in the world, used as early as the Warring States Period, the side of the plate is 17.8cm long, the ladle is 11.5cm long

The hanging compass (model), Song Dynasty

The steps of making paper in Song Dynasty

The tomb of Cai Lun in Longting town, Xiyang County, Shanxi province

Canon (from Wu Jin Zong Yao)

Printing books, Ming Dynasty

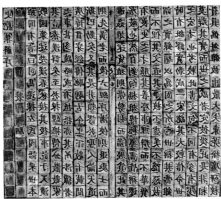

Movable type in Northern Song Dynasty, 43cm long, 37cm wide

Puncture vine pottery tomb, pottery shell with gunpowder inside, the earliest explosive firearm

Bronze shotgun with inscriptions, Yuan Dynasty

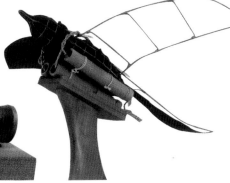

Shen Huo Fei Ya, the fire bomb made according to the principle of rocket launching (reproduction), Ming Dynasty, the wing is 64cm long, the body is 56cm long

Flowing compass, reproduced according to Sketchbook of Dream Brook and Ben Cao Yan Yi

Compass turtle (model), Yuan Dynasty (1260-1368 AD)

Compass, Qing (1644-1911AD)

第七篇

竞争与统一

10. Genghis Khan and the Great Empire in the Yuan Dynasty

Emperors in Yuan Dynasty

Emperor Taizu, Genghis Khan (1206-1227AD)

Emperor Taizong, Wokuotai (1229-1241AD)

Emperor Dingzong, Guiyou (1246-1248AD)

Emperor Xianzong, Mengge (1251-1259AD)

Emperor Shizu, Boerzhijin Hubilie (1260-1294AD)

6. Emperor Qindingdi, Yesun Tiemuer (1323-1328AD)

7. Emperor Tianshundi, Asujiba (1328AD)

3. Emperor Wuzong, Haishan (1307-1311AD)

8. Emperor Mingzong, Heshila (1329AD)

9. Emperor Wuzong, Haishan (1329-1332AD)

10. Emperor Ningzong, Yilingzhiban (1332AD)

11. Emperor Shundi, Tuohuantiemuer (1307-1311AD)

4. Emperor Renzong, Aiyulibalida (1311-1320AD)

5. Emperor Yingzong, Shuodebaci (1320-1323AD)

2. Emperor Chengzong, Tiemuer (1294-1307AD)

The Mausoleum of Genghis Khan (1162-1227 AD), 15 km south of Atangxilianzhen Town, Yijinholoqi, Inner Mongolia

Pioneers between the East and the West, two regions that were more or less cut off from each other, were not rare. However, it wasn't until the 13th century that there was a true connection between them. The outstanding achievements of Genghis Khan(namely, Timujin,1162-1227) and his descendants have been an amazing wonder to later generations up to now.

Ancestors of Genghis Khan originated from *Monwushiwei*, a tribe which lived in the northern region of the Great Xin'an Mountains during the period of Tang regime, and which wasn't also called Mongolse, Mongoli or Mongol in the Song, the Jin and the Liao period. Together with other tribes, it was sometimes called Tartar. During the period of the Liao regime, the Mongol tribes reached a new stage of development. Then, Timujin, chief of a small tribe distinguished himself in wars among the tribes. Having fought and marched for more than ten years, he unified all the Mongol tribes in the early 13th century. In 1206, he had a clan conference held on the bank of the Onon River (modern Enen River, Mongolia), at which he was proclaimed the Great Khan, with the honorific title of Genghis Khan. Thus a unitary Mongol Khanate (also known as Great Mongolia) was established and he was later known as Emperor Tai Zu of the Yuan Dynasty.

After the founding of the Mongol Khanate, Genghis Khan drew up a complete set of military and administrative rules and regulations. Then he made a Uygur scholar, Tatatonha, who had been captured by the Mongols create the ancient Mongolian language by modeling on the Uygur language, in which he compiled the legal documents *da zha sa*.

The Situation of Yuan Dynasty

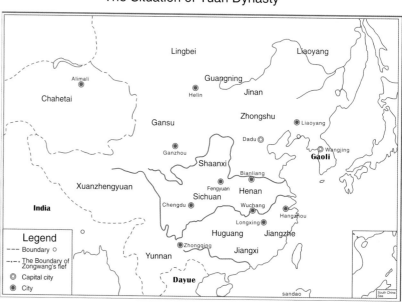

Lingbei

Liaoyang

Alimali

Guangning

Helin

Jinan

Chahetai

Zhongshu

Gansu

Liaoyang

Dadu

Ganzhou

Wangjing

Shaanxi

Gaoli

Bianliang

Xuanzhengyuan

Fengyuan

Henan

Chengdu

Sichuan

Wuchang

India

Longxing

Hangzhou

Huguang

Jiangzhe

Zhongqing

Jiangxi

Yunnan

Dayue

sandao

South China Sea

Legend
- - - Boundary ○
- · - · The Boundary of Zongwang's fief
- ◎ Capital city
- ◉ City

Silver lian-toilet box with posy design, Yuan Dynasty (1271-1368 AD)

Around the time when the Mongolia was established, Genghis Khan began his expansion and plunder in neighboring regions. In 1219, commanding 200,000 men, he personally led a western expedition to Hualazimo (to the east of modern Caspian Sea, west of modern Aral Sea, and south of modern Irtysh River) and the Mongol forces drove straight on to the northwest reign of India. Troops on the other front marched towards Caucasus, with its sphere of influence stretching as far as to the northern coast of the Black Sea and further into the Crimea Peninsula. Genghis Khan divided the newly occupied area into many fiefs of Khan. The fief of Juji, the eldest son of Genghis Khan was called Kipchak Khanate; the fief of Jagatai, the second son of Genghis, was named Jagatai Khanate and the Ogdai Khanate was the fief of Ogdai, the third son of Genghis Khan. After Genghis Khan died in 1226, his successors made another two expeditions to the west. In the second western expedition from 1235 to 1244, the Mongol forces took Russia and marched into Persia, Hungary and Austria. In the third time of their expedition from 1253 to 1259, the Mongols conquered Muciyi, part of modern Iran and *Black Dashi*, then marched into Damascus and other places in Syria, pressing on towards Egypt. Thanks to the third western expedition, the Il- Khanate was established. Apart from the metropolitan territory of the Mongol Khanate, the Khanates described above formed the four Great Khanates. Bringing the west and the east under one centralized rule, the Mongol Khanate that was powerful and prosperous for a time created a miracle in the world history, and thus promoted worldwide economic and cultural exchanges.

In 1234, the Mongol forces destroyed the Jin. In 1260, Kublai succeeded as Great Khan and in 1271 he called his regime Great Yuan. The next year, Kublai

Longquan porcelain plate with dragon design, Yuan (1271-1368 AD)

Tie Guai, Yuan (1260-1368 AD), by Yan Jun, silk scroll, ink and wash, 14.6cm wide, 72.5cm long

Silver mirror stand, Yuan Dynasty (1271-1368 AD)

Standing male figure with object in hands, Yuan Dynasty (1260-1368 AD), 26.8cm high, unearthed at Xi'an, Shaanxi province

Pottery female figure, Yuan Dynasty (1260-1368 AD), 29cm high, unearthed at Xi'an, Shaanxi province

第七篇

竞争与统一

Emperor Shi Zu of Yuan Dynasty, Hubi Lie (1215-1294 AD)

The Queen of Emperor Shi Zu of Yuan

Openwork jade pendant, Yuan (1260-1368 AD), 6.6cm long, 5.3cm wide, 1.3cm thick

Emperor Shi Zu of Yuan hunting, partial, Yuan, by Liu Guandao, 182.9cm high, 104.1cm wide

A porcelain pot with phoenix's head, Yuan (1260-1368 AD), 18.5cm high

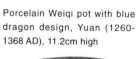

Porcelain Weiqi pot with blue dragon design, Yuan (1260-1368 AD), 11.2cm high

Longquan porcelain pot with lotus leaf lid, Yuan (1260-1368 AD)

Chizhou jar with baby design, Yuan (1260-1368 AD)

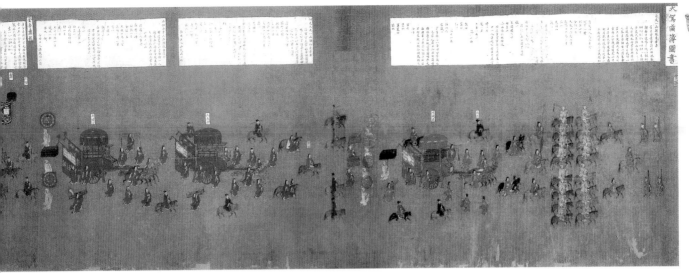

Procession, Yuan (partial)

designated Dadu (now Beijing)as capital. The Yuan government established the Secretariat, an organ that exercised control over six departments and took charge of all the national administrative affairs. Besides, the Military Council was established, which was invested with the power to direct military activities. There were also Censorate and Council of Buddhist affairs, with the former supervising all government officials and the latter dealing with Buddhist affairs and administrative work of Tufan. Under the Yuan regime, people of the country were divided into four categories: the Mongols, the Semu people, the Hans and the "southerners". In central as well as many local government organizations, the Mongols and the Semu people were appointed to be garrison officials, whose duty was to solidify the rule of the Mongol nobles. In 1279, the Yuan exterminated the Southern Song and thus accomplished the task of unifying the country, which laid a foundation for China's vast territory. Then huge armies were dispatched in succession by Kublai to go on expeditions to Japan, Annan, Zhan Cheng, Myanmar and Java, but all the attempts failed in the end. From 1294 when Kublai died in Dadu to the time of Emperor Shun Di's reign, it was a period of fierce internal struggles for the throne that lasted forty years, which saw the reigns of nine emperors.

Showy blue porcelain Adalokiteavara, Yuan (1260-1368 AD), 67cm high

With a broad scale and complete arrangements, Dadu was an international metropolitan and a masterpiece of ancient urban construction of China. In Dadu, there were well-laid -out buildings and wide streets with complete drainage system inside the city. Besides, numerous and jumbled bureaucratic apparatus and large population could be found in city proper. The Yuan government set up a *zhanchi* system, under which Dadu was the core and there were as many as over 1,500 *zhanchis* established all over the country. In addition, a kind of pothouse called *ji di pu*, which specialized in transmitting official dispatches, was established and thus a close connection between the central government and local authorities was guaranteed.

There were people of different ethnic groups in Dadu, including Han Chinese, Mongols, the Hui, Uygurs, the Hani, the Yudian and the Tibetan people, among whom were bureaucrats, army men and their families, handicraftsmen and merchants. The handicraft industry then consisted of manufacturing of felt rug, gold, silver and agate processing, silk weaving, weaponry making and mining, of which a large proportion was of the government, and thus there were numerous craftsman families. Markets of rice, iron, furs, horses and cattles, camels, pearls, and shalas (corals) could be found everywhere and various kinds of goods were sold in Dadu, the northern commercial center. Foreign trade was brisk then. Chinese merchants could be found in East Asia, South Asia, West Asia, East Africa and continent of Europe which was linked up by land routes. Meanwhile, one after another, merchants from foreign countries came to Dadu as well. Being the educational center of the nation, Dadu was a city where the institution of highest learning, known as Imperial College, located and where the general examinations for candidates of the imperial civil exams were held after the middle era of the Yuan Dynasty. The Yuan regime adopted a policy of toleration towards all religions. Buddhism, Taoism, Islam and Christianity spread in Dadu. Many foreign emissaries, merchants, scientists and missionaries came to Dadu in succession and thus promoted economic and cultural exchanges between China and other countries in Asia, Africa and Europe. Among the visitors was Macro Polo (1254-1324), an Italian who made extensive tours in China and lived for a long time in Dadu and wrote a remarkable book entitled *Journey to the East and Records of knowledge about the East*. Other visitors such as the Italian traveler Odorico, the Moroccan traveler Ibn Batuta, the envoy named Marignolli that was sent by Pope of Europe and several Korean emperors had all been to Dadu. In brief, Dadu of the Yuan Dynasty deserved the title of "capital of the world".

Potala Palace — Jokhang Monastery in Lhasa, Tibet

11. Art and Literature, Science and Technology

The Yuan opera was one of the outstanding achievements in ancient Chinese art and literature, which consisted of *san qu* and *za ju*. San qu was a new poetic form that derived its origin from the *shi* or *ci* poetry. While *za ju*, a comprehensive dramatic art, was originated from the song and dance drama during the Tang and Song period, the drama script in the Jin and the ballad form of the song and Jin dynasties called *zhugongdiao*. *Za ju* included singing, storytelling and acting, but it mainly took the form of singing a tune, thus also being called the Yuan opera. *Za ju* in the Yuan Dynasty was so flourishing that many works were produced. There were over 500 pieces of *za ju* works that had been recorded and still 162 ones that have been handed down to this very day. Besides, there were more than 200 dramatists,

Reclusion (partial), Yuan Dynasty, by Qianxuan

including Guan Hanqing, Ma Zhiyuan, Bai Pu and Zheng Guangzu, who were jointly known as "Four Great Dramatists". Among dramatists of the Yuan, Guan Hanqing and Wang Shifu were the two who exerted a comparatively great influence on later generations and whose works were of rather high artistic quality.

Guan Hanqing (c.1220-c.1300) wrote more than 60 pieces of drama in his life, among which over ten pieces were preserved intact. He wrote about a wide range of subjects, including legends of heroes, talented scholars and beautiful ladies, household chores and complicated legal cases. In particular, most of his works gave expression to the lives of the oppressed women. In his drama, tunes and words were succinct and beautiful, and every figure had a distinctive personality. The representative works of Guan Huanging were

Rescuing a Prostitute, *Wangjiang Pavilion*, *Baiyue Pavilion* and *Dandao Hui*, but the most outstanding one was *Snow in Midsummer*. Up to now, many of his works have long been lively on stage in various forms. Wang Shifu wrote fourteen pieces of drama but only two pieces, namely *Cui Yingying Awaiting the Moon in the West Chamber* and *Lichun Tang* have survived. Being noted for the literary grace, his works were compared to "the beauty in flowers" by ancient Chinese.

In the Yuan Dynasty, paintings by scholars and officials sprang up. Besides their pursuit of splendid and exquisite workmanship, and lifelike portrait, they put emphasis on the expression of personal feelings and emotional appeal in writing. Further combining calligraphy with drawing, such paintings in the Yuan Dynasty required painters to have a good mastery of literature. It is the combination of shi poetry, elligraphy and drawing that makes Chinese paintings full of more literary taste. What is called "the paintings of the Yuan Dynasty advocating artistic mood"is just the great development in China's painting history.

Landscape painting was the most popular in the Yuan Dynasty. Painters such as Zhao Mengfu, Qian Xuan. Gao Kegong and the so-called "four masters of the Yuan Dynasty", namely, Huang

Abridged armilla (model), the 2nd to 7th year of Zhengtong Period of Ming Dynasty (1437-1442), reproduced according to the abridged armilla designed by Guo Shoujing in Yuan Dynasty, now preserved at the observatory in Zijinshan Mountain, Nanjing province

Gongwang, Wang Meng, Ni Zan and Wu Zheng all made relatively great achievements. Among them, Zhao Mengfu, who detested and avoided the school of thought that had lost its original coloring in the imperial art academy of the Southern Song Dynasty, under the pretext of upholding traditions, brought forth new ideas of combining calligraphy with drawing and writing in an effective way. Thus all the mountains and waters, flowers and birds, figures, saddles and horses, trees and grass, bamboos and stones that were drawn by him were extremely exquisite. The four master painters of the Yuan Dynasty modeled themselves after Dong Yuan of the Five Dynasties and Ju Ran of the Northern Song Dynasty and were influenced by Zhao Mengfu. Among them, Huang Gongwang made greatest accomplishments and thus was called "the best of the four masters of the Yuan Dynasty". Others such as Ni Zan, noted for the tranquility and desolation in his works, Wang Meng whose works had a profound and elegant charm, and Wu Zheng, whose works were gloomy, delicate and handsome, all demonstrated a noble and lofty style of painting. In the field of flower-and -bird painting, flowers and birds painted in Chinese ink became the popular subjects. Besides Qian Xuan and Zhao Mengfu, important flower -and -bird painters included Wang Yuan, Ke Jiusi, Wang Mian and so on.

There were remarkable religious frescos in the Yuan Dynasty. In the Yongle Palace, Ruicheng County of Shanxi province, a Taoist fresco, imposing and magnificent, with as many as 286 figures in it, drawn in straight and forceful lines and rich colors, could be rated as a masterpiece of frescos.

In addition, outstanding achievements could be found in astronomy in the Yuan Dynasty. Guo Shoujing was a well-known scientist who was proficient in astronomy, calendar making and water conservancy. He created more than ten kinds of astronomical equipments, including *Jianyi, gaobiao, yangyi* and *zhengfangyi*. During the early years of the Yuan Dynasty, he presided over the astronomical observations in 27 regions all over the country, an area extending as far south as

Guan Hanqing (c. 1220-1300 AD)

the South China Sea which located at the 15th parallel of north latitude, and as far north as the North Sea at the 65th parallel of north latitude, a place close to the Arctic Circle. In Dengfeng County, Henan Province, the observatories and heliometers that were built in those years have been preserved up to now. He built an observatory in Dadu to observe and measure heavenly bodies and based on large amount of observational data, he compiled and edited a new calendric system *the Time-Telling Calendar* in which he determined that 365.2425 days constituted a year, a time that was only 26 seconds less than the actual period the earth takes to revolve around the sun. His figure was as accurate as that of the present Gregorian calendar. But the former was 300 years earlier than the latter. In brief, he was a scientist that stood in the forefront of the contemporary scientific and technological world. In 1970, the International Astronomers Society named a lunar crater on the reverse side of the Moon Guo Shoujing Mountain.

Thanks to the large territory of the Yuan Dynasty, conditions were created for the development of geography. Important accomplishments in geography included survey of the Constellation Sea which was the source of the Yellow River, *Territorial Map* drawn by Zhu Siben and *Unified Domain under the Yuan Regime* compiled by Bo Lanxi and Yue Xuan. Due to

Brick statue, Yuan Dynasty (1206-1368 AD), 34cm high
The illustration in Snow in Midsummer

the extensive contacts with foreign countries in the Yuan Dynasty, there were other great works such as *Local Conditions and Customs of Cambodia* by Zhou Daguan and *Records of Islands by* Wang Dayuan.

As cotton was widely planted, progress was made in cotton textile industry. In the Yuan Dyansty, water-driven spinning wheels were used in spinning, which was about 400 or 500 years earlier than that in Europe. A woman weaver named Huang Daopo, a native of Wunijing of Songjiang County (in Shanghai), learned the skills of spinning and weaving from the Lis when she wandered homeless to Yazhou (modern Hainan), the home of a minority people called the li. After she went back to her hometown, she improved the backward textile technique and created a set of tools used for ginning, fluffing, spinning, and weaving. She interlocked the yarn to mix colors in the right proportion. She turned out quilt covers with various designs and patterns, the colors being bright and pleasing, and as beautiful as paintings. For some time, "Quilt Covers from Wunijing" were famous all over the world and Songjiang County once became the cotton textile center of China.

In the field of agricultural science, the Agriculture Department of the Yuan Dynasty compiled *Summary of Farming and Sericulture*, which were promulgated all over the country. In 1313, an other book entitled *On Agriculture* wrote by Wang Zhen was issued, consisting of *the General Formula of Farming and Sericulture, 100-Character Guide* and *Agricultural Implements Illustrated*. This book was an agricultural encyclopedia of the Yuan Dynasty.

Washing Horses, Yuan Dynasty, by Zhao Mengfu

12. The life in Song and Yuan Dynasties

The development of the Song Dynasty stimulated the uprising of cities. The population in many cities grew by leaps and bounds. Dongjing (Kaifeng), the capital of Northern Song Dynasty, had more than a million inhabitants. Most of the high-rising buildings in the streets were on hire. Stores, wine shops and restaurants of all scales scattered around. Vendors' stands could be seen everywhere. There were lots of "*Wazi*" in Dongjing, which were public places for entertainment. "*goulan*" or "*peng*" were places for performance. There were night fairs and brothels around the 24-hours *Wazi* fairs. The night fairs started when dusk fell and ended until the third or fourth watch. On the mid-autumn day, they lasted all night long.

When the Song government moved to south, the development of population and economy in the new capital Lin'an (Hangzhou, Zhejiang province) quickly caught up with and surpassed Kaifeng. There were all sorts of jewelry, jade articles and other precious wares in the market. Even the catering trade paid special attention to delicacies and foods in season. The night fairs in Hangzhou were prosperous, and they densely gathered along both sides of the imperial road. The catering trade was the most popular business in the night fairs. Toys and articles of everyday use changed from season to season. The increase of cities around the nation was unprecedented. More than ten cities had over 50,000 inhabitants. Towns flourished everywhere.

As the imperial civil examination system became mature in the Song Dynasty, scholar-official bureaucratic class rose. The successful candidates in the early Song Dynasty were 4 or 5 times more than that of the Tang Dynasty. The government tried every means to perfect the official selection system in order to enlist talented people. Scholar-official bureaucratic ruling class played a very important role in the society, politics and culture.

The development of economy gave rise of the change of farmers' consciousness. The spread of customs and ideas became faster. In the late Song Dynasty, every city had a town god's temple, and many cities also had Wenchang Temple. Wenchang was originally a horrible ghost in Sichuan, but in the Song Dynasty it was regarded as the patron saint for all the students. In many regions, family became a crucial power in the local political life.

The development of print and extend of the scholar-official class made more women familiar with literacy. Owing to the prosperous economy, women's dowries were increased. The markets of buying and selling women as maidservants,

Gray cotton coat with golden embroidery, 135.5cm long, unearthed from the tomb of Jinqi King, Acheng, Heilongjiang province

Gray kneepad with golden embroidery of plum flower pattern, 86.5cm long, unearthed from the tomb of Jinqi King, Acheng, Heilongjiang province

Embroidered gauze shoes (115-1234 AD)

Riding, Yuan, by Wu Kuan

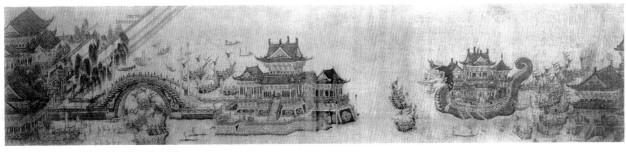

Dragon-boat Race, Yuan (1271-1368 AD)

concubines and prostitutes were also broadened. Families that provided a lot of dowries expected profits from the marriage. In the Song Dynasty, it was emphasized that men and women were different. Widows were encouraged to preserve chastity and not to remarry. Women must cover their heads whenever they went out, even seeing a doctor.

In Liao, Xia, Jin and Yuan Dynasties, the government stipulated in explicit terms the difference between the nationalities to protect the privilege of the conquerors. Sometimes the rulers were most concerned with how to avoid their own nationalities being assimilated by Han nationality; sometimes they placed more emphasis on preventing Han people from learning their languages and acknowledging their cultures. Although the intermarriage between nationalities happened occasionally, it was not encouraged. Han people didn't like to be ruled by other nationalities, but all the classes tried to adapt to the new life. The customs of Hu and Han mixed together. In Yuan Dynasty, the country had a vast territory. The cultures and customs of different nationalities influenced and infiltrated each other. The Mongolian nobles accepted the ruling methods of Han nationality in different degrees in every aspect of the social and economic life, but they still remained the distinct characters and customs of the northern nomadic nationalities. The Mongolian cavalry fought in one place after another. It not only connected the transportation of East and West, but also strengthened the communication between the two sides. The rise of this prairie nationality was called "Mongolian Tornado" by historians.

Mosque on Niujie Street, Beijing, established in the fourth year of Tonghe Period of Liao Dynasty (996 AD)

Arhats Northern Song Dynasty (960-1127 AD), 50-58cm high

Coffin with grass pattern, Song and Liao Dynasty

竞争与统一

148

Chapter 8

Centralization of State Power and Transformation of Social Pattern
--The Ming Dynasty

Wish always runs counter to the reality. The Ming Dynasty was an era of absolute autocratic monarchy. Imperial Guard, Western and Eastern Depot emerged as the times required. However, the Ming Dynasty was also an open age. Unified ideology and autocratic rule, Gave birth to new trend of thought and fresh atmosphere. Wherefrom started culture enlightenment and China began to move towards modern times.

The Great Wall of Ming Dynasty

1. Zhu Yuanzhang

Towards the end of the Yuan Dynasty, the whole nation was thrown into disorder, with armed struggles against the Yuan regime broke out one after another throughout the country. The Red Turbau rebellion was one of the anti-Yuan forces. Zhu Yuanzhang (1328-1398), a man of Zhongli of Haozhou (modern Fengyang County, Anhui), was born and brought up in a peasant's family. When young, driven by poverty, he went to a temple and became a monk. Later, he went to the Red Scarves led by Guo Zixing for shelter and gradually became a leader of it. In 1356, Zhu Yuanzhang and his men took Jiqing (modern Nanjing), which was then renamed Yingtianfu, and made it his base area.

Under the circumstance that the nation was carved up by rival warlord regimes, Zhu Yuanzhang adopted the proposal made by a Confucian scholar named Zhu Sheng, which was 'building high city walls, accumulating numerous food grains and being slow in proclaiming himself emperor'. Thus, Zhu Yuanzhang revered the "Longfeng" title of the Great Song, an anti-Yuan regime. And his force kept growing steadily in complicated struggles between separatist warlords. Famous scholars such as Liu Ji, Ye Chen, Zhang Yi and Song Lian were invited in succession to his troops. In 1361, Zhu Yuanzhang was conferred the title of "Duke of Wu" by Han Liner, the King of Xiaoming of Great Song.

In 1364, Zhu Yuanzhang made himself King of Wu. In 1366, he dispatched his men to throw the King of Xiaoming into the Yangtze River. Thus, the Great Song was exterminated and the Longfeng title was abandoned. One after another, he first destroyed the Han regime set up by Chen Youliang and the Wu regime by Zhang Shicheng. Then he conquered Fang Guozhen who controlled the coastal regions of Zhejiang and Chen Youding in Fujian. Later, he divided forces to march into Guangdong and Guangxi and appointed Xu Da as General of Expedition to go on a northern expedition to the Central Plains. In 1368, Zhu Yuanzhang proclaimed himself emperor and titled his dynasty Great Ming. Then he changed the designation of his reign into Hongwu and renamed Yingtianfu as Nanjing and changed Kaifeng to Beijing.

As the Ming troops took Dadu (modern Beijing), Emperor Shun Di of the Yuan Dynasty fled northward to Shangdu (to the east of modern Zhenglan Qi, Inner Mongolia). In 1371, the Ming forces exterminated the Xia and dominated Sichuan. In 1381, they marched into Yunnan and the Prince of Liang of the Yuan Dynasty committed suicide after he suffered a defeat. In 1387, the Ming forces marched eastward and

Emperor Tai Zu of Ming Dynasty, Zhu
Yuanzhang (1328-1398 AD)

The Territory of Ming Dynasty

Emperors in Ming Dynasty

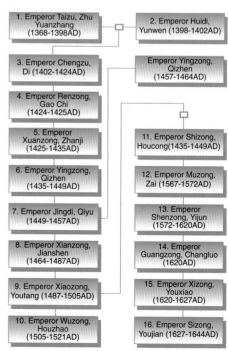

took Liaodong, where the Prime Minister of the Yuan Dynasty named Naha surrendered himself. So far, Zhu Yuanzhang generally accomplished the task of unifying the whole country.

At the beginning, the Ming government adopted the Yuan system of administration, including the Secretariat and the executive secretariats. Later, Zhu Yuanzhang replaced the executive secretariats by the Administrative Commissioner's office, Judicial Commissioner's Office and Military Commissioner's office, jointly known as "Three Offices". The heads of the three offices took charge of executive, judicial and military affairs respectively and they weren't subordinate to one another. All together thirteen Administrative Commissioner's Offices were established in succession across the country. Placed under the Administrative Commissioner's office were some municipalities and prefectures under which were counties. Concerned with organizations at the basic level, a li-jia system was adopted. The li and jia were organized on the basis of households: 110 households made up a li and a li were divided into ten jia.

The prime minister was established in the Secretariat, commanding all the other officials. However, they wielded too much power. In 1380, Zhu Yuanzhang executed Prime Minister Hu Weiyong for the latter had schemed for a rebellion. Thus, the Secretariat was abolished and all the significant state affairs were handled by the emperor.

In the Ming Dynasty, the Censorate that was headed by the Left and Right Censors, the Supreme Court that was the highest judicial organ of the country, and the Board of Justice were jointly called the "Three Justices". All the key cases should be Handed over to the "Three Justices" to conduct a joint trial. Laws of Great Ming was a complete statute book that was modeled on the laws of Tang. Meanwhile, Zhu Yuanzhang compiled some important cases into a book entitled Admonition, which, together with another book, The Laws, became the basis for decision on the sentence. In addition, prisons were established by the Security Department, an organ placed under the direction of Guards in Embroidered Coats that was a branch of the Imperial Guards. These prisons were set to try important national criminals and were not bound by state laws, just being accountable directly to the emperor.

During the early years of the Ming Dynasty, the General Command was established to take charge of the Ming troops. At the time when the Secretariat was abolished, the General Command was divided into five Military Commands-Left, Right, Central, Front, Rear-which were in charge of the troops in the capital and those of each dusi as well. While the five Military Commands handled such affairs as officials' provisions, training of soldiers, weapons and so on, the selection and appointment of military officers were entrusted to the Board of War and the Board of Civil Office. At the time when there were significant military actions, it was the emperor that appointed provincial military governors, dukes, marquises and earls as generals and grand generals to command the troops. As for the establishment for army units, a wei-suo system was adopted. Both wei and suo were set up in communication centers and every du si had several wei under its jurisdiction.

In order to arrogate all power to himself, Zhu Yuanzhang eliminated in succession a large group of influential officials and persons who had rendered outstanding services to him. After Hu Weiyong was executed, many people were killed as "members of Hu's gang". In 1393, the Grand General Lan Yu was killed and another group of people were implicated. In the two

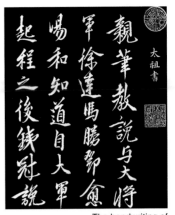

The handwriting of Zhu Yuanzhang, Emperor Tai Zu of Ming

Blue and white porcelain plate, Hongwu Period of Ming Dynasty (1368-1398 AD), diameter 58.2cm

cases of murder, which were known to historians as "Persecution of Hu-Lan," more than 50,000 persons were killed in succession, including nearly forty dukes and marquises. Zhu Yuanzhang did not scruple to use stern laws and severe punishments to uphold rules and disciplines as well as to stamp out political corruptions, which he paid particular attention to. In order to rope in talented persons, Zhu Yuanzhang gradually set up the civil service examinationination system as a means to elevate scholars and established Imperial College in the capital and schools in prefectures and counties throughout the country, at the same time when virtuous talents were recommended.

Zhu Yuanzhang kept a close lookout for court officials and claimed to take eunuchs under strict constraint. However, from the Hongwu period, eunuchs actually played an important role in political life. For instance, they were responsible for transmitting government decrees, supervising ministers, investigating officials and they were sent on diplomatic missions as well. All of this left behind a hidden danger for later generations.

Zhu Yuanzhang showed concern for the people's livelihood and laid stress on agricultural development. He encouraged peasants to reclaim wasteland and promoted the cultivation of cash crops, such as cotton and others. Water conservancy projects were constructed in all parts of the country. Zhu Yuanzhang based the registration as well as organization of population and requisition for taxes and rents on huang ce and yulin tuce, so as to guarantee the national revenue. The state economy thus stepped from a long-term destruction caused by war towards gradual recovery and prosperity

In 1398, Zhu Yuanzhang died at a venerable age of seventy-one and was buried at Xiao Mausoleum on Mountain Zhong in Nanjing. He was given the posthumous title of "Emperor Gao" and a temple name of Tai Zu.

Stone statue of civil official in the mausoleum of Ming Dynasty

第八篇

集权与转型

2. Emperor Yongle

Emperor Cheng Zu of Ming Dynasty, Zhu Di (1360-1424 AD)

To preserve and perpetuate the rule of China by the Zhu family, Zhu Yuanzhang, from 1370, began to appoint his twenty-four sons and grandsons to vassalages scattered across the country, and the designed purpose of these vassalages was to "protect the royal house in the capital". Upon his death, Zhu Yuanzhang was succeeded by his grandson, Zhu Yunwen, because the crown prince named Zhu Biao died young. The title of his reign was Jianwen. Fearful of the powerful vassalage, Zhu Yunwen decided to reduce vassal states.

In 1399, just when Zhu yunwen prepared to weaken the vassalage of Prince of Yan, the latter, whose name was Zhu Di, revolted publicly. Zhu Di, the forth son of Zhu YuanZhang, coveted the throne a long time ago. He and his supporters rallied to pledge resolution before launching an armed revolt and claimed to "stabilize the situation and pacify the country". Ever since, began the Campaign to Restore Order. In 1402 Zhu Di led his troops to Nanjing and Emperor Jianwen disappeared without a trace. Zhu Di thereby ascended the throne. The next year, he changed the reign title to Yongle.

Once upon the throne, Zhu Di massacred tens of thousands of persons in succession, among who most were honest and righteous men as well as civil and military officials of Emperor Jianwen. The event was known to historians as "Catastrophe of Renwu". He also declared that regulations that once were altered by Emperor Jianwen should all be restored. In addition, he renewed all the severe punishments and re-established prisons under the control emperors which was abolished by Zhu Yuanzhang. In addition, he established the Eastern Depot which was staffed by eunuchs. It was an intelligence agency specializing in spying on the privacy of the bureaucracy and the populace. Zhu Di also dispatched them to supervise the army, to garrison towns and to

Huayan Bell, the big bell in Juesheng Temple in Beijing, built in the Yongle Period of Ming (1403-1424 AD)

Hall of Prayer for Good Harvests in the Temple of Heaven in Beijing, built in the 18th year of Yongle Period of Ming (1420 AD)

go on expeditions so as to raise the status of eunuchs. During the early years of his reign, Zhu Di made some inexperienced but capable civil officials participate in important affairs. Among them were Xie Jin and Hu Guang, companions to the emperor in study; Huang Huai and Yang Shiqi, imperial compilers; Yang Rong, an editor; Jin Yiuzi and Hu Yan, inspectors. They were all appointed to work in Wenyuan Hall. Waiting upon for the emperor day and night, they became his advisers and formed a new agency called Inner Depot, with the duty of Handling official documents, maintaining law and order as well as issuing imperial mandates. With the passage of time, it became an administrative center.

In 1403, Zhu Di changed Beiping into Beijing. In order to rebuild the city, he mobilized workers

The letter from Yongle Emperor of Ming to Shangshihalima

Pray to Buddha, partial, Ming Dynasty, fresco in Gugegu town, Zhada County, Tibet

to dredge the Grand Canal, which linked the north and the south. In 1420, a new palace was constructed in Beijing. The next year, the capital was formally moved to Beijing. Being huge in scale and a project of great magnitude, the city of Beijing was divided into inner city, imperial city and Forbidden City. All the walls and moats, palaces and mansions, altars and temples in Beijing were masterpieces of China's ancient architecture. During his reign, Zhu Di recruited more than 3000 scholars, working for years, to compile the largest leishu in China's history, which was entitled *Great Encyclopedia of Yongle*.

Zhu Di was diligent in state affairs. In order to business boundaries, he personally led his troops to the frontier areas for five times on punitive expeditions against the Mongols, and established there local governments of different levels. In addition, he sent Chen Cheng, and Li Da to the Western regions, Hou Xian to Tibet and Zheng He to the Occident on diplomatic missions. To put a stop to the disturbance caused by the Annan he dispatched troops to inflict punishment. Pioneered and managed by Zhu Di, the Ming Dynasty came to the most glorious period.

In 1424, in his fifth northern expedition, Zhu Di died at the age of 65 in Yumuchuan and was buried at the foot of Mountain Tianshou in Changping of Beijing. His tomb was known as Chang Mausoleum. Zhu Di was given the posthumous title of Emperor Wen and a temple name of Tai Zu, which was changed into Cheng Zu in 1538.

Buddhist convent of White Pagoda, according to legends it preserved the mantle of Emperor Jian Wen, outside the gate of Bucheng, Beijing, 25m high

Front gate of the Imperial Palace in Beijing, built in the 18th year of Yongle Period of Ming Dynasty (1420 AD), rebuilt in the 4th year of Shunzhi Period of Qing Dynasty

第八篇

集权与转型

Great Encyclopedia of Yongle of the Ming Dynasty, compiled from 1403 to 1408AD

A pair of mandarin ducks, Ming Dynasty (1368-1644 AD), diameter 9.5cm, 1.5cm thick

Blue and white porcelain octagonal candle-stick, Yongle Period of Ming Dynasty (1403-1424 AD)

Jade ornament in openwork, Ming (1368-1644 AD), diameter 4.7cm, 2.3cm high

Pottery cart, Ming (1368-1644 AD), 70cm high

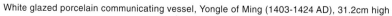

White glazed porcelain communicating vessel, Yongle of Ming (1403-1424 AD), 31.2cm high

Former Confucian Worthies and Sages, Ming, Baoning temple in Youyu county, Shanxi province, 118cm high, 62cm wide

Filial descendants, Ming, Baoning temple in Youyu county, Shanxi province, 118cm high, 62cm wide

Ancient city of Pingyao, Shanxi province

第八篇

集权与转型

3. Zheng He's Voyages to the Occident

Zheng He (1371-1435 AD)

200 vessels. Among them were 62 large ships that had a length of 130 and a width of 53. Able to carry aboard more than 1000 passengers, it was equipped with nine masts that flew 12 sails. Those who participated in the navigation were as many as more than 27,000. Being the most advanced fleet in the contemporary world, the ships were provided with sea charts, compasses and experienced sailors as well as quartermasters. The fleet sailed to Zhancheng, Java and Guli, and returned to Nanjing in 1407, with a voyage lasting two years and three months.

Since then, Zheng He had, six times in succession, sailed on long voyages in 1407,1409,1413,1417,1421 and 1431. The fleet sailed along over 30 countries and regions in Asia and Africa and the longest voyage carried him all the way to the eastern coast of Africa and the littoral of the Red Sea. The voyages strengthened the contacts between the Ming Dynasty and other countries in Asia and Africa and gave an impetus to cultural and economic exchange between them.

Zheng He (1371-1435), whose original surname was Ma and whose childhood name was Sanbao, also known as "three treasures", was a native of Kunyang of Yunnan (modern Jinning). During the Hongwu period, he was selected and retained in the imperial palace. Later, he was in the attendance of Prince of Yan named Zhu Di. As he performed great feats in the Campaign to Restore Order, he was promoted to eunuch and was conferred the surname of Zheng.

The fleet under the command of Zheng He were supplied with large quantities of cargo, including porcelain, silk goods, iron implements, silver and copper coins, so they were also referred to as "ships of treasure". Wherever he went, he publicized the national power and influence of the Ming Dynasty and invited the host sovereign to send emissaries to present tribute to China. As for economy, the Ming government pursued a policy of "stressing grants, not gains". Therefore, no matter what country he visited, Zheng He presented it with large number of rewards and carried out fair trade with local officials and civilians.

Being a feat in the history of navigation of mankind, Zheng He's expeditions manifested the intelligence and ability of the Chinese people.Compared with the discovery of America in 1492 by Columbus of Italia and the navigation around the Cape of Good Hope by Vasco da Gama of Portugal, Zheng He's first long

The year of 1405 saw a world-shaking event in China's transportation history. By imperial edict, Zheng He, a eunuch, leading all the sailors, set to sea from the Port of Liujia in Suzhou. It was a vast fleet of all together over

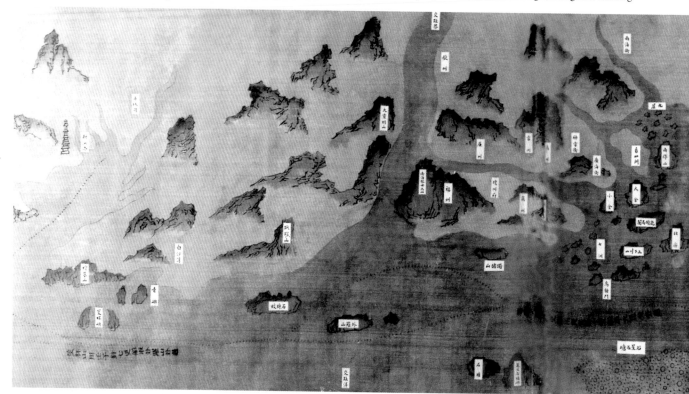

voyage was greater in scale and approximately eighty or ninety years earlier. Seeds of the friendship between the people were sowed wherever he went. In Southeast Asia today, there are towns, wells, ports and places of interest named after Sanbao. Many emissaries, merchants, and even rulers of the land came to China either on board of Zheng He's fleet or by the sea route opened by him.

One of Zheng He's retainers named Ma Huan wrote a book entitled *Vision in Triumph in a Boundless Sea*. Fei Xin also wrote a book entitled *Vision in Triumph: Ships Sail Under Starry Sky*. And Gong Zhen wrote *A Record of Alien Nations in the West* as well. All books recorded people and things in the country they visited and thus enriched the Chinese people's knowledge of the world. Besides, names and locations of the places on his route, which was from Nanjing, then along the South China Sea and the India Ocean, and eventually to the eastern coast of Africa, were drawn and demonstrated in *Zheng He's Nautical Charts*. Summing up the experience of his navigating practice, Zheng He also wrote a book entitled *Indication of Direction by Compass*, which provided precious data for long-voyage navigation. Before he set to sea again in 1431, Zheng He had erected a stone tablet in Tianfei palace in Changle County of Fujian province, recording the course of his former six-time sailings. Such tablet was an important cultural relic in China's navigation history.

The Routes of Zheng He's Voyages to the Western Seas

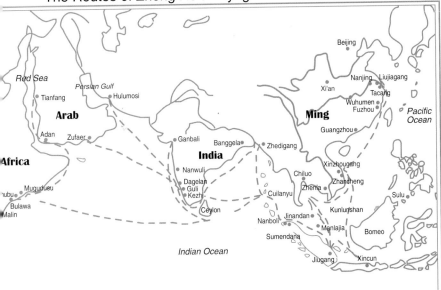

White glazed porcelain pot, Ming (1368-1644 AD), 19.7cm high

Blue and white porcelain pot, Hongwu Period of Ming Dynasty (1368-1398 AD), 38cm high

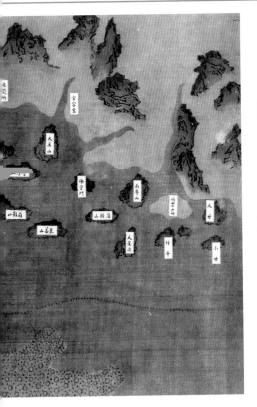

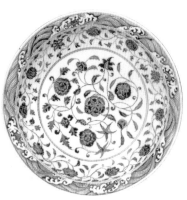

Blue and white porcelain plate with peony design, Xuande Period of Ming Dynasty (1426-1435 AD)

The Nautical Chart (partial reproduced), the 5th year of Xuande Period, Emperor Xuan Zong of Ming (1430 AD), used by Zheng He in his 7th voyage to the Western Seas

Dehua three-dragon porcelain pot, Ming Dynasty (1368-1644 AD), 12.9cm high, bottom diameter 4.8cm

第八篇

集权与转型

4. From Tumu Incident to Conferment on Altan Khan

The Great Wall of Ming Dynasty

The Mongols in the north of the Gobi desert was the major threat to the Ming regime. During the reigns of Emperor Hongwu and Emperor Yongle, the Ming court dispatched time and again troops to go beyond the Great Wall on a northern expedition against the Mongols and established many *wei* and *suo* there for stationing troops. At that time, all the Mongol tribes presented tribute to the Ming court. During the reign of Renxuan, the stern and ruthless state policy became relaxed and the frontier defending force in the north was like to draw back. In Xuande's reign (1426-1435), the Oirats unified all the Mongol tribes and gradually took control over a vast region that extended from central Asia in the west to Korea in the east. Time and again, they sent troops to harass the border and pressed on towards frontier fortress.

In Zhengtong's reign (1436-1449), an eunuch named Wang Zhen wielded political power of the state. In 1449, on the pretexts that the Ming court deliberately forced down prices of their horses, insulted their emissaries and broke off a marriage contract, the Oirats dispatched the troops along four routes to attack Datong, Xuanfu (modern Xuanhuan, Hebei), Chicheng (in modern Hebei), Liaodong and Ganzhou (modern Zhangye,Gansu). The defending forces of the Ming Dynasty were routed repeatedly and the situation became critical. Wang Zhen did his utmost to incite the emperor to lead   an army of 500,000 soldiers personally to meet the invaders head-on, despite the admonition not to do so of Kuangye, a minister of the Board of War and Yu Qian, the left Deputy Minister of War. Before arriving at Datong, however, the Ming troops withdrew hastily. In a place called Tumubao (twenty *li* west of modern Huailai County, Hebei), the Ming troops were surrounded by the Oirats and Ying Zong of the Ming Dynasty was captured alive; Wang Zhen, was also killed by rioting soldiers. More than half of 500,000 Ming soldiers were killed as a result. Such was the well-known "Tumu Incident".

After the Ming troops suffered a crushing defeat in Tumubao, the situation in Beijing tended to be in imminent danger. Some ministers suggested to move the capital southward, which was opposed by Yu Qian, the Left Deputy Minister of War and some others. Then he was appointed as Minister of War and was ordered to defend the capital. Meanwhile, Prince of Cheng named Zhu Qiyu was designated emperor (Emperor Jingtai), and thus the minds of people were set at ease. Thanks to the corporation of soldiers and civilians, Yu Qian routed the Oriat troops time and again and compelled Esen to break camp and run away.

In August of the very next year, Esen had no option but to send an envoy to return Ying Zong and requested to restore tribute and trade between the Oirats and the Ming. Towards the Jiajing period (1522-1566), the Tartars, another Mongolian group, under the leadership of Tayan Khan, became powerful after having conquered all the other Mongolian groups. It posed a new threat to the Ming regime. In 1550 (year of Geng Xu), Altan Khan (1506-1582), the grandson of Tayan Khan, raised an army in Gubeikou, then marched into Hebei proper and pressed on towards Tongzhou. The invaders then burned, killed, and plundered in the suburbs of Beijing, such as Miyun, Sanhe and Changping and this event was known to historians as "Catastrophe of Geng Xu".

Later on, the Altan tribe invaded and harassed the hinterland from time to time, and the Ming government repeatedly imposed a curfew in the capital. After the reign title of the Ming Dynasty was changed into Longqing (1567), the frontier defense was strengthened, due to the fact that Gao Gong, Senior Secretary of the Grand Secretariat and Minister of Rites, as well as other officials paid a relative attention to the construction of boarder areas. Meanwhile, the Tartars increasingly felt it more favorable to have a friendly relationship and trade with the Ming than to launch a war against it.

In 1571 (the fifth year in Longqing period), Altan entreated the Ming court to confer a title on him and wanted to pay tribute to the Ming as well as to restore trade with it. Governor-general named Wang Chonggu, who was in charge of defense affairs of the northern regions, and the governor of Datong named Fang Fengshi, submitted a written statement to the Ming court for approval,

Emperor Xuan Zong of Ming Dynasty, Zhu Zhanji
(1398-1435 AD)

Emperor Shi Zu of Ming Dynasty, Zhu Houcong
(1522-1566 AD)

which won supports of Zhang Juzheng and Gao Gong, the Senior Secretary of the Grand Secretariat. Thus Altan Khan and the Ming government negotiated peace and the latter conferred upon the former the title of the "Prince of Shunyi". Besides, trades and tribute were permitted by the Ming government; the city where Altan Khan lived was given the name of *Guihua*; all the brothers, nephews and descendants of Altan Khan were awarded positions; and markets were opened in Datong, Xuanfu and other places. All of the grants by the Ming government were known to historians as "Conferment on Altan Khan". In 1587, a woman leader of the Tartars named San Niangzi, was conferred the title of "Zhongshun Lady." As she held power for more than 20 years, the Tartars and the Ming maintained a friendly relationship with each other. Moreover, they presented tributes to each other and carried out trade between them. Thus, the situation in the region from Xuanfu and Datong to Gansu became stable and calm.

Glazed screen wall with nine dragons design in front of the residence of Prince Gui

5. Japanese Pirates and Ming's Resistance Against the Japanese Pirates

Qi Jiguang (1528-1587 AD)

In the last years of the Yuan Dynasty and the early years of the Ming Dynasty, Japan was then in the Southern and Northern Dynasties which were featured with division and tangled fighting. Many defeated and dispersed generals and soldiers and samurai that emerged in the tangled warfare, went to some islands after an exile. They usually, in the collusion with lawbreaking merchant ships and bandits on the sea, raided and pillaged China's coastal areas. In the meantime, some separatist regimes in Japan often dispatched samurai to trade or plunder on the sea. The crowds mentioned above constituted the "Japanese pirates."

In the early years of the Ming Dynasty, the Japanese pirates had a simple constitution, formed mainly by Japanese sea rovers. As private foreign trade gradually expanded from the middle era of the Ming Dynasty, some powerful gentry, in order to reap colossal profits by shaking off the restraint of the Ming government, even pretended to be pirates or collaborated with or incited them to pillage and slaughter people in coastal regions, resulting in serious disasters. During the Jiajing period, the composition of pirates became complicated day by day, and thus the trouble made by pirates got worse evidently.

In 1547, the Ming court specially appointed Zhu Wan (1494-1550) as governor of Zhejiang, to rectify military affairs in Zhejiang and Fujian so as to defend against the Japanese pirates. Zhu Wan then strengthened the coastal defense and rigorously ordered people not to put to sea. Besides, he searched and arrested those unscrupulous merchants as well as those rich and powerful people who had collaborated with the Japanese. By doing so, he was opposed by all the bureaucracy in coastal areas of Zhejiang and Fujian, who were concerned in foreign trade. As a result, he was dismissed from office and was investigated by the Ming government. Eventually, he was forced to commit suicide by taking poison. After his death, the Japanese pirates became more and more wild and unrestrained. In 1553, the Japanese pirates invaded and harassed China's coastal areas on a large scale, killing and pillaging the people. The next year, they went into South China again, burning countless houses and killing innumerable persons. Governor of Zhejiang named Wang Yu (1507-1560) conducted Yu Dayou (1504-1580) and others to resist the Japanese pirates and then won a battle on Putuo Mountain. In 1555, Zhang Jing (?-1555), Minister of War in Nanjing and military Supreme commander of the provinces in southeast China, commanding the soldiers and civilians of the Han, Zhuang, Miao and Yao nationalities, routed the Japanese pirates in Wangjiangjing (to the north of modern Jiaxing, Zhejiang). In that battle which was known as Victory at Wangjiangjing, about 2,000 enemies were killed and countless were burned or drowned. Before long, Zhang Jing, framed by the henchmen of Yan Song (1480-1565), was put to death in prison.

In the same year when the Ming troops won the battle in Wangjiangjing, Qi Jiguang (1528-1587) was transferred from Shandong to fight against the Japanese pirates. Qi Jiguang, who styled himself Yuanjing and whose alias was Nantang, was a man of Penglai, Shandong. Born and brought up in a hereditary family

Penglai Pavilion (in Penglai, Shandong province), Qi Jiguang once trained his army to fight the Japanese pirates

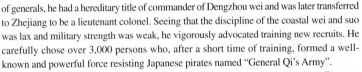

Mounted man guard of honor, Ming Dynasty (1368-1644 AD), 32.5-39cm high, unearthed from the tomb of Zhu Gongdu in Chang'an, Shaanxi province

Enameling bronze horse harness, Ming

of generals, he had a hereditary title of commander of Dengzhou wei and was later transferred to Zhejiang to be a lieutenant colonel. Seeing that the discipline of the coastal wei and suo was lax and military strength was weak, he vigorously advocated training new recruits. He carefully chose over 3,000 persons who, after a short time of training, formed a well-known and powerful force resisting Japanese pirates named "General Qi's Army".

In 1561, General Qi's Army got a resounding victory of a battle in Taizhou. The next year, they fought to Fujian. In 1563, cooperating with Yu Dayou, Qi Jiguang won a battle in Pinghaiwei. By the spring of 1564, all the Japanese pirates in Zhejiang and Fujian had been mopped up. Then General Qi's Army turned to Guangdong. In the meantime, General Yu's Army established by Yu Dayou, also achieved miraculous feats in battles against the Japanese pirates. They demonstrated their martial prowess especially in suppressing the pirates in Guangdong. In 1566, the Japanese pirates in coastal areas of southeast China were wiped out completely. Before long, the Ming court lifted the ban on maritime trade and allowed private trade on sea.

Terra Cotta warriors, Ming Dynasty (1368-1644 AD), 51cm high

Chariot, Ming Dynasty, 350cm long, 320cm wide

Iron canon of Ming Dynasty in Shanhai Pass, Chongzhen Period of Ming Dynasty (1621-1644 AD)

6. The Transforming Society

The Ming Dynasty was established in turbulent times. But after the establishment of the Ming Dynasty, officials and civilians then scrupulously abided by the norms of etiquette. The prevailing custom of the people was simple and honest. Society of that time was featured with a natural and plain practice. After the reign of Zheng De, however, yielding themselves to the temptation of commodities and money, people went beyond social etiquette and upheld an extravagant life style. Therefore, changes took place in all respects such as people's daily life, weddings and funerals, as well as habits and customs of bureaucracy and scholars.

Every social member vied for personal gain and worshipped money. Not only did numerous merchants and handicraftsmen stint no effort in seeking profit, but also a tendency towards engaging in trade and business appeared in the countryside. While social status of merchants went up day by day, the traditional moral principles and ethics fell into a decline. Zhu Zaiyu (1536-1611) wrote in *Sheep on Hillside-Money Talks*, "Everybody opens his eyes and sees clearly. Nothing but money is true. Having it, you could be always happy, while without it, nobody could move even a single step. Rich cripples' walk is stylish and wealthy dumb persons could sign elegantly. Now, what people admire is nothing but money".

All the landlords and squires also competed in seeking money and engaged in malpractices and perverted the law for personal gains. Many bureaucrats regarded the official career as a short cut to amassing a fortune, thus it became a common practice to flatter and solicit others for help. Such matters as the strong bullying the weak, and the many insulting the few were also popular. Besides, it was a prevailing custom to contest a lawsuit, to be litigious and to gamble. Proper regard for precedence and seniority met an unprecedented challenge. The younger generation of prostitutes, actors, actress and yamen runners, who used to be low in social status, now tried to raise their position by pursuing profits. Such emerged in an endless stream that the lower level overrode the higher level and that the young insulted the old, which aggravated the instability in social class development.

Practices of officialdom and habits of scholars also underwent an utterly different transformation. In the middle as well as the last periods of the Ming Dynasty, eunuchs meddled in state affairs; political struggle and factional strife broke out time and again; discipline and order were lax; and bureaucrats took it as honor to indulge in pleasures as well as to fish for fame and compliments. All the factors mentioned above made the politics of the Ming Dynasty depraved. Besides, customs in

Gilded bronze filigree enameling incense burner with two loop-handles, Ming Dynasty (1368-1644 AD), 28cm high, rim 19cm, bottom diameter 14cm

Gem laid leaf-shaped gold ornament, Ming (1368-1664 AD), 7.9cm high, 6.7cm wide

Dehua porcelain statue of Avalokitesvara, Ming Dynasty (1368-1644 AD)

Painted porcelain figures of standing men (2 pieces), Ming Dynasty (1368-1644 AD), 33.4cm and 34cm high

Green-glazed pottery figures of standing men (2 pieces), Ming Dynasty (1368-1644 AD), 38.5cm and 38cm high

Women guard of honor (7 pieces), Ming Dynasty (1368-1644 AD), 21-23cm high, unearthed from the tomb of Zhu Gongdu, Chang'an, Shanxi province

the academic world went from bad to worse, and came into a state of decay. Being no more pragmatic as well as energetic and promising, scholars tended to be deceitful, overambitious and showing malicious joy.

As for the life style, people all broke the norms of etiquette and social stratum to quest for spacious houses, splendid furnishings as well as bright and beautiful clothes. Influenced by the prevailing customs, even ordinary citizens regarded luxury as honor. Such a general mood reflected that traditional society had been affected by commodity economy. Those that upheld traditions sighed with regret that "people had gone beyond proper bounds" and "customs and education had degenerated." However, in an actual fact, it was to breed traditions and to make it clear to all that a new era was coming.

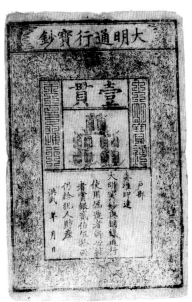
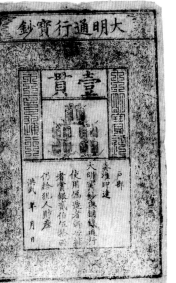

Paper currency of Ming Dynasty, 33cm long, 22cm wide

A set of square silver cups, Ming Dynasty (1368-1644 AD), 12 pieces, diameter of rim 4.1-8.6cm

Five-colored plate with dragon and phoenix design, Ming Dynasty (1368-1644 AD), 4.3cm high, rim diameter 25.8cm, bottom diameter 15.7cm

The performance scene in the illustration of Plum in the Gold Vase

Writing brush with black clouds design, Ming Dynasty (1368-1644 AD), 20cm long

Ink stone of the 6th year of Zhengde Period, Ming Dynasty (1368-1644 AD), 34cm long

Black wooden desk, Ming Dynasty (1368-1644 AD), 87cm high

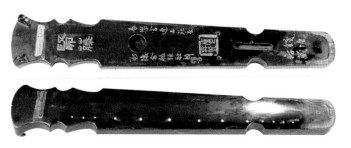

A lacquer instrument, Ming Dynasty (1368-1644 AD), 120cm long

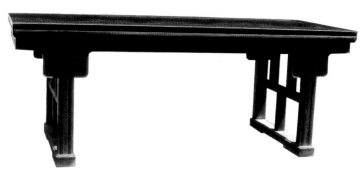

Red sandlewood drawing desk, Ming Dynasty (1368-1644 AD), 85cm high

Exponents from various schools of thought, Ming Dynasty, Baoning Temple, Youyu County, Shanxi province, 118cm high, 62cm wide

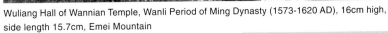

Wuliang Hall of Wannian Temple, Wanli Period of Ming Dynasty (1573-1620 AD), 16cm high, side length 15.7cm, Emei Mountain

Round chair with eight legs, Ming Dynasty, 49cm high

Chair, Ming Dynasty, the seat surface 58.5cm x 119.5cm

The illustration in Stories to Enlighten the World, one of three collections of short stories in Ming Dynasty

Huang Juan Spring Outing, bingzi year of Chongzhen in Ming Dynasty (1636 AD), ink and color on silk scroll, 38cm x 311.2cm

第八篇

集权与转型

7. Country Harmed by Fatuous Rulers and Dictatorship of a Eunuch Clique

Emperor Shenzong of Ming Dynasty, Zhu Yijun (1563-1620 AD)

Zhang Juzheng (1525-1582 AD)

During the reigns of Zhengde (1506-1521) and Jiajing (1522-1566), calamities and chaos broke out in profusion. Wuzong loved pleasure and indulged in dissipations and Shizong, believed in Taoism. The whole ruling class had become completely corrupt and degenerate. Japanese pirates in the south, barbarians in the north and peasant uprisings all posed threats to the Ming regime. Ministers in the Grand Secretariat struggled fiercely for the leading position. Chief Secretary of the Grand Council, equal to the Prime Minister, was of crucial importance in national policy making..

In order to emphasize that he was the legitimate heir and to strengthen his imperial authority, Emperor Jiajing initiated the "disputation on rites between Ministers", under the pretext of presenting Prince of Xing Xian, his father-in-law, with a posthumous title. Such movement led all the ministers to factional strife. Those who obeyed imperial orders would be assigned to key posts; otherwise, they would be retaliated. Yan Song (1480-1565), who was good at writing prayers of the Taoists, tried to please the emperor and eventually, was appointed as head of the Inner chancery with the support of influential officials and eunuchs. Towards the end of Jiajing's reign, some insightful people rose to reform court affairs. On the local level, Pan Jixun (1521-1595) and Pang Shangpeng (?-c.1582) initiated reforms of taxes and levies. Besides, Qi Jiguang won a resounding victory in his fighting against the Japanese pirates. During the Longqing period (1567-1572), Hai Rui (1514-1587) and Gao Gong recognized domestic affairs and Qi Jiguang as well as Wang Chonggu strengthened border defense.

At the beginning of Wanli period (1573-1620), Zhang Juzheng, succeeding to be head of the Inner Chancery, pushed the reforms to a climax. In order to stamp out political corruption, he introduced a strict comprehensive check-up system. To measure the land of the whole country, he carried out "Integrated Cash Tax Law". As for water conservancy works, he charged Pan Jixun, an expert in water control, with the duty of harnessing the Yellow River and Huaihe River. In addition, frontier defense in the north was also strengthened.

After the death of Zhang Juzheng, Shen Zong of the Ming Dynasty assumed the reins of government. However, being given to a corrupt and luxurious living, he didn't pay attention to state affairs for years and he rarely met his ministers. Most of the memorials presented by ministers were laid aside. Moreover, Shenzong even didn't go personally to offer sacrifices to ancestors, which was the most sacred and solemn matter for the monarch. At this time, court officials were either dismissed or compelled to resign from theirs posts, thus many key positions in the government were left vacant. On the one hand, the central government organization nearly came to a standstill. On the other hand, however, many superintendents and tax collectors were dispatched in succession to all parts of the country to extort money and valuables.

As Shenzong's queen had no son, he wanted to make the son of his favorite imperial concubine whose family name was Zheng, crown prince. For this, court officials formed different cliques and thus factional strife broke out one after another. Gu Xiancheng, a Senior Secretary of the

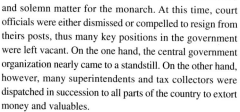

"Jin Yi Wei Yin" Seal, Ming Dynasty

Painted statue of eunuch, Ming Dynasty

Gu Xiancheng (1550-1612 AD)

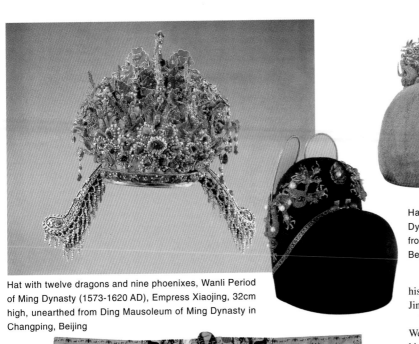

Hat with gold wing, Wanli Period of Ming Dynasty (1573-1620 AD), 24cm high, unearthed from Ding Mausoleum of Ming Dynasty in Changping, Beijing

Hat with black gauze wing, Wanli Period of Ming Dynasty (1573-1620 AD), 23.5cm high, unearthed from Ding Mausoleum of Ming Dynasty in Changping, Beijing

Hat with twelve dragons and nine phoenixes, Wanli Period of Ming Dynasty (1573-1620 AD), Empress Xiaojing, 32cm high, unearthed from Ding Mausoleum of Ming Dynasty in Changping, Beijing

Imperial robe in Kesi fabric (restoration of the one unearthed from Ding Mausoleum of Ming Dynasty)

Board of Civil Office, was dismissed from his post for he vigorously advocated making Shen Zong's eldest son named Zhu Changluo crown prince. Then Gu Xiancheng, together with his younger brother Gu Yuncheng and others, rebuilt and repaired the Donglin Academy in his hometown Wuxi, where he joined with Gao Panlong and other persons to deliver lectures. Not only did those scholars "speak candidly on current affairs," but they "criticized contemporary leaders as well". Thus the Donglin Academy once became a public opinion center. Some upright officials who were still in office also "coordinated with them from afar." People of that time called them Men of the Donglin Party. They wanted political reforms to be carried out in the government and opposed the ruthless plunder of many superintendents and tax collectors. They advocated laying stress on agriculture as well as industry and commerce. They wanted to strengthen the defense force in Liaodong so as to guard against the Manchus to march southward. Those that opposed to the Donglin Party were Zhe Party, Qi Party, Xuan Party, and Kun Party. During the Tianqi period of Emperor Xizong's reign (1621-1627), a eunuch clique headed by Wei Zhongxian, a eunuch of the Office of Rites, took shape. They ruthlessly suppressed the Donglin Party. Many members of Donglin Party were either dismissed from office, exiled or harassed to death in prison.

In the Ming Dynasty, organizations that were staffed by eunuchs were the so-called twenty-four yamen, including twelve imperial offices, four departments and eight bureaus. Among them Office of Rites were invested with the greatest power. The eunuchs who wielded a brush in the Office of Rites were responsible of writing comments to show approval or disapproval. Therefore, they often acted for the emperor to write comments on petitions and memorials. In addition, Office of Rites controlled such intelligence agencies as the Eastern Depot, the Western Depot and the Imperial Guard. There were several extremely arrogant eunuchs who manipulated state affairs in the Ming Dynasty, such as Wang Zhen, Liu Jin and Wei Zhongxian. During Zhengde period of Wu Zong's (Zhu Houzhao) reign, Liu Jin established a new intelligence agency called "Inner Depot" that was invested with even greater power, watching and supervising the activities of both the Eastern and Western Depot as well as the Imperial Guard. He alone made arbitrary decisions on significant affairs and dealt with the memorials and documents from all parts of the country at home. Every day, there were a lot of officials waiting for him at

his house gate to handle official business. Thus Liu Jin was then called "the standing emperor."

Wei Zhongxian (1568-1627), who originally named Wei Jinzhong, came to the imperial palace by castrating himself. When Xizong (on the throne from 1621 to 1627) came to throne, Wei Zhongxian became the emperor's confidant. With the help of Xizong's wet nurse with whom Wei was on friendly terms, he was quickly promoted to the eunuch wielding a brush in the Office of Rites. Then he formed a clique and discriminated against anybody who didn't belong to his coterie. In the name of "training the eunuchs", he chose some eunuchs to learn martial arts and to make firearms so as to build up his military force and control the whole nation by special and secret means. Many ministers bartered away their honor for the patronage of Wei and thus formed the eunuch clique. They were particularly antagonistic towards the Donglin Party. All those who held different views were labeled Men of the Donglin Party. In order to get rid of the dissidents, Wei Zhongxian ordered to prohibit and destroy the Imperial Academies throughout the country. Although he committed misdeeds and crimes, and claimed himself to be "Nine Thousand Years" (Note: a deferential allusion to a prince that was next to the emperor), Emperor Xizong conferred him the highest honorable title of a minister, called "Superior Duke". Besides, he was bestowed an inscribed metal pledge of the emperor that no matter what crime he would commit, he would not be given death penalty, and he was also given one thousand qing of farmland by Xizong. The governor of Zhejiang, named Pan Ruzhen, built a memorial hall for the living Wei and thus for a time governors of all parts of the country competed to do likewise, leading to such a wide spread indignation and discontent that he was spat on and cursed by all the people.

Then Xizong died and was succeeded by Emperor Sizong of the Ming Dynasty (named Zhu Youjian) (reigned from 1628 to 1644), who resolutely eliminated Wei Zhongxian. However, Sizong was so opinionated that before long he once again assigned eunuchs to key posts. Therefore, the force of eunuchs grew wild and unrestrained for another time. They were dispatched on all missions such as defending, going on expedition, supervising soldier's pay and provisions, taking military command of battles and so on. Such a situation continued till the end of the Ming Dynasty.

8. Cultural Enlightenment

Song Lian (1310-1381 AD)

Fang Xiaoru (1367-1402 AD)

Wang Shouren (1472-1528 AD)

Li Zhi (1527-1602 AD)

Before the Chenghua and Hongzhi periods of the Ming Dynasty, the orthodox school of Neo-Confucianism represented by Zhu Xi was the ruling ideology that dominated the scholar. However, the social changes in the middle era of the Ming Dynasty, made some scholars feel the straits and restraint of the Neo-Confucianism pioneered by the Cheng Brothers and Zhu Xi. Therefore, these scholars rose to explore the path to new ideology. Among them was Chen Xianzhang, who styled himself Gong Fu and had an alias of Shi Zhai. As he was a man of Baishali of Xinhui Country, a place close to Jiangmei City, his theory was known as Jiangmei School. He laid stress on self-existence and self-value as well as subjective perception. Facing the copying style of the orthodox school of Neo-Confuciasm in the early years of the Ming Dynasty, he advocated a new learning style, which regarded it commendable to question authoritative works and to be self-confident about one's own views. Besides, he promoted independent thinking and spirit of emancipating the mind, that is, one should not only echo the views of the saints without thinking. His theory caused a sensation in the ideological and academic world of that time and thus broke a path for "the Theory of the Mind" of the Ming Dynasty.

During the Hongzhi and Zhengde periods, "all the bachelors in the nation loved the new and loathed the old". A native of Yuyao of Zhejiang, named Wang Shouren initiated Yaojiang School. He advocated his new theory and caused a sensation throughout the land. Thus the theory of the mind of the

Ming Dynasty was developed and spread widely. Wang Shouren (1472-1528), whose alias was Wang Bo'an, was also referred to as Master Yang Ming for he had lectured in his hometown named Yangmingdong. In 1499, he became a successful candidate in the highest imperial civil service examination. However, as he had offended the eunuch named Liu Jin, he was relegated to Longchangyi of Guizhou. Later, he made great contribution to the quelling of Prince of Ning, so he was promoted to Minister of War of Nanjing and was conferred the title of Count of Xinjian. Wang Shouren was the most important thinker in the Ming Dynasty and his writings were compiled into *The Complete Works of Wang Shouren* by his disciples. Two treatises in this book, *Record of Learning* and *Questions on the Great Learning* are his major contributions to the philosophical studies.

Wang Shouren advocated the theory of "there is no object, no word, no reason, no righteousness and no benevolence beyond the mind", which was known as "the theory of the mind". The gist of this school of philosophy is the theory of "innate knowledge" and that "mind is reason". "Agreement between knowledge and action" is its theoretical base. He inherited and developed Lu Jiuyuan's philosophy.Thus the theories of these two persons were jointly called the "Lu-Cheng School". Having an evidently opposing attitude towards traditions, Wang Yangming's theory of the mind stressed man's nature and respected individual thinking, which was the beginning of a rebellious trend of thought that people should pursue the liberation of individual personality. His theory built up its own system in the early years of Jiajing's reign and was soon in full bloom, thus becoming an essential aspect of academic thinking.

Li Zhi (1527-1602), was the offspring of

Tao Village and Thatched Abode, Ming Dynasty, Xiu Ying (?-1552 AD), silk scroll, green and blue, 150cm high, 53cm wide

Carved lacquer box with pavilion and people design, Ming (1368-1644 AD), 4.5cm high, rim diameter 12.9cm

Carved bamboo figure of fishman, Ming (1368-1644 AD), by Zhu Sansong, 13.5cm high

Bronze figure of Bodhidharma , Ming (1368-1644 AD), 16.5cm high

Dehua Buddha, Ming (1368-1644 AD), He Chaozong, 21.5cm high

Lotus leaf-shaped jade bowl, Ming (1368-1644 AD), 5.3cm high, rim diameter 9.4cm

Mynas on a Pine Tree, by Emperor Wu Zong, Zhu Houzhao (?-1521 AD), silk scroll, 187.8cm high, 96.5cm wide

Celebration of Lunar New Year, Ming (1368-1644 AD), by Zhou Daoxing, 184.5cm high, 94.7cm wide

Cranes on a Pine Tree, Ming (1368-1644 AD), by Wang Weilie, silk scroll, 187.8cm, 96.5cm wide

the Taizhou School initiated by Wang Xuezhong and a thinker who opposed traditions in the last years of the Ming Dynasty. He violently attacked in sharp and forceful words the Confucian ethnical codes as well as three cardinal guides and five constant virtues elucidated in Cheng-Zhu's Neo-Confuciasm. He even pointed criticisms against Confucius who was regarded as "the Sage". He advocated developing human's "common nature" and wished people to develop their individual personalities freely. In addition, he advanced the idea of equality between men and women and some other views, which were regarded as "heterodoxy in the extreme" in the Ming Dynasty.

During the time from Wang Shouren to Li Zhi, it was popular throughout the country to free oneself from the fetters of traditional ideas as well as to quest for individual liberty and to regard selfish desire as positive. Thus formed a trend of thought to rebel against traditions in the middle as well as the last period of the Ming Dynasty. Such a trend of thought was of enlightening significance.

9. Science Being on the Way to Modern Times

Li Shizhen (1518-1593 AD)

Xu Guangqi (1262-1633 AD)

Xu Guangqi and Li Madou (1552-1610 AD)

During the Jiajing and Wanli periods, the development of society and economy and overseas trading demanded expanded production and technological reform of traditional commodities. As a result, an innovation as well as a summation of science and technology was needed urgently. The novel and pragmatic feature of Western science and technology, such as astronomy, calendar making, the manufacture of firearms, mechanical principle, water conservancy, architecture and cartography, which were passed on by European Jesuits, evoked the thirst for knowledge of those scholar-officials who were particular about real learning. The science and technology of the Ming Dynasty thereby started heading for modern times.

After the middle era of the Ming Dynasty, evident progress could be found in natural science. The outstanding scientific achievement in the Ming Dynasty was *Outline of Herb Medicine* compiled by a pharmacist named Li Shizhen (1518-1593). His alias was Li Dongbi and he was a native of Qizhou of Huguang (modern Qichun County, Hubei). His family had practiced medicine for generations. From 1552, he started his compilation of *the Outline of Herb Medicine*. It took him twenty-seven years to complete the book, which had been revised three times in succession and consisted of fifty-two chapters. In *the Outline*, he recorded 1,892 herbs, which were 374 ones more than those in his original draft; he listed 11,097 prescriptions, which were five times as much as those done by predecessors; and included more than 1,100 illustrations. Besides, he gave an accurate account of the manufacture, appearance, smell, indication and application of all the medicine. The Outline summarized all the knowledge on medicine and the experience of pharmacology of the last 2,000 years in China, and proposed a new understanding of many medicines. It also touched on such subjects of natural science as chemistry, mineralogy, crystallography, environment and organism as well as inheritance and variation. It was from the Outline that Darwin Charles (1809-1882), a British scientist, drew his inspiration to establish the theory of evolution.

Zhu Zaiyu (1536-1611) was Ren Zong's decedent in the sixth generation and the eldest son of Prince of Zheng by his princess. After the death of his father, he would inherit an imperial title according to the established practice. However, he declined the conferment repeatedly. Being diligent in study in his whole life, he was proficient in astronomy, calendar making, temperament, drawing, poetry and dance. His works included *Complete Collection of Temperament*, *Jialiang Mathematical Manuals*, *Pythagorean Illustration of Circles and Squares*, *Aphorisms to Awaken the Public* and others. He completed the calculation of twelve-mean-tones and the manufacture of the wind of twelve-mean-tone, thus solved the thorny theoretical problem of modulation that had existed for over 2,000 years in the history of music. Such was his distinguished accomplishment in temperament. Ricci Matteo, who, being adept in music and mathematics, came to China to do missionary work, passed on the two achievements mentioned above to Europe. Up to now, they have still been adopted in music circles all over the world. In addition, Zhu researched into astronomy and calendar. He computed the accurate length of a tropical year and measured the geographical latitude of Beijing and the oblique angle of geomagnetism.

Xu Guangqi (1562-1633), a native of Shanghai, styled himself Zixian and had an alias of Xuanhu. He became a successful candidate in the highest imperial civil service examinationination in Wanli period. His highest official position was Minister of Rites and Secretary of East Hall. He devoted his whole life to the research on practical science and was eager to learn and introduce western science and technology. In those years, Catholic Jesuits came to China to do missionary work, among whom an Italian named Ricci Matteo (1552-1610) and a German named Schallvon Bell Adam (1591-1666) were most well known. Xu Guangqi learned from them western mathematics as well as calendar and firearms. In mathematics, he translated in collaboration with Ricci Matteo Euclidean *Geometry* written by Euclid and introduced the geometric system in western mathematics. In *Similarities and Dissimilarities of Measurements* and *Pythagorean Theorem*, he compared the Chinese way with the western way and tightened up the ancient testifying method. In astronomy, Xu laid emphasis on inspection with instruments. Adopting advanced instruments as well as way of calculation, he conducted members of the calendric department to draw up the Stellar Chart, including all the celestial bodies, which was quite developed at that time. Besides, he was ordered to supervise the revision of calendar making and to employ such westerners as Longobardi.N., Terrenz.J.,Schallvon Bell Adam and Rho.J, who were well versed in astronomy and calendar making. After having worked together with them for five years, Xu Guangqi finally compiled *the Chongzhen Almanac*.

A Compendium of Farming written by Xu Guangqi was the most important book on agriculture in the Ming Dynasty. This book consisted of sixty chapters, and was divided into twelve subjects, namely, cost of farming, land system, farm work, water conservancy, agriculture, growing mulberry and raising silkworms, sericulture, cultivation, animal husbandry, manufacture and relief policy in years of famine. His book covered a wide range of things, including agriculture, as well as those policies, regulations and measures relating to agriculture, farm implements and agricultural technology. Not only did he summarize the agricultural science of forefathers, he also took in foreign knowledge. He was eager to know the world. He advocated developing trade between all the countries, as well as making canons by western means to resist the Manchu troops and promoting agriculture to make his country wealthy and strong. He was a great scientist who had entirely new ideas in the contemporary world and was also an important person who inherited the past and ushered in the future in the history of China's ancient science and technology.

The Travel Notes of Xu Xiake is the rarest of all books on science. Its another named Xu Hongzu (1586-1641), also known as Xu Xiake, styled himself Zhengzhi. He was a man of Jiangyin (modern Jiangyin, Jiangsu). Beginning at a time when he was still young, he went out to travel. He carefully observed and recorded each of the areas he had visited ---- its rivers and streams, its geomorphology and geology, its climate, its ecology and the distribution of animals and plants. *The Travel Notes*, a summation of his thirty years' inspection, consisted of 20 chapters and contained nearly 400,000 words. It was a work of importance in the world history of geography. In particular, the recording of the distribution, type and cause of formation of lava in China's southwest and his initiative scientific research that was carried out on the basis of such materials, were the earliest achievements in lava inspection.

Expositions of the Works of Nature is an encyclopedia on agriculture and handicraft industry. Its author was Song Yingxing (1587-1661), a man of Fengxin of Jianxi Province, who styled himself Changeng. The book consisted of three chapters and eighteen treaties. Being rich in content, the book first discussed the cultivation as well as the harvest and processing of crops. Second, it elaborated on the making of salt and the refining of sugar, the pressing of oil, the making of wine, production of clothing and the making of dyes. Third, it expounded the manufacture of such items as bricks and tiles, porcelains, boats and vehicles, the manufacture

Shu Ying—printed paper that indicates the content of the book Feng He Yuan Ben

Xu Xiake (1586-1641 AD)

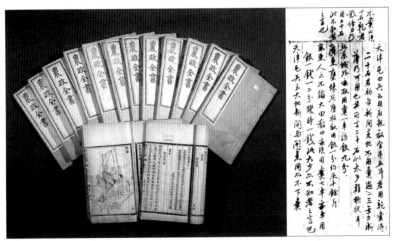

The manuscript and Shu Ying of A Compendium of Farming

Xu Xiake's manuscript, wrote in his travel in Yunan province

The illustration in Expositions of the Works of Nature

of military weapons, and the making of red and black dyes. Lastly, it discussed the mining, smelting and forging of metals and the utilization of lime, sulphur and coal. What was the most commendable was that Song Yingxing adopted ways of research that were similar to those employed in the modern times. For instance, he not only went to great detail in recording the raw materials to be used and the process of production for each item elaborated in his book, but also described it vividly by using illustrations, which were 123 in his book. Besides, he paid particular attention to using data to explain the production quality and efficiency as well as to compare the good and bad tools of production and the differences between crops. Thus the sizes of many tools were recorded in his book.

Contemporary scientists were Li Zhizao (1565-1630), Wang Zhi (1571-1644), Fang Yizhi (1611-1671) and others. They all made fruitful efforts in the pursuit of western advanced science and technology as well as in the promotion of Chinese ancient science and technology. From them, a ray of modern science came into view.

第八篇

集权与转型

Chapter 9

The Brilliant Setting Sun

--The Qing Dynasty

History seems to always follow the beaten track.

The Manchus crossed the Great Wall to China proper,

and ruled China in an even more autocratic way.

Nevertheless, they were unable to evade their fate of destruction.

It was also in this dynasty that Western solid warships and powerful cannon defeated the self-esteemed celestial Empire.

Doomed forever, the monarchy was on the wane.

Summer Palace, an Imperial Garden in Beijing

1. Rise of the Manchus and the Qing

Emperors in Qing Dynasty

Emperor Tai Zu of Qing Dynasty, Aisin Gioro
Nurhachi (1559-1626 AD)

Emperor Tai Zong of Qing Dynasty, Aisin Gioro
Huangtaiji (1592-1643 AD)

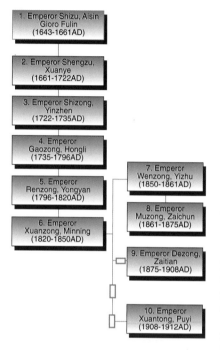

1. Emperor Shizu, Aisin Gioro Fulin (1643-1661AD)

2. Emperor Shengzu, Xuanye (1661-1722AD)

3. Emperor Shizong, Yinzhen (1722-1735AD)

4. Emperor Gaozong, Hongli (1735-1796AD)

5. Emperor Renzong, Yongyan (1796-1820AD)

6. Emperor Xuanzong, Minning (1820-1850AD)

7. Emperor Wenzong, Yizhu (1850-1861AD)

8. Emperor Muzong, Zaichun (1861-1875AD)

9. Emperor Dezong, Zaitian (1875-1908AD)

10. Emperor Xuantong, Puyi (1908-1912AD)

During the Ming Dynasty, the Nuzhens that inhabited the Northeast once maintained good relations with the Central Plains over a long period of time. They had three groups: Jianzhou, Haixi and Yeren. At one time, the Ming government established a local government called *Nuergan Dusi* in Telin on the estuary of the Heilongjiang River. Besides, more than 380 *wei* and *suo* (place of garrison) were distributed over the vast northeastern region. In the last years of the Ming Dynasty, however, the Northeast gradually got out of the hand of the Ming court. Having migrated several times, the Jianzhou Wei and Jianzhou Left Wei of the Nuzhen tribe, finally reached the Suzi rivers. In Shen Zong's reign, Nurhachi (1559-1626), who was the descendent of Mongtimur, the chief of Jianzhou Left Wei, inherited the leadership. They had a clan name of Aisin Gioro, which meant family of the deceased Nuzhen.

In 1583, Aisin Gioro Nurhachi, with thirteen sets of amour and weaponry that were handed down by his ancestors, began a war of unification of all the Nuzhen groups. In 1588, he subjugated the Jianzhou group by force. From then on and for nearly thirty years, he finally unified the Haixi group and controlled most of the territories of Yeren group. As his power increased steadily, the Ming court conferred in succession on him ranks of commander, commander-in -chief and grand commander, with the title of General of Longhu.

In 1601, Nurhachi introduced an Eight Banner System, under which 300 able-bodied men constituted a *niulu* (arrow); 5 *niulu* formed a *jiala* (team), and 5 *jiala* became a *gushan* (banner). There were altogether eight banners, each of which was identified by a specific color of its flag. At the beginning, there were only four banners of different colures: yellow, red, blue and white; later, four more banners were added: the yellow-bordered, the red - bordered, the blue-bordered and the white -bordered. The chief of each banner was called *gushan ezhen*, and each *jiala* as well as each *niulu* also had its own *ezhen*. The Eight Banners were an integration of army and government and the Nuzhen people were both producers and warriors. Therefore, *ezhen* was not only the military commander but also an executive head. As for Nurhachi, he was the patriarch as well as the supreme commander of the Eight Banners. The head of each banner was one of his sons or nephews, who was called "heshuo King of *Gushan*" (or King of Gushan). Heshuo beile was the supreme leader of each Banner and all the significant state affairs were discussed and decided jointly by the eight kings. In the meantime, Nurhachi constructed the Hetuala City (present Xinbin, Liaoning Province) and adopted such measures as selection of talents, enactment of statutes and invention of a written language. In 1616, Nurhachi established in

Yuan Chonghuan (1584-1630 AD)

Hetuala the regime Great Jin, known as Later Jin to historians, with the reign title of Tianming. Nurhachi was called Great Sagacious Khan.

In 1618, Nurhachi first listed "seven hatreds" against the Ming Dynasty and then launched an attack on the Ming under the pretext of these 'seven hatreds'. The Ming government thus assembled 100,000 soldiers and appointed Yang Hao as High Commissioner of Liaodong to prepare for an offensive action. The next year, the Ming troops marched towards the capital of Later Jin along four routes. However, the Ming army was decisively defeated in the battle fought at Sarhu (to the east of Fushun City, Liaoning). From then on, the Ming Dynasty was on the defensive. In 1621, Nurhachi conquered the strategic Liaoyang and Shenyang, and controlled the whole region of the east of the Liaohe River. In 1625, the capital of Later Jin, which had once been moved to Liaoyang, was then moved to Shenyang, which was renamed Shengjing.

The conflicts between the Ming and Later Jin became more and more intense. However, the eunuch clique monopolized power during Xi Zong's reign. They wanted to abandon all the areas outside the Great Wall and compelled the inhabitants to move southward. Nevertheless, the military governor of Jiliao, Yuan Chonghuan (1584-1630) would rather die than comply with the request. He and his followers put up a heroic resistance at the isolated Ningyuan (modern Xingcheng, Liaoning). In 1626, at the head of 130,000 men, Nurhachi attacked the Ming Dynasty on a large scale. Yuan Chonghuan and his army fought back with great bravery. As a result, the Jin troops failed to take Ningyuan and suffered serious injuries in the battle. Nurhachi, wounded by canon, had to withdraw and died from sorrow shortly afterwards. This battle was known as "Victory in Ningyuan".

After Nurhachi died, Huangtaiji, his eighth son, succeeded him. Setting up a trap to sow discord and distrust among the Ming camp, Huangtaiji made Emperor Chong Zhen condemn Yuan Chonghuan to death and thus he gradually took control over the whole Northeast. Besides the Manchu Eight Banners, Mongolian Eight Banners and Han Eight Banners were also established in Nuzhen army. In 1636, Huangtaiji declared himself emperor in Shenyang and named his new regime "Great Qing". He changed the reign title to Chongde and called the Nuzhen "Manchu". Huangtaiji established Three Inner Chanceries (Inner Secretariat, Inner Institution in charge of the writing of history and Inner Institution in charge of commenting historic losses and gains, issuing and carrying out certain systems) and six Boards. Later new organs such as the Censorate and the Board of Minorities Affairs were added. These organizations of government were jointly known as Three Chanceries and Eight *yamen*, through which Huangtaiji pinned down the force of the Eight Banners and centralized the state power.

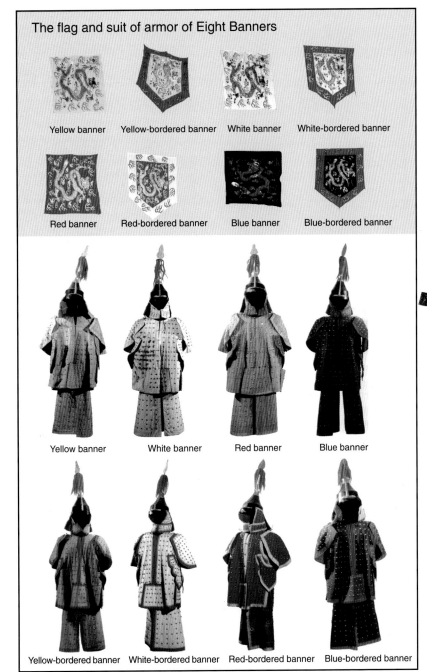

The flag and suit of armor of Eight Banners

Yellow banner

Yellow-bordered banner

White banner

White-bordered banner

Red banner

Red-bordered banner

Blue banner

Blue-bordered banner

Yellow banner

White banner

Red banner

Blue banner

Yellow-bordered banner

White-bordered banner

Red-bordered banner

Blue-bordered banner

The treasured sword of Aisin Gioro Nurhachi

Iron canon, Qing Dynasty

"Unconquerable General" Canon, Qing Dynasty

第九篇

辉煌落日

2. Success and Failure of Li Zicheng

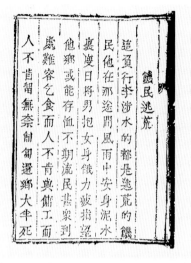

The content of poor people's lives, inscription, Ming Dynasty

Beginning from the middle era of the Ming Dynasty, mutinies, peasant uprisings and slave rebellions broke out one after another in all parts of the country. And such revolts were much broader in scale than before. In 1627, peasant Wang Er was the first to start revolt in Chengcheng, Shaanbei. Then in succession, Wang Jiayin staged an uprising at Fugu, and Gao Yingxiang and Zhang Xianzhong (1606-1647) did likewise in Ansai and Yan'an, respectively. In 1630, Li Zicheng (1606-1645), a man of Mizhi, joined the peasant army. In 1631 the Ming government dispatched Hong Chengchou (1593-1665) to command the military affairs in frontier areas and to suppress the insurgents. As Gao Yingxiang's military force was the most powerful among peasant armies, he was elected to be the Dashing King. As for Li Zicheng, he was the Dashing General. In 1635, Hong Chengchou was transferred to his new post as military governor of five provinces to encircle and suppress peasant revolts. GaoYingxiang and others, altogether thirteen military groups and seventy-two battalions joined forces in Yingyang,

Bronze seal of Li Zicheng's Da Shun regime

Li Zicheng's Entry into Beijing City

Henan Province. Then they divided forces to meet the Ming troops head-on. The peasant army led by Gao Yingxiang and others conquered Fengyang, original home of Zhu Yuanzhang, where they burned and destroyed the tombs of the reigning emperor's ancestors. Such actions stunned the Ming court. The next year, Gao was captured and subsequently executed. Li Zicheng then succeeded to be the Dashing King. From then on, two major forces led by Li Zicheng and Zhang Xianzhong respectively, gradually took shape.

In 1637, the Ming government dispatched the Minister of War named Yang Sichang (1588-1641) to suppress the peasant army. Zhang Xianzhong and his men, pretending to surrender to the government, rested and recognized. Li Zicheng and his followers, having suffered extremely heavy losses, hid themselves in the Shangluo Mountains. In 1639 Zhang Xianzhong rose again and broke through the encirclement of the Ming troops. In 1643, he declared himself King of Da Xi and set up his regime. The

Shi Kefa (1601-1645 AD)

Wu Sangui (1612-1678 AD)

next year, he proclaimed himself emperor at Chengdu and called his regime "Da Xi" ("Great West"), with the reign title of Dashun. Then Li Zicheng also went out of Henan in 1640 and rose again with force and spirit. The peasant army expanded quickly to hundreds of thousands. At that time, Niu Jinxing and Li Yan (?-1644), juren of the Ming Dynasty, also enlisted under Li Zicheng's banner. They offered to Li Zicheng such advice as "equalization of landownership" and "freedom from taxation". The next year, Li Zicheng attacked and seized Luoyang, and killed the Prince of Fu-Zhu Changxun. As such, the morale of the peasant army was greatly boosted. In 1642, Li Zicheng captured Xiangyang. The next year, he changed Xiangyang to Xiangjing and declared himself King of Xinshun and established positions for civil and military officials. Shortly afterwards, Li Zicheng, leading his army, marched northward. He passed through Tongguan and then captured Xi'an. On the lunar New Year's day of 1644, Li Zicheng

established his regime in Xi'an and titled his dynasty Great Shun, with the reign title of Yongchang. Then he changed the name of Xi'an to Xijing. Then he perfected government organizations, made calendars, made Yongchang coins and introduced the civil service examination system as a means to elevate scholars. In February, Li Zicheng led million bold warriors across the Yellow River and marched towards Beijing. On March 18, Li's army entered Zhangyi Gate and succeeded in seizing the outer city of Beijing. Early the next morning, Emperor Chong Zhen hung himself on the Coal Hill (modern Jing Hill, Beijing) to the north of the imperial palace.

At the time when the peasant army led by Li Zicheng entered Beijing, Wu Sangui, the Ming garrison commander at the Sanhaiguan Pass, seduced the Qing troops launching a counter offensive. Li Zicheng, at the head of his men, went beyond the Great Wall to meet the enemy head-on. Having been defeated, he withdrew and returned to Beijing. On April 29, Li was inaugurated as emperor in a rush and left Beijing the very next day. Then Li Zicheng passed through Shanxi and moved to Xi'an. Later he fought from Shaanxi to Huguang and other places. The Great Shun army led by Li Zicheng and the Great West army by Zhang Xianzhong, fought a bloody war against the Qing troops. Nevertheless, Zhang Xianzhong was killed in action on Fenghuang Mountains, Xichong and Li Zicheng, after having been defeated, was also killed by the enemy in an ambush on Jiugong Mountains, Tongshan County. However, it was said by some others that Li, after being defeated, withdrew from secular life and became a monk in Jiashan Temple in Shimen, Hubei, where he, commanded in the name of Monk of Fengtianyu the remainder of the Great Shun army to fight against the Qing Dynasty in alliance with the Southern Ming.

Shanghaiguan Pass (northeastern of Qinghuangdao in Hebei province)

第九篇

辉煌落日

3. Zheng Chenggong's Might on the Sea

Poem written by Zheng Chenggong

After Li Zicheng had captured Beijing, the Ming ministers in Nanjing supported the Prince of Fu (Zhu Yousong) to assume the imperial title and changed the reign title into Hongguang. The next year, Nanjing was conquered and the former Ministry Counselor of Punishments, Qian Suyue and other people supported Prince of Lu(Zhu Yihai) as "National Supervisor" in Shaoxing. The Annan Count Zheng Zhilong(1604-1661) and Huang Daozhou(1585-1646) supported the Prince of Tang(Zhu Yujian) as emperor in Fuzhou, with the reign title of Longwu. In the summer of 1646, the Prince of Tang was captured and died shortly afterwards. Then governor of Guangxi named Qu Shisi(1590-1651) and governor-general of Guangdong and Guangxi, named Ding Kuichu(?-1647) supported the Prince of Gui(Zhu Youlang) as emperor at Zhaoqing, Guangxi, with the reign title of Yongli. Among all the Southern Ming regimes, Emperor Yongli's regime lasted for the longest period of time, which was seventeen years. The armed forces on the sea, which was led by Zheng Chenggong, first esteemed Emperor Longwu's reign and then Yongli's reign. They carried through the fights against the Qing government to the end.

Zheng Chenggong(1624-1662), with the original name of Zheng Sen, styled himself Damu. Emperor Long Wu of the Southern Ming conferred on him the surname of Zhu and changed his name into Chenggong. He was the son of Zheng Zhilong. After his father had surrendered to the Qing, Zheng Chenggong threw aside the writing brush and joined the army. He pledged to fight against the Qing and Emperor Long Wu conferred on him the title of General of Zhaotao, who was the commander-in-chief. From 1647-1649, taking Nan'ao as his base of operation and leading his righteous naval army, Zheng Chenggong captured Tong'an, Haicheng and Quanzhou in succession, and finally marched into Jinmen and Xiamen. He renamed the Left and Central *Xiamensuo as Simingzhou*, where he established six officials to handle various affairs of the government separately and improved administrative organs. As such, Emperor Yongli conferred on him the title of Prince of Yanping.

Time and again, Zheng Chenggong went on northern expeditions and fought battles in Fujian and Guanggong. In 1659, he and Zhang Huangyan(1620-1664), the Minister of War, at the head of an army and a navy of 83 battalions, altogether 170,000 men, pressed on towards Nanjing. Then northern expedition army advanced by both land and water. Shortly afterwards, they conquered Jiaoshan, Guazhou and then captured the important gateway on the Yangtze River, Zhengjiang as

Dutch army's surrender

well as all the counties under its jurisdiction. Nanjing was close to fall. However, because of Zheng's mis-commanding, his troops lost the best opportunity for combat and the northern expedition eventually ended in defeat

In order to back his protracted anti-Qing activities, Zheng Chenggong promoted a large -scale maritime trade. He controlled all the trading passageways leading to China and thus all the arrived merchant ships from Europe, including those of the Dutch, had to pay a certain amount of tax. The Chinese on the sea also received political as well as military protection from Zheng when they were persecuted or unfairly treated by the domineering Europeans. In order to curb power of Zheng Chenggong, the Qing government, repeatedly issued order that neither official nor civilian ships could put to sea without permission. Besides, it moved the costal inhabitants several miles inland so as to cut their relations to Zheng's army.

In order to set up a new base of operation against the Qing regime, Zheng Chenggong determined to capture Taiwan. In the late period of the Ming Dynasty, the early western colonialists came to China and took in succession some places in China as well as in Southeast Asia as strongholds to carry out trading activities. In 1557, the Portuguese seized Macao of China and in 1624, the Dutch entered Taiwan.

In spring of 1661, Zheng Chenggong and his men marched towards Taiwan. On the first day of the 4th lunar month they arrived at Luer Gate and conquered Chikan City (modern Anping Port, west of Tainan, Taiwan). People in Taiwan warmly welcomed the arrival of Zheng's army. Thanks to the support given by the Taiwan people, Zheng Chenggong gradually took control over the whole territory of Taiwan. On February 1, 1662, the head of the Dutch colonialists in Taiwan, a man named Coyett, was forced to sign on the instrument of surrender. Zheng Chenggong released all the prisoners of war and allowed Dutchmen to leave Taiwan with necessaries that were needed on their homeward journey. After the recovery of Taiwan, Zheng still adopted the reign title of Yongli. Then he changed Taiwan City to

The Statue of Zheng Chenggong (1624-1662 AD),

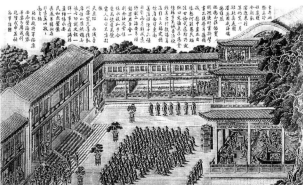

Anping Town, Chikan City to Chengtianfu and established the two counties of Tianxing (modern Jiaxingli of Jiayi County, Taiwan) and Wannian(Xinglongli of Gaoxiong County, Taiwan). Under his leadership, officials were appointed and production was developed. He ordered not to harass Tushe (also Gaoshan national minority) and solicited agronomists from the coastal regions of China's mainland to pass on production technology. Thus the management of Zheng Chenggong promoted the exploration and construction of Taiwan.

In April 1662, when the news of the death of Emperor Yong Li reached Taiwan, Zheng Chenggong was deeply grieved. In the meantime, the son of Zheng Chenggong named Zheng Jing extended his influence with military power on mainland of China.

Being exhausted both mentally and physically and in mixed feelings of grief and indignation, Zheng Chenggong died of illness on the 8th day of 5th lunar month (June 23rd). After the death of his father, Zheng Jing came to Taiwan. In 1683, the Qing government dispatched General of Jinghai named Shi Lang to conquer Taiwan and eventually completed the task of unification. The very next year, the Qing government established Taiwanfu, which were subordinate to Fujian Province. According to the request of the offspring of Zheng's family, Zheng Chenggong's tomb was moved to Nan'an, Fujian. Besides, the Qing government constructed a memorial hall for Zheng Chenggong and offered sacrifices to him. In 1874, the Qing government built another memorial temple for Zheng Chenggong in Taiwan, named Memorial Hall to Prince of Yanping. It gave him a posthumous title of "*Zhongjie*" and held a memorial ceremony for him every spring and autumn.

Success in suppressing Taiwan, 53rd -55th year of Emperor Qian Long (1788-1790 AD)

第九篇

辉煌落日

4. Peace and Prosperity of Emperors Kang Xi and Qian Long

Emperor Shi Zu of Qing Dynasty, Aisin Gioro Fulin (Emperor Shunzhi 1638-1661 AD)

Emperor Sheng Zu of Qing Dynasty, Aisin Gioro Xuanye (Emperor Kangxi 1654-1722 AD)

In 1644 when Wu Sangui let the Qing troops cross the Great Wall, Emperor Shun Zhi (Fulin)moved his capital from Shengjing to Beijing. In 1661, Emperor Shun Zhi died of smallpox and was succeed by his third son, Xuanye who was then eight years old. The reign title of Xuanye was Kangxi. Ao Bai and other three ministers in ruling the country assisted the new emperor. However, Ao Bai became arrogant because of his achievements. He built up his coterie, pushed aside people of different views, and recklessly enclosed people's land. In 1667, Xuanye assumed the reins of government. Two years later, he eliminated Ao Bai and thus strengthened his rule.

Emperor Kang Xi didn't advocate vain control of the country, but strived for practical and effective ways to run the state. He paid attention to the recruitment of Han scholars to the government organs at various levels so as to mitigate the contradictions between the Hans and the Manchus. He renewed the Inner Chancery and Imperial Academy of the Ming Dynasty, which were once abolished by Ao Bai and other ministers. He ordered the Imperial Academy to teach him Confucian classics and history daily. In 1677, Emperor Kang Xi ordered Zhang Ying, Gao Shiqi and others to be on duty in the southern study in the Palace of Heavenly Purity. They were responsible for drafting imperial edicts as well as giving advice on state affairs. Emperor Kang Xi broke free from the conventions in Shun Zhi's reign that most governors were the Manchus, and issued an order that able and virtuous persons should be selected from either the Manchus, or the Chinese of Han Eight Banners, or the Han Chinese. In 1674, he set up the contribution system and the examination system for scholarship and literature in succession to scout around for talents. Besides, he made three inspection tours to South China, where he paid his homage at Xiaoling Mausoleum of the Ming Dynasty, offered sacrifices to the Confucian temple, and acquainted himself with conditions of the people as well as political situation so as to win the hearts of the people in South China.

Emperor Kang Xi paid attention to agricultural production. He explicitly ordered twice that the government should never annex farmland of the people. In addition, he returned the land annexed by the princes of the Ming Dynasty to those who had tilled it before. Land of this kind was changed to be civilian household and became people's permanent family property, and was thus called as Renamed Land. Emperor Kang Xi also inherited from Shun Zhi the policy of rewarding people for reclaiming wasteland and took the reclamation of abandoned land as an important criterion for officials' political achievements. In addition, he carried out a policy of remitting taxation. In 1712, the Qing government

The Territory of Qing Dynasty

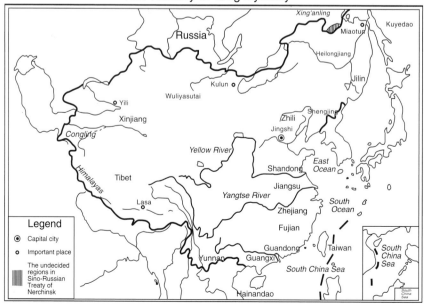

declared "no increase in tax during a prosperous era when population increases", and the population figure in the year of 1711would serve as the base for taxation. Such measures taken by the Qing government lightened the peasants' load. Emperor Kang Xi stressed on harnessing the Yellow River. He appointed Jin Fu and Chen Huang to harness rivers for more than ten years, the transportation of grains to the capital were thus unimpeded and that the inundated fields turned to fertile farmland again.

In the early years of Emperor Kang Xi's reign, the country was in turmoil. As Prince of Pingxi (Yunnan) Wu Sangui, Prince of Pingnan (Guangdong) Shang Kexi and Prince of Jingnan (Fujian) Geng Zhongming who had contributed a lot to Qing's entrance into China proper, became more and more powerful, they gradually set up their separatist rule. In order to defend national unification, Emperor Kang Xi quelled the "Rebellion of the Three Feudatories", which, from 1673 to 1681, lasted eight years. Two years later, the Qing government eliminated Zheng's regime in Taiwan and thus unified the whole nation. However, Galdan, an aristocrat of the Jungar tribe which inhabited China's northwest, maintained illicit relations with Tzarist Russia and started a rebellion. The Jungar army annexed all of the three tribes of the Eleut group, attacked the Hui tribe and harassed the Khalkha Mongolians. Emperor Kang Xi personally led troops to meet the enemy three times and eventually put down the revolts. Early in 1644, Russia's Expedition Army invaded into the areas in Heilongjiang Province and, was resisted indomitably by the local Chinese. In 1682, Emperor Kang Xi made an eastern inspection tour to Shengjing (modern Shenyang) and Wula (modern Jilin City), and dispatched persons to investigate Yacsa, Heilongjiang. In 1685, he sent troops to expel Tzarist Russia's aggression army that forcibly occupied Yacsa. In 1689, the Qing court concluded a treaty with Russia, which was known as the *Sino-Russian Treat* of Nerchinsk. It fixed the eastern section of the Sino-Russian border and curbed Tzarist Russia's aggression on China.

Emperor Kang Xi was on the throne for sixty-one years. In 1722, he passed away and was succeeded by his fourth son Yin Zhen, known as Emperor Yong Zheng. Diligent in state affairs, Emperor Yong Zheng established the Privy Council. Serving in such organ were trusted and influential ministers of the emperor's own choice that helped to handle military affairs. In this way he strengthened his control over local areas.

Emperor Yong Zheng was determined to reorganize finance and taxation. In 1723, he accepted the suggestion of Li Weijun, a governor directly affiliated to the central government, and carried out the policy that "poll tax is incorporated into land tax", that is, corvees and tax were portioned according to the amount of land a family had, and "land and population merged into a single whole. " Therefore, labors enjoyed a relatively greater freedom. In order to rectify local administration as well as to put an end to corruption, he introduced the measure of changing the additional fee into regular and fixed taxes so as to lessen the burden of the people and lead to clean politics. Local officials were permitted to levy from each tael of silver two or three more fen of the additional fee as a result of loss of silver when cast, which was used as currency at that time, and the money raised in this way was given to the officials in order to promote clean politics.

Emperor Yong Zheng followed the policies of the Ming Dynasty. He "brought the aboriginal chieftains in southwest ethnic areas such as Yunnan, Guizhou and Sichuan, under the jurisdiction of the central government by giving them regular official titles". He replaced the hereditary headmen with magistrates in such areas. The Qing government placed ministers-in-residence in Tibet and thus greatly strengthened its control over Tibet. Besides, it sent troops to suppress the rebellion of the aristocracy of the Eleut group in Qinghai and the revolt of the nobles of the Jungar tribe. It concluded with Tsarist Russia the

Emperor Shi Zong of Qing Dynasty, Aisin Gioro Yin Zhen (Emperor Yongzheng 1678-1735 AD)

Emperor Gao Zong of Qing Dynasty, Aisin Gioro Hong Li (Emperor Qianlong 1711-1799 AD)

Hat, Qing Dynasty, 20.5cm high, rim diameter 30cm

第九篇

辉煌落日

Emperor's Robe, Qing Dynasty, 113cm high

Emperor's Court Attire, Qing Dynasty, 138cm high

Emperor's Boots, Qing Dynasty, 46.5cm high

Close in and hunt

Incense burner, Qing Dynasty, 104cm high

Spittoon, Qing Dynasty, 104cm high

Sino-Russian Blinski Border Agreement and *Sino-Russian Qiaktu Border Agreement*, which delimited the central section of the Sino-Russian border. As a result, the tension between the two countries eased off. Seeing that all the princes seek to destroy each other for the throne in the late years of Emperor Kang Xi's reign, Emperor Yong Zheng, shortly after he ascended the throne, established the system of secret appointment of the crown prince, which was followed by later emperors.

In 1735, Emperor Yong Zheng died and was succeeded by his fourth son, Prince of Baoqin named Hongli, known as Emperor Qian Long. The distinguished achievement of Emperor Qian Long was his management of the frontier areas in China's northwest. In 1755 as well as in 1757, he sent troops to suppress the rebellions of Dawach and Amrsala of the Jungar tribe. Then from 1757 to 1759, he put down the revolts of Da Hezhuo as well as that of Xiao Hezhuo, heads of the Uygurs in the south of

Throne, Qing Dynasty, 220cm high

Carved lacquer screen with the design of landscape and people, Qing (1643-1912 AD), 37.9cm high, 22.2cm long, 3cm thick

Sixth Panchen

One of the eight temples in Chengde

Xi and Emperor Qian Long". However, the autocratic government of the Qing Dynasty became depraved day by day. Relying on his "outstanding martial arts skills", Emperor Qian Long became arrogant and conceited and lacking in enterprising spirit. In his late years, he placed his trust on an influential minister named He Shen. Moreover, it was in vogue at that time that official posts and titles were sold and government officials took embezzlement and bribe. As a result, the political crisis sharpened and the Qing Dynasty was on the wane.

Summer resort, Qing Dynasty, by Leng Mei, silk scroll, 391cm high, 209cm wide

the Tianshan Mountains. In 1762, the Qing government placed the General of Yili in Xiajiang to manage all the military as well as civil affairs. In such cities as Ujurngin, Kashgar, Yinjishar, Yerqiang, Hetian, Aksu, Wushi and Kalashar, the Qing government set up commander-in-chief, assistant ministers and managing ministers to take charge of the military affairs in the areas under its jurisdiction and to defend the frontier regions.

Emperor Qian Long also strengthened up the administration in Tibet. He abolished the Tibetan hereditary system and created *ga xia* (local government of Tibet). He appointed three high officials, one layman and two clergymen, to handle political affairs. Besides, he promulgated *the Imperial Tibetan Constitution*, in which the respective authorities as well as positions of the ministers-in-residence in Tibet, Dalai Lama and Panchan Lama were explicitly stipulated. In 1791, the Qing troops, under the commandership of General Fu Kangan, crushed the intrusion of Kuorke (modern Nepal) on Tibet, which was manipulated by Britain. Meanwhile, the Qing government continued carrying out the policy of "replacing tribal chiefs with government officials" in such areas as Yunnan, Guizhou, and Guangxi, Sichuan, Hunan and Hubei that were governed by chieftains, and quelled the rebellions launched by the chiefs of Da Jinchuan and Xiao Jinchuan.

Towards the end of Emperor Qian Long's reign, Chinese people accounted for 1/3 of the world's population and the economic power was the greatest in the world. Besides, the country had a balance of exports for such a long period of time that even Britain, an important trading country in the world, was unable to put an end to the balance -of-trade deficit. The Qing Dynasty was at its zenith in more than 100 years from Emperor Kang Xi's reign to that of Emperor Qian Long, when there were great achievements. It was a time of great prosperity, known as "peace and prosperity in the reigns of Emperor Kang

第九篇

辉煌落日

5. Autocracy and Door-Closing Policy

Emperor Gao Zong of Qing Dynasty, Aisin Gioro Hong Li in his battle dress (Emperor Qianlong 1711-1799 AD)

Cheng-Zhu School of Neo-Confuciusm. The "eight-legged essays" were still prescribed for the imperial civil service examination in the Qing Dynasty. The questions in the examinations were derived from the Four Books and the Five Classics, and the compositions must be based on the authorized comments and must be phrased in a strictly prescribed form. After Emperor Kang Xi assumed the reins of the government, it had the special examination system, in addition to the civil service examination system. Under the special system, there were three categories: "scholarship and literature", "study of Confucian classics" and "virtuous conduct", which were peculiarly given in the reigns of Kang Xi and Qian Long. In Qian Long's reign, examinations for "scholarship and literature" and "government" were also held to rope in talents as well as to win people's hearts.

In order to brag about achievements in running public affairs, emperors in the early Qing Dynasty collected, compiled and annotated ancient books and records on a large scale. China's extant largest leishu, *A Collection of Books of Ancient and Modern Times*, consisted of 10,000 chapters. This great undertaking started in Emperor Kang Xi's reign and finally completed in the reign of Emperor Yong Zheng, lasting twenty-four years. The largest collection of books, *entitled The Complete Library of the Four Treasuries*, had its beginning in Qian Long's reign and was completed fifteen years later. Consisting of 79,016 juan that were bound into more than 36,000 volumes, it included all together 3,470 books. The compilation of these two books mentioned above, helped the preservation of many books and records. Nevertheless, in the name of collecting and editing books, the government either destroyed those books or deleted their contents that were deemed harmful to itself and forged some literary works. As such, many ancient works and records were seriously damaged.

In order to strengthen the cultural as well as ideological control, the Qing government employed various kinds of measures, the most merciless of which was literary inquisition. At that time, some surviving ministers of the Ming Dynasty, seeing the newly established regime, usually

In the reigns of Kang Xi, Yong Zheng and Qian Long, it was a time when imperial authority was unprecedently strengthened. The system of the Conference of Princes Regent, under which the Manchu aristocracy discussed state affairs together, was eventually abolished. The establishment of the Privy Council had greatly weakened the power of the Inner Chancery; thereby the absolute authority of the emperor was more firmly set up. After the Qing Dynasty was established, the government started paying attention to civil affairs. In 1645, it introduced the civil service examination system and advocated reverence for Confucius as well as the study of classics. In particular, it promoted the

Complete Library in the Four volumes of Literature

Imperial banquet in Wanshu garden, partial

trade. Later, as Zheng Chenggong's anti-Qing force was active in southeastern coastal areas, the Qing government even more strictly prohibited putting to sea. In 1656, it issued a "ban on maritime trade", under which merchant ships couldn't put to sea without permission. In 1661, "an order of moving away from sea" was issued, leading to a scene of desolation in an area of thirty to fifty li off the sea. Towards the reign of Emperor Qian Long, the Qing government once more strictly enforced the ban on foreign trade and in1757, it confined the trading port to Guangzhou alone. In 1759, the Qing government issued *the Foreign Merchants Norms and Foreign Trade Regulations*, which consisted of six articles. In 1831, another eight articles of the regulation were enacted and then in 1835, eight more were added. With the passage of time, there were more and more diverse and complicated rules and regulations as well as strict restrictions. The main purpose of such efforts, however, was to prevent foreign merchants from contacting with the Chinese.

Jade scepter, Qing Dynasty, 43.5cm long

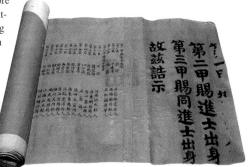

List of successful candidates in the palace examination, pasted outside the gate of imperial palace. Palace examination is the final imperial examination. Being on this list is a happy event for the students. In order to come first in the examination, the students read thousands of books, but only a few can succeed.

wrote some essays to express their nostalgic memories of their native land, which was unbearable to the Qing government. In the early years of Kang Xi's reign, a native of Guian(modern Wuxing County, Zhejiang) named Zhuang Tinglong block-printed *the History of the Ming Dynasty*, written by Zhu Guozhen of the late period of the Ming Dynasty. In one of palace stories that happened in Emperor Chong Zhen's reign, the author criticized much the Manchus. As a result, more than seventy persons that were concerned with the matter, including booksellers and print-workers, were all executed, while all the women were punished by exile. Though Zhuang Tinglong had already died, the Qing government dug his body out and cut it into pieces. In Emperor Yong Zheng's reign, Zha Siting presided over the imperial civil service examinations in Jiangxi. Just because he set a topic of "*wei ming suo zhi*", which was tentatively interpreted as to remove the head of "Yong Zheng", he was then killed. In Emperor Qian Long's reign, there was much more strict ban on free expression of thought. It was quite often that a person was killed just because of a single word. For instance, Hu Zhongzao was killed because he used "to tell good from evil" in his poem, which could be tentatively interpreted in Chinese as "On the corrupted Qing Dynasty". And Xu Shukui, his grave was dug and his body was destroyed, because he wrote "I'm flapping the winds and soaring high towards Qing capital", which was interpreted as "The Ming Dynasty will prosper again while the Qing capital will be destroyed". Things like this are legion.

Under such high-handed cultural policy, a new form of academic study, which concerned mainly with textual research, took shape in the period of Qian Long and Jia Qing. Different from the Neo-Confuciusm in the Song Dynasty and the Ming Dynasty, it did scholarly research in the way adopted by the Han Confucianists, thus it got the name of Han learning or Pu learning, generally known as School of Qian-Jia. As a result, both the sphere of learning and the style of study underwent a transformation among the literati.

At the same time when cultural autocracy was employed, the Qing government once again closed down customs houses and carried out a door-closing policy. In the early period of Shun Zhi's reign, the Qing court did not allow foreign merchant ships to come to any city of China, except Macao, for

Water basin and dipper, diameter 9.3cm

Ink stone, 32cm x 24cm

Jade ink stand 3.3cm, ink stick 12.2cm

Writing set

Brush tube, 15.2 x 9.3cm

第九篇

辉煌落日

Top-rank, Crane (xianhe)

Second-rank, Golden pheasant (jinji)

Third-rank, Peacock (kongque)

Fourth-rank, Wild goose (yunyan)

Fifth-rank, Silver pheasant (baixian)

Sixth-rank, Egret (lusi)

Seventh-rank, Mandarin duck (xichi)

Eighth-rank, Quail (anchun)

Ninth-rank, Paradise flycatcher (lianque)

The door-closing policy obstructed the proper growth of China, leading to a dull, unenlightened, stagnant and retrograde situation and resulting in the loss of opportunity to synchronize China's development with that of the world. In the 17th and the 18th centuries, West Europe had walked out of dark cage of the Middle Ages, which gave rise to quick development in culture and ideology as well as in natural science. However, being out of touch with reality, Chinese literati indulged in Neo-Confuciasm, eight-legged essays, textual research and arts of writing, and remained where they were. During Emperor Kang Xi's reign, in Beijing as well as in other cities, there were some Jesuits who brought with them certain western science and technology. However, such knowledge was just enshrined in the inner court. Because of government prohibitions, the lively and dynamic scene that advanced intellectuals worked hard to learn from the West was all gone. Towards the end of Kang Xi's reign, the Qing court took issue with the Vatican, which obstructed the missionary work. In the early period of Yong Zheng's reign, Catholicism was totally prohibited, therefore the only weak connection between Chinese culture and western culture was eventually cut off. In 1792 and 1816, the British government sent in succession the Magcni and Amshed diplomatic corps to China. However, both because of disputes over

Gilded bronze lion, Qing Dynasty, Imperial Palace in Beijing

The prisoners in the jail in Qing Dynasty

Eight rank insignia for military officers, Qing Dynasty

Top-and Second-rank, Lion (shizi)

Third-rank, Tiger (hu)

Fourth-rank, Leopard (bao)

Fifth-rank, Bear (xiongpi)

Sixth-and Seventh-rank, Tiger cat (biao)

Eighth-rank, Rhinoceros (xiniu)

Dukes and marquises, emperor's son-in-law and earl, Unicorn (qilin)

Ninth-rank, Sea horse (haima)

Elephant, Qing Dynasty, 40.3cm high, 28.5cm long

Auspicious animal, 43cm high, 32cm wide

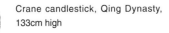

Crane candlestick, Qing Dynasty, 133cm high

protocol, relations between China and Britain reached insoluble deadlock. In the imperial edict to the British monarch, Emperor Qian Long rejected all the requests made by the British diplomatic corps, which showed the ignorance of the world situation as well as the arrogance and self-importance of the Qing government. The fact that the Qing government excluded itself from the world trend, caused China to fall immediately behind the West. By 1840, per head grain yield in China was merely about 200 kilograms, while in America, the figure almost reached to 1,000. China's annual iron output was 20,000 tons, less than 1/10 of that in France and 1/40 of that in England.

第九篇

辉煌落日

6. The Opium War

Emperor Xuan Zong of Qing Dynasty, Aisin Gioro Minning (Emperor Daoguang 1782-1850 AD)

Opium den in Qing Dynasty

Opium, commonly known as *dayan*, is a kind of drug. In the early period of the Qing Dynasty, no more than 200 chests (nearly 120 *jin* of opium per chest) of opium were imported every year as medicine. Before the 19th century, China had always had a balance of exports over imports in Sino-Western trade. In order to put an end to the unfavorable balance in Sino-British trade, from the late period of the 18th century, however, Britain sold large quantities of opium to China to seek exorbitant profits. The importing of opium created such social problems as a widespread opium addiction, a severer corruption among officials in opium-smuggling, the rapid drain of silver from China, soaring prices and financial difficulties.

In 1838, Emperor Dao Guang (Min Ning) appointed Lin Zexu as imperial commissioner, who was empowered to "act at his discretion" as well as to command the navy of Guangdong, to take charge of banning the drug in Guangdong. Early in1839, Lin Zexu arrived in Guangzhou. Under his direction, from the 22nd of the 4th lunar month to the 15th of the 5th lunar month (from June 3 to 25), 2,376,254 *jin* of opium was burned in public on the Humen Beach. After hearing the news, the British government intensified preparations for an aggressive war against China. In Feburary1840, the former commander of the fleet that had navigated around the Cape of Good Hope, George Elliot (1784-1863) as commander-in-chief of the "Eastern Expedition Army" and plenipotentiary, led forty-eight warships carrying more than 4,000 soldiers to China. In June, the British army reached the seacoast of Guangdong and blockaded the estuary of Zhujiang River. Thus the Opium war broke out.

After the failure in attacking Guangdong, the British forces sailed northward. They bombarded Xiamen and then started invading Zhejiang, where they captured Dinghai. Later, they divided their forces and sailed northward to Baihekou, Tianjin. At that time, they put pressure on the Qing government for negotiation. In January 25, 1841 the British army occupied Hong Kong by force. Emperor Dao Guang sent a punitive expedition against the British forces. However, the latter launched a pre-emptive attack on the fortress outside Humen. The Admiral of Guangdong named Guan Tianpei (1781-1841) led his men to hold fast to their position and died heroically. In May, when the British captured Guangzhou, the Qing troops were forced to conclude *the Convention of Guangzhou* at the fortress outside the city, agreeing to pay indemnity and to withdraw from Guangzhou. The aggressors

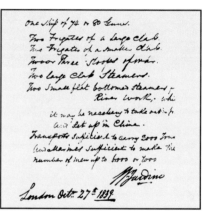

A letter from an English merchant dealing with opium to an English diplomat in 1839

The Situation of the First Opium War

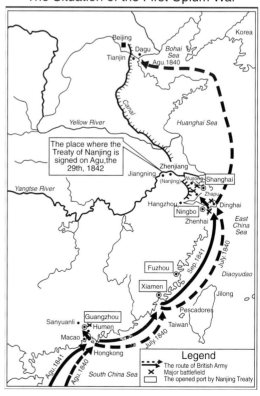

did every evil conduct in Guangzhou area, burning, killing, raping and looting, which made the people in Sanyuanli rise up to resist against the enemy In August, British forces captured Xiamen, later Dinghai, and Ningbo. In the meantime, Admiral of Dinghai Ge Yunfei (1789-1841) died on the battlefield. Governor-General of Jiangnan and Jiangxi and imperial commissioner Yu Qian (1793-1841) threw himself into the sea and died at his post. Thus the enemy captured three strategic cities in Zhedong. In spring of 1842 the British troops invaded the fortress in Wusong and Admiral of Jiangnan Chen Huacheng (1776-1842) died in action. Then the British occupied Wusong, Baoshan and Shanghai. In August, British warships arrived at the Yangtze river off Nanjing. On August 29, 1842 imperial envoys Qi Ying (1790-1858) and Yilibu (1772-1843), accepting all the provisions made by the British, signed *the Treaty of Nanking with the British* plenipotentiary Henry Pottinger(1789-1856) on a British warship anchored at Xiaguan, Nanjing. The treaty provided an indemnity of twenty-one million silver dollars, the cession of Hong Kong, opening of five trading ports-Guangzhou, Xiamen, Fuzhou, Ningbo and Shanghai; and traffic on export and import customs on British goods to be fixed by mutual agreement; and no intervention by the Qing government in opium trade. In the following year (1843), China and Britain signed *the General Regulations* under which British trade was to be conducted at the five ports and the *Supplementary Treaty of Hoomun Chai*, giving British the privileges of consular jurisdiction, unilateral most-favored-nation treatments in China and the privilege of renting land as well as constructing houses at the five ports. Such unequal treaties severely infringed on the sovereignty and territorial integrity of China.

Lin Zexu (1785-1850 AD)

Canon on Humen fort

The American and the French rushed over on hearing about the success of the British troops. Threatened by force, Qi Ying signed *the Treaty of Wang-hea* with the American envoy extraordinary and minister plenipotentiary, Caleb Cushing (1800-1879), and *the Treaty of Whampoa* with the French special envoy Marie Melchior Joseph de Lagrene. Under these treaties, the United States and France both gained all the privileges that were enjoyed by Britain. Moreover, their consular jurisdiction was extended and they were permitted to carry out freely missionary activities at the trading ports. Eventually, the Qing government was forced to lift the ban on Catholicism, which was issued more than 100 years ago.

The ancient empire in the East was forced to open its door, however, the western powers were far from satisfaction. In 1856 the Chinese navy searched off Guangzhou a Chinese vessel, the larch arrow, which was registered in Hong Kong and captured two pirates and ten sailors who were suspected of piracy. The British consul in Guangzhou seized the

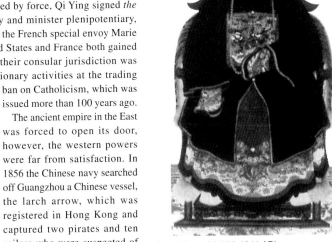

Guan Tianpei (1780-1841 AD)

The Situation of the Second Opium War

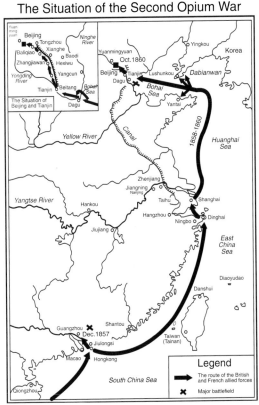

opportunity to make things difficult and attempted to aggravate the situation. On October the 23rd, British warships attacked under orders all the fortresses near Guangzhou and even marched into the inner city. Shortly afterwards, they withdrew because of inadequate strength. In spring of 1857, Britain sent an expedition army to China once again; while France, making use of the killing of a French Catholic priest Manai who illegally carried out missionary activities in Guangxi as an excuse, sent troops to China and joined Britain. As such, the Second Opium War broke out. The Anglo-French forces captured Guangzhou and Tianjin and once advanced to Beijing. Along their way, the invaders looted, burned and killed. They even set fire on the Yuan Ming Yuan Summer Place, the most magnificent palace and treasure -house of Eastern arts. As such, the Qing government had no way but sign the unequal treaty *Convention of Peking*, with Britain, France, America, and Russia respectively. In addition, Russia compelled Yishan (1790-1878) Chinese general in Heilongjiang, to sign *the Treaty of Aihui*. From then on, the western powers spread out their invasions of China in all directions and aspects, from south to north, from the seaside to inland, from economy to politics, and from merchandise to culture. China thus walked step by step to the chasm of colonization.

7. Taiping Heavenly Kingdom

Hong Xiuquan (1814-1864 AD)

"the world one family to enjoy peace in common". Preaching in succession in Guixian County as well as in Zijinshan, Guiping County, Guangxi, Hong Xiuquan and his country fellow Feng Yunshan (1815-1852) attracted many impoverished peasants and coal workers, and thus their force grew rapidly. On January 11, 1851when Hong Xiuquan was just thirty-eight, he started a revolt and called his organization the Heavenly Kingdom of Taiping and named himself Heavenly King. Hong then gave titles to several leaders: Yang Xiuqing (1823-1856), Eastern Prince; Xiao Chaogui (1820-1852)Western Prince; Feng Yunshan, Southern Prince; Wei Changhui (1826-1856) Northern Prince; and Shi Dakai (1831-1863), Prince of Wing. The Eastern Prince was placed in charge of all the other princes. The Taiping Army swept across several provinces, such as Jiangxi and Anhui. In March 1853 the Taiping Army captured Nanjing and made it the capital of its kingdom.

The Taiping Heavenly Kingdom proclaimed *the Heavenly Land System*, which centered on the reform of land system. By practicing this system, the Heavenly Kingdom hoped to establish an ideal society in which "land, food, clothes and money should all be shared equally, and all under Heaven should be well fed and clad". The system called for land to be distributed equally according to family size. The income of each family was to be turned over to the state and all the expenses were disbursed by the State Treasury, or the "Holy Treasury". Private industry and commerce was abolished and it was the state that organized handicraft production and distributed goods. Monogamy was introduced and orders were issued to prohibit prostitution. Besides, women could enjoy the right to participate in managing the state. Nevertheless, *the Heavenly Land System* was no more than an idealist proposal that could never be realized.

In May 1853 the Heavenly Kingdom sent its army on northern and western campaigns. Commanded by the deputy Prime Minister of the Heavenly Office Lin Fengxiang (1825-1855) and the Marquis of Dinghu Li Kaifang (1826-1855), the northern expedition army of over 20,000 men marched straightly towards Beijing. In less than half a year, the vanguard of the army reached the outskirts of Tianjin. However they had to withdraw shortly afterwards since they fought single-handed and lacked reinforcements as well as winter clothing. In the end, they were totally destroyed. Meanwhile, the western expedition army, under the leadership of Hu Yihuang, Lai Hanying and Zeng Tianxing, advanced westward along the Yangtze River. The purpose of the western expedition was to recover the areas of the middle and lower Yangtze River Valley and to safeguard the capital Nanjing. The Taiping Army scored a great victory over Zeng Guofan's Hunan army and captured Wuchang three times. Later they took Jiujiang and Anqing, and put most parts of Anhui, Jiangxi, Hubei, and Jiangsu under their control. In 1856, the Taipings removed the threat to the capital Nanjing by crushing in succession the Great Southern Camp and the Great Northern Camp of the Qing forces. At that time the Heavenly Kingdom reached the zenith of its power.

In September 1856, the leaders of the Taiping Kingdom scrambled for power, which resulted in the "Incident of Nanjing". As Yang Xiuqing, the Eastern Prince, had been of great service in the establishment of the Taiping

The gun used by Taiping Army

The canon used by Taiping Army

Copper coin of Taiping Heavenly Kingdom

The rottenness on the part of the Qing government caused people to constantly stage uprisings across the country. For instance, there were some local secret anti-Qing organizations, such as the Heaven and Earth society, Three Points Society and Three Joints Society. Under such circumstances, Hong Xiuquan, a rural intellectual born into an impoverished peasant family, who adopted a combination of Christian ideas of "equality" and "fraternity" and ancient Chinese ideal of "Great Harmony" as his guide, started a revolution -the Taiping Peasant War. Most of the participants in the war were poor peasants and the revolution aimed at setting up an equal and mutually loving heaven on earth.

Hong Xiuquan (1814-1864) was a man of Huaxian Country, Guangdong. Having several times failed the civil service examination, he became a tutor in a village school. In 1843 inspired by a book entitled *Good Words for Exhorting the Age*, which propagated Christianity, he created the Society for the Worship of God. In his works like *Doctrines on Salvation* and *Doctrines on Awakening the World*, he claimed God to be the only true divine being and put forward the idea to make

Heavenly Kingdom, he became arrogant. He demanded that Hong Xiuquan give him the title of "Wan Sui"(His Majesty). Hearing about the news, Wei Changhui, the Northern Prince, returned from Jiangxi to the capital with troops and killed Yang Xiuqing as well as his whole family and all of his followers, over 20,000 people in all. Then Shi Dakai, Prince Wing, hurried back from Wuchang front to denounce Wei for his indiscriminate killing of innocent people, which only caused Wei to kill his whole family. Hong Xiuquan then executed Wei Changhui and thus put an end to the internal strife. In June the next year, Shi Dakai, sensing that Hong did not trust him, was forced to leave Nanjing, with his troops fighting alone. They fought in Jiangxi, Sichuan and Guizhou. In June 1863 he was surrounded by the Qing troops at a natural barrier, the Dadu River in Sichuan and he and his entire army were destroyed.

After the Nanjing Incident, the Qing forces seized the opportunity to launch counterattacks and laid siege to Tianjin again. At that time, many young commanders came to the fore. In 1858, Li Xiucheng(1823-1864), Prince Zhong, Chen Yucheng(1837-1862), Prince Ying and others went on eastern campaigns to Susong and southern expeditions to Zhejiang, and eventually lifted the blockade of Nanjing by the Qing's Great Northern Camp. As such, the Heavenly Kingdom reestablished its prestige. In 1859, Hong Rengan(1822-1864), Hong Xiuquan's cousin who had lived in Hong Kong for refuge for seven years, came to Nanjing on a roundabout trip, was given the title of Prince Gan and was placed in charge of the kingdom's state affairs. Hong Rengan wrote *New Guide to Government*, which was the first programmatic document in China's pursuit for development of capitalist economy. Nevertheless, as he could neither solve the land problem, the most basic one for peasants, nor put his ideas into practice, his proposals were just best of wishes that could never be realized.

Zeng Guofan (1811-1872 AD)

Early in 1860, Li Xiucheng, leading his troops, captured Hangzhou. Then his troops returned to Nanjing to join the Prince Ying Chen Yucheng. They marched along five fronts to attack the Great Southern Camp, and finally crushed it. Shortly afterwards, Li Xiucheng led his troops to march towards Suzhou and Hangzhou areas, and pressed on towards Shanghai. Meanwhile, the Anglo-French forces were attacking the Qing's capital in the North, however, the Qing officials as well as the gentry and compradors in the South asked Britain and France for help to suppress the Taipings. In 1860, a comprador in Shanghai named Yang Fang employed an American, Frederick Townsend Ward(1831-1862) to recruit over 200 foreign sailors, drifters and deserters, who were organized into a "Foreign Rifle Detachment". The Foreign Rifle attempted to attack the Taipings who were then on their eastern expedition to Jiangnan. However, Li Xiucheng defeated them. In Li Xiucheng's attack on Shanghai, the Anglo-French forces and their warships resisted the Taiping army, resulting in extremely heavy losses of the Taipings. As Hong Rengan and Li Xiucheng still cherished illusion about "foreign brothers" who held the "same religious belief", they were not determined yet to fight against them and decided to withdraw. In 1861, Emperor Xian Feng(Yi Zhu) died of illness at the Summer Mountain Resort in Chengde and was succeeded by his six-year-old son, Zai Chun, known as Emperor Tong Zhi. Zai Chun's own mother, Yehe Nala (Empress Dowager Ci Xi) (1835-1908) then collaborated with the emperors' uncle Prince Gong named Yi Xin(1833-1898) to stage a coup d'etat, known as "Xinyou Coup". Thus Empress Dowager Ci Xi had the supreme authority in the Qing government. Ever since then, foreign powers formally started its collaboration with the Qing court. They helped the Qing government train soldiers, presented it with arms and ammunition, and established mixed army, called Chang Sheng Jun, Chang Jie Jun and so on, to encircle the Taiping Army. In collusion with foreign aggressors, Zeng Guofan's branch of Hunan army, Li Hongzhang's Anhui army and Zuo Zongtang's branch of Hunan army, marched from Anhui, Jiangsu, Zhejiang and Shanghai to launch a full-scale attack against the Taiping Army. The Taipings fought against the enemy with great courage. They killed Ward, the commander of Chang Sheng Army at Cixi, Zhejiang and captured alive its deputy leader Farced at Qingpu.

Emperor Wen Zong of Qing Dynasty, Aisin Gioro Yizhu (Emperor Xianfeng 1831-1861 AD)

Then some wavering elements in the Heavenly Kingdom turned traitor one after another. The Heavenly King didn't deal with concrete matters but groundlessly conferred titles on people to win their hearts, leading to as many as more than 2,700 princes in the kingdom. Besides, the TaiPings were lax in discipline and thus gradually lost the hearts of the people. As Li Xiucheng's plan "to rescue the South by marching to the North" failed, the capital Nanjing fell into a tight encirclement. In June 1864 Hong Xiuquan died of illness and was succeeded by his eldest son Hong Tianguifu. Several months later, Nanjing fell. Li Xiucheng, Hong Rengan, and the Young Heavenly King Hong Tianguifu were killed in succession. Thus, the Taiping peasant revolution that swept across eighteen provinces and lasted for fourteen years failed in the end. After the fall of Nanjing, Lai Wenguang, Prince Zun, the remainder of the Taiping Army, joined Zhang Zhongyu Prince Liang and Ren Huabang, Prince Lu who both were leaders of the Nian Army in the North, and continued their anti-Qing struggles. At one time, this peasant army completely destroyed Sengelinqin, a famous Qing general and his army. Not until August 1868, did the Qing forces eventually defeat these peasants.

New Guide to Government, by Hong Renxuan (1822-1864 AD)

8. Official Westernization Movement

Li Hongzhang (1823-1901 AD)

Zhang Zhidong (1837-1909 AD)

idea of "learning from the west" to "make foreign implements" and advocated "relying mainly on Chinese feudal ethnical codes and adopting foreign techniques to make the country rich and strong", which were later summarized by Zhang Zhidong(1837-1909) as the so-called "Chinese learning as the base, Western learning for application". The Qing court and its officials therefore engaged in such activities as buying foreign arms, importing machines, recruiting foreign technicians, opening up mines and factories, employing foreign officers to train armed forces and sending students to study abroad to achieve China's rejuvenation. Those who managed such foreign affairs were called Westernization group, including Prince Gong, Yi Xin and Minister of the Board of Civil Service Wen Xiang, and those who rose in suppressing the Heavenly Kingdom of Taiping, such as Zeng Guofan, Zuo Zongtang, Li Hongzhang and the later Zhang Zhidong.

According to the Westernization group, "military force is the most critical factor to make a country strong, and advanced weapons must be produced first to arm military forces. " Thus they set up in succession the Anqing Arsenal, Kiangnan Machine Building Works, Fukien Dockyard, Tianjin Machinery Factory and other war factories to produce new weaponry, which, to a certain extent, played a positive role in improving the equipment of the Qing forces and their fighting competence. However, the military industries of the Westernization group were monopolized by the bureaucracy and managed in a yamen way and overstaffed. Moreover, they depended completely on foreign personnel from design and construction, machinery equipment and production technology to the supply of raw materials, and thus the arms and warships produced by them were of very low quality. Before long, more problems emerged, such as the shortage of fund and the lack of support by basic industries, which made them gradually realize that the wealth and strength of the West depended not only on advanced warships and arms but also on economic power. Thus under the slogans of "striving for wealth"and "strength and prosperity is based on wealth", the Westernization group set up some civilian industries.

Zuo Zongtang (1812-1885 AD)

洋务项目	年 代	创办情况
江南创造局	1865 年	李鸿章创办于上海
金陵机器局	1865 年	李鸿章创办于南京
福州船政局	1866 年	左宗棠创办
天津机器局	1867 年	崇厚（满族）创办
湖北枪炮厂	1888 年	张之洞等办于广州 次年张之洞调任 迁汉阳
上海轮船招商局	1872 年	李鸿章创办
上海机器织布局	1876 年	李鸿章等办 1890 年投产
甘肃织呢总局	1876 年	左宗棠开办于兰州 1880 年投产
开平矿务局	1878 年	李鸿章开办 1881 年投产
天津电报总局	1880 年	李鸿章开办

After the failure of the Second Opium War, some people believed that it was "strong warships and sophisticated weapons" that made Britain and France powerful. In order to "strive to become strong" and to "resist invasion", they wanted to buy foreign warships and cannon as well as to learn to make machines and firearms. Feng Guifen (1809-1874) put forward the

Hubei Munitions Factory (Wuhan, Hubei)

Jinling Machinery Plant (Nanjing, Jiangsu)

Former site of Tong Wen Guan (Beijing), the earliest school built in Official Westernization Movement in Qing Dynasty

At the beginning, most civilian industries were government-supervised and merchant-managed. Among them were the China Merchants Steamship Navigation Company, Kaiping Coal Mines, China Telegraphs Office and Shanghai Textile Mill. Later, there were enterprises of co-management by government and merchants and some private industries. All of these civilian industries were beneficial to the resistance to foreign economic aggression and the privately-owned industries were the harbinger of China's national industry.

Besides setting up modern industry, the Westernization Movement also included building up modern navy and army, opening up various technical schools, creating Department of Translation and Interpretation, translating books on western science and technology and selecting and sending students studying abroad. It is beyond doubt that the Official Westernization Drive played a positive role in broadening the outlook of Chinese people at various levels as well as in promoting China's social civilization.

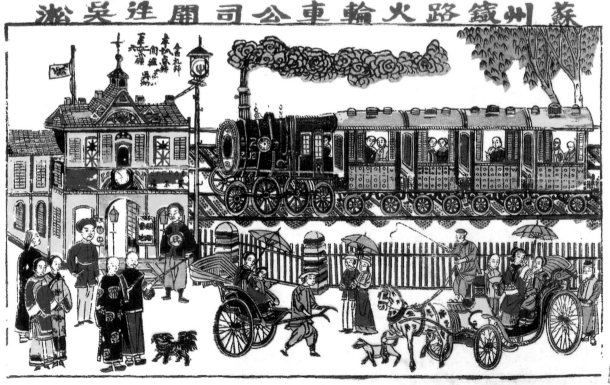

Train from Suzhou to Wusong, New Year Picture, Qing Dynasty

第九篇

辉煌落日

9. Sino-French War and Sino-Japanese War

Liu Yongfu (1837-1917 AD)

Feng Zicai (1818-1903 AD)

After the Second Opium War, the Western powers, backed by arms, forced the Qing government to sign a great many unequal treaties and demanded from it various kinds of privileges. The Tax Inspector-General, a post with full power of customs administration of the whole nation, however, had been dominated by foreigners for more than forty years. At the beginning, it was a British named Lay Horatio Nelson (1832-1898) that took up the post. After 1863, another British Hart succeeded him. Sir Robert (1835-1911). After the 70s of the 19th century, these imperialists quickened their steps to invade China. For instance, Russia sent troops to occupy the Ili region and coerced the Qing court into the cession of more than 70,000 square kilometers of territory in China's northwest Having long coveted Xinjiang, Britain made inroads into Tibet form India, and Yunnan from Burma. As for France, it attempted to use Vietnam as a foothold to intrude into China's hinterland. In 1882, French forces captured Hanoi, the capital of Vietnam and tried to cross the Honghe River to pry about Yunnan. However, they met with resistance from the Vietnamese civilians and the Black Flag Army led by Liu Yong Fu (1837-1917).

From 1883 to 1885, the French troops outrageously attacked the Qing army in the North of Vietnam and the ship-building yards in the sea areas of Fujian, thus provoking the Sino-French War. The Chinese army and civilians, under the commandership of an old general Feng Zicai (1818-1903) and Liu Yongfu, won decisive victories at Zhennanguan and Lintao, which reversed the critical trend on Vietnam's battlefield and which caused the French cabinet headed by Ferry Jules to fall from power. Nevertheless, the Qing court negotiated peace with the French despite its own winning position, and signed a cease-fire agreement which stipulated that the Qing government recognized the capture of Vietnam by France and that France could carry out trading activities as well as build railways in China.

After the Meiji Reform in 1868 Japan rose to be a powerful country and thus began to put its expansionist policy into practice. In 1874 Japan intruded into Taiwan, China. Later, it invaded Korea and advanced southward to annex Ryukyu islands (changed into Okinawa Country). In 1885, Japan sent Ito Hirabumi (1841-1909), the first Prince Minister to China and forced the Qing government to sign the Special Clause of Tiantisen Conference, which stipulated that both sides should inform each other before dispatching troops to Korea.

After the capture of Taiwan, the Qing court started to set up Beiyang Navy in 1875. In 1885 it created a naval *yamen* and in 1888 it established the Beiyang Fleet, which possessed two giant warships, the Dingyuan and Zhenyuan, eight cruisers, six gunboats and six auxiliary vessels, with its headquarters at Liugong Island, Weihai and the garrison commander of Tianjin named Dingruchang as the admiral. At the beginning when the fleet was established, its scale was almost second to none in the Far East. Later, however, it did not add new warships any more and after 1891, it even ceased to buy arms and ammunition. Moreover, most of the military expenditure for the fleet was either embezzled by officials or diverted by Empress Dowager *Ci Xi* to rebuild and

Battleship Zhenyuan of the Beiyang Navy

repair the Summer Palace. Japan, on the contrary, hasted to make all kinds of warships in dealing with Beiyang Navy and thus its naval force quickly surpassed that of Beiyang Navy.

In 1894 (the year of Jiawu according to Chinese lunar calendar), a rebellion started by the Dongxue Party occurred in Korea. The Korean ruler appealed to the Qing government to send troops and help it suppress the revolt. Taking the advantage of the strife, Japan dispatched troops to Korea and occupied Asan. In the middle of July, the Japanese fleet attacked Chinese warships near Korean Peninsula, sinking a merchant ship Gaosheng leased from Britain for the transportation of troops and causing the deaths of more than one thousand Chinese soldiers as well as officials on board. On the very day, the Japanese army attacked the Qing troops that garrisoned at Yashan Mountain south of Asan. On August 1st, directed by Emperor Guang Xu (Zai Tian), the Qing court declared war against Japan and on the same day Japan also proclaimed war against China.

The Japanese land force marched northward along four routes and laid siege to Pyongyang. The Qing commander Zuo Baogui died heroically while General Yi Zhichao fled first. In October, the Japanese crossed the Yalu River and marched into Liaodong.

On the sea route, on September17 the Beiyang Fleet escorted from Dalian the Qing troops to Dadonggou at the estuary of Yalu River. At the time when the fleet began to return to the base, the Japanese warships flying the American flag, launched a sudden attack on the Beiyang Fleet. As such, the sea warfare broke out. The fighting lasted for more than five hours. The mast-head of the flagship Dingyuan of the Beiyang Fleet was destroyed and the Zhiyuan was sunk by an enemy torpedo, and Deng Shichang, captain of the Zhiyuan lost his life. As for the Japanese fleet, the Jiye, Chicheng, and Birui were seriously damaged, the flagship Songdao lost its fighting capacity; and the Xijingwan was almost sunk.

In October, the Japanese troops landed at Huayuankou, Liaodong Peninsula, and advanced directly towards Lushun and Dalian. Shortly afterwards, Lushun fell and the naval base of the Beiyang Fleet also fell into the hands of Japanese. At the end of the year, a Japanese land force of nearly 20,000 men took all the fortresses north and south of Weihaiwei and thus the Beiyang Fleet fell into an encirclement. The Japanese troops bombarded intensively the Beiyang Fleet that defended against the siege at the port. In the end, the Beiyang Fleet was totally destroyed and Admiral Ding Ruchang also died.

Deng Shichang (1855-1894 AD)

Zuo Baogui (1837-1894 AD)

Japanese troop's massacre in Lushun

During the whole war, Empress Dowager Ci Xi and the Beiyang Minister Li Hongzhang had always tried to avoid fighting, and sue for peace under humiliating circumstances. The Qing troops thereby were doomed to failure. On April 17, 1895 Li Hongzhang signed the *Treaty of Shimonoseki* with Ito Hirabumi at Shimonoseki, Japan, which stipulated that China would recognize the "independence" of Korea (In fact, it was to recognize the control of Korea by Japan); cede to Japan the Liaodong Peninsula, Taiwan as well as the islands under its jurisdiction, and Penghu islands; pay an indemnity of 200 million taels of silver; open Chongqing Shashi, Suzhou and Hangzhou to foreign trade; and give Japan the right to open factories in China. After the conclusion of the Sino-Japanese War, China sank into the danger of being partitioned by the imperialists.

Li Hongzhang signed the Treaty of Shimonoseki in Japan in 1895

第九篇

辉煌落日

10. Reform Movement of 1898

Emperor De Zong of Qing Dynasty, Aisin Gioro Zaitian (Emperor Guang Xu 1871-1908 AD)

Kang Youwei (1858-1927 AD)

Calligraphy in cursive, by Kang Youwei

The Reform Movement of 1898, was also known as the "Modernization Movement of 1898". From the 60s of the 19th century, influenced by Western capitalist ideas and the Official Westernization Movement as well as inflicted by domestic trouble and foreign aggression, some Chinese intellectuals wanted reform to be carried out. After the Sino-Japanese War, China was beset by national crisis. At that time, a modernization group, represented by Kang Youwei (1865-1898), Liang Qichao (1873-1929), Tan Sitong (1865-1898) and Yan Fu (1854-1921), mounted the political arena. They realized that reform must be carried out to make China rich and strong. They demanded a constitution, civil rights, parliament, and constitutional monarchy so as to abolish the autocratic monarchy.

In May 1895, Kang Youwei and Liang Qichao led 1,300 scholars who had passed the provincial examination and were now in Beijing for the metropolitan examination to submit a memorial to Emperor Guang Xu, opposing *the Treaty of Shimonoseki*. Such was the noted "Joint Petition of Imperial Examination Candidates to the Emperor". In August, initiated by Kang Youwei, the modernization group established the Qiang Xue Hui (Learn-to-be-strong Society), which published *Zhong Wai Ji Wen (World Bulletin)*, *Qiang Xue* Bao and other periodicals recommending reform and modernization and calling for fight for the survival and salvation of the nation. Kang Youwei also wrote *A Study of the Forged Classics* and *An Inquiry into Confucius' Reform* to advocate reform. Liang Qichao edited *the Shi Wu Bao (Contemporary Affairs)* and wrote *Exposition on Institutional Reform* and some other articles, expounding the necessity of reformation. Yan Fu created *the Guo wen Bao (National News)*, and translated a large amount of Western theoretical works, among which the most important one was Huxley's (1825-1897) *Evolution and Ethics*. Yan Fu laid great emphasis on such ideas as "organic evolution and natural selection" and "the victory of the strong over the weak", which supplied a theoretical basis for the reform. Tan Sitong wrote *On Benevolence*, in which Tan attacked violently the autocratic monarchy. As such, the tide of reform surged forward day by day.

The propositions of the modernization group were supported by Emperor Guang Xu and his teacher Weng Tonghe (1830-1904) and other officials who formed a small group of political force, known as the "Emperor's Party"; while the other group attaching themselves to Empress Dowager Ci Xi were called the "Empress Dowager's Party". With the intense conflict between Emperor Guang Xu's faction and that of Empress Dowager, the modernization movement reached its climax. On June 11, 1898 (the year of Wuxu) Emperor Guang Xu issued an imperial edict of "Reformation of State Affairs" and declared new policies to be carried out. With the plan and preparation of Kang Youwei and others, the Qing court issued from June to September a series of new decrees and declared to follow the example of Japan for reform and national revival. The main contents of the reform edicts were: to encourage the expression of opinions through memorials to the throne; to reduce unnecessary administration organs; to dispatch princes and ministers to inspect abroad; to set up a general bureau of agriculture, industry and commerce to encourage industry and commerce; to train soldiers in the Western way and strengthen national defense; to reform the civil service examination system and establish the Metropolitan College; to abolish the "eight-legged essays"; to select and send students to study abroad; and some measures to liberate people's mind, such as to forbid exaggeration in writing and foot-binding of women; and to cut men's braids. However, among the provincial officials, only the governor of Hunan Chen Baozhen carried them out seriously, and others just ignored the decrees.

Members of the Emperor's party intended to take the real power from Ci Xi's hand by carrying out new policies, which was unbearable to those of the Empress Dowager's party. Five days after the reform edict was issued, Ci Xi expelled Wing Tonghe from Beijing and thus eliminated the backbone element of the Emperor's party. Later she appointed her trusted follower Ronglu (1836-1903) as Viceroy of Zhili and in this way, she took control over the capital and its environment. However, Emperor Guang Xu also dealt certain counter blow at Ci Xi. He broke a rule to promote Tan Sitong, Lin Xu (1875-1898), Liu Guangdi (1859-1898) and Yang Rui (1857-1898) to the fourth official rank officers to help in the

Liang Qichao (1873-1929 AD)

Poem with five characters in a line, regular script, by Liang Qichao

Privy Council on matters relating to institutional reform. In addition, Emperor Guang Xu called in Yuan Shikai officially since the former wanted to enlist the help of the latter's newly-established modern army to strengthen his force. However, Yuan Shikai played a double game. On the one hand, he showed his "loyalty" to the emperor and on the other he informed Ronglu about the secrets of the reformists immediately after he returned to Tianjin.

Hearing about the news from Ronglu, *Ci Xi* took actions at once. On the early morning on September 21, *Ci Xi* staged a sudden coup d'etat and imprisoned Emperor Guang Xu at Yingtai near the South Middle Sea. Then Empress Dowager *Ci Xi* proclaimed in the emperor's name to the public both at home and abroad that the emperor was seriously ill and

Tan Sitong (1865-1898 AD)

On Benevolence
by Tan Sitong

supported the reform were either imprisoned or banished. After the coup d'etat, most new policies were abolished except the establishment of the Metropolitan College. Thus hardly had the modernization reform been carried out for no more than 103 days when it ended in defeat.

that he requested Empress Dowager to "take charge of state affairs" again. Shortly afterwards, she dispatched persons to search and arrest the reformist leaders. As Kang Youwei received in advance a confidential imperial edict, he left Beijing for Shanghai the day before the coup d'etat and then escaped to Hong Kong with the help of Britain. Protected by the Japanese, Liang Qichao left Beijing by putting on make-up. Later, he escaped from Tianjin to Japan. Tan Sitong, however, was unwilling to escape. On September 28, Tai Sitong, Yangrui, Lin Xu, Liu Guangdi, Kang Guangren (1867-1898) and Yang Shenxiu (1849-1898), known to historians as "Six Virtuous Men in the Year of WuXu", were executed at Caishikou, Beijng. The officials who had

Rong Lu (1836-1903 AD)

Yan Fu (1853-1921 AD)

11. *Yi He Tuan* Movement and Aggression of Eight-Power Allied Forces Against China

Foreign missionaries in China

Men and women in Yi He Tuan

Banner of command and the banner of Yi
He Tuan

After the Sino-Japanese War, China fell into the serious crisis of partition by imperialists. Imperialist economic aggression badly damaged the natural economy in the countryside, resulting in more difficult living conditions for peasants and other labors. Meanwhile, foreign missionaries swarmed into China. Among them some aroused successive rebellions since they forcibly took people's farmland, coerced government, monopolized legal practice, and incited scoundrels to ride roughshod over the people. As such, peasants began their struggles against imperialist aggressors and *Yi He Tuan* became an organization for the anti-imperialist struggle.

Yi He Tuan, first known as *Yi He Quan*, originated in a place where Shandong and Zhili met. It attracted people to join in by establishing the organization of "*tan*", where people were taught to practice boxing. In autumn of 1898, the Catholics in Liyuan Village of Guanxian County, Shandong, destroyed the Yuquan Temple in order to build a Catholic church. Villager Yan Shuqin invited the leader of *Mei Hua Quan* of Weixian County (modern Hebei) Zhao Sanduo to lead people to protect the temple. The villagers then set fire to the Hongtaoyuan church and hoisted the flag of "support the Qing to expel foreigners" in Jiangjia Village of Guanxian County (in modern Weixian County, Hebei). Then Zhu Hongdeng, the monk Xincheng and others rose in response in Chiping County (in modern Shandong) and raised the slogans of "assisting the Qing to destroy the foreign aggressors" and "making Qing strong to destroy foreigners". They destroyed churches and attacked Catholics and drove away missionaries, and thus won support of the populace from the low stratum. On the second half of 1899, *Yi He Quan* and other similar organizations renamed themselves in succession as *Yi He Tuan*. By 1900, *Yi He Tuan* had spread all over the Beijing and Tianjin areas and it could even be found in the northeast, northwest as well as the southwest regions. The composition of *Yi He Tuan* was complicated and it lacked a unified organization either, with separate *tan kou*, *tan chang* and *quan chang* acting on their own. They held discussions only when absolutely necessary and took joint actions only by sending notes to inform each other. Such posts as master, eldest fellow apprentice, second fellow apprentice were established in each *tan*, who took charge of boxing training and commanded actions. There were similar organizations like the Red Lantern Detachment and the Blue Lantern Detachment, composed mainly of women. *Yi He Tuan* abstained from corruption and sex and wanted to kill corrupt officials as well as foreigners. They worshipped Chinese traditional gods; believe in magic power and thought that no weapon could harm their bodies. So the organization was featured with distinctive defects.

There were two different opinions in the Qing court towards *Yi He Tuan*. Some held that *Yi He Tuan* members were rebels that should be eliminated, while others believed that they were righteous people who could destroy foreign aggressors. As for Empress Dowager Ci Xi, she bore a grudge to Japan and Western countries for protecting reformists and supporting publicly Emperor Guang Xu and thus wanted *Yi He Tuan* to destroy those foreigners to vent her spite. Then large number of *Yi He Tuan* members entered Beijing and Tianjin, spreading all over the streets and lanes of the city.

In early April 1900, envoys of the four countries, United States, Britain, France and Germany, jointly presented a note to the Qing

Eight-Power Allied Forces enter the Forbidden City

Relics of "Xie Qi Qu" in Yuanmingyuan

government and pressed it to crush *Yi He Tuan* within two months. On May 28th all the foreign envoys in Beijing held a meeting and decided to send an allied force to suppress *Yi He Tuan*. They first dispatched over 400 soldiers to enter Beijing by force and then assembled their warships at Dagakou. Under the leadership of Seymour. E. H, a British Vice-Admiral, an army of more than 2,000 men organized by Britain, the United States, German, France, Russia, Japan, Italy and Austria advanced towards Beijing by train. However, the allied army was defeated by *Yi He Tuan* and the Qing army and retreated hastily to Tianjin. At this time, the foreign warships attacked and occupied Dagu Fort. Thus Dowager Ci Xi decided to declare war against foreign powers. She appointed Prince Zhuang, Zai Xun (? -1901) and the Associated-Secretary of the Grand Council, Gang Yi (1837-1900) as commanding officers of *Yi He Tuan* and rewarded it with 100,000 teals of silver and 20,000 *dan* of rice.

Several thousands of additional allied troops were sent to attack Tianjin, while the Beijing branch of *Yi He Tuan* laid siege to the foreign legations and attacked the *Xishiku* church. Both sides fought violently on the battlefield. However, Ci Xi went back on her words shortly after she declared war. In addition, when the Qing court declared war, the governors-general in the South, Zhang Zhidong, Liu Kunyi (1830-1902) and others refused to obey the imperial order and on the other hand, reached an agreement of "the South and the North defending together" with the foreign consuls in Shanghai, which aimed at preventing *Yi He Tuan* from spreading to the Southeast. Shortly afterwards, the allied army attacked and occupied Tianjin, where it set up Governor's Office and organized an army of 20,000 men to advance towards Beijing. The allied forces entered Beijing when Empress Dowager Ci Xi fled hastily westward, taking Emperor Guang Xu with her. On her way, she decreed to extirpate the *Yi He Tuan* and instructed Li Hongzhang to go northward to negotiate peace.

Under the leadership of the commander-in-chief Walderse. A. Von, a German, the eight-power allied army burned, killed, looted and committed all kinds of atrocities in Beijing and Tianjin areas. After they occupied Beijing, the troops were allowed to loot for three days in the capital, but in fact, they looted for eight days. They plundered everything on their way, from imperial palace to civilian houses and the field was strewn with dead bodies. Early in1900, Britain, the United states, Germany, France,

One of the pictures of the 40 sceneries in Yuanmingyuan, the tenth year of Emperor Qian Long (1745 AD)

Japan, Italy, Russia, Austria and those that proclaimed war against China but didn't send troops to fight, such as Spain, Belgium and Holland presented an outline of peace negotiation to the Qing Government. Empress Dowager Ci Xi instructed negotiating ministers Yi Kuang and Li Hongzhang to try to appease the foreign aggressors. In 1901 (the year of Xinchou), the Qing court signed the International Protocol of 1901 with the foreign powers. By the terms of the treaty, the Qing court would pay an indemnity of 450 million taels of silver (principal and interest amounted to 980 million taels of silver); establish in Beijing a "legation quarter" where foreign troops were to be stationed and Chinese barred from residence, dismantle the fortress along the way from Dagukou to Beijing, forbid Chinese troops to be stationed twenty li off Tianjin and allow foreign troops to be stationed along the way from Beijing to Shanhaiguan; punish the officials who favored war against them; ban any popular anti-imperialist activities under penalty of death ; and change *Zongli Yamen* into Ministry of Foreign Affairs which was to be placed before the Six Boards. At that time, China turned to a semi-colony under the joint-jurisdiction of foreign powers.

Yi Kuang and Li Hongzhang signed the International Protocol of 1901 with the representatives of foreign countries

第九篇

辉煌落日

12. Empress Dowager Ci Xi and New Administration in the Late Qing Dynasty

Empress Dowager Ci Xi, with a family name of Yehe Nala (1825-1908 AD)

Prince Gong Yi Xin (1833-1896 AD)

Empress Dowager Ci Xi (1835-1908), with a family name of Yehe Nala, was a concubine of Emperor Xian Feng, and the actual ruler in the reigns of Tong Zhi and Guang Xu towards the end of the Qing Dynasty. In 1856, as she gave birth to a boy child, she was made a highest-ranking imperial concubine by Emperor Xian Feng. In 1860 when the Anglo-French forces entered Beijing, she fled to Rehe (modern Chengde, Hebei) with Xian Feng. The next year, Emperor Xian Feng died of illness and was succeeded by his six-year-old son Zai Chun, with a reign title of Qixiang. As such, she was respectfully called Goddess Empress Dowager, with a glorious title of Ci Xi, thus she was also known as "Empress Dowager Ci Xi". Living in the western palace, she was also called "Western Empress Dowager". As she had a strong desire for authority, she collaborated with Prince Gong Yi Xin to stage a coup d'etat in November, known to historians as "Coup of Xinyou". Then she changed the reign title to "Tong Zhi" and began to take charge of state affairs "behind the screen". Ever since then, she seized the imperial power. Though Emperor Tong Zhi was on the throne for 13 years, he assumed the reins of government only in the last two years. In 1874, Emperor Tong Zhi died of illness. Since he had no son, Empress Dowager Ci Xi designated Zai Tian, son of Yi Xuan, Prince Chun as emperor to facilitate her control over the state. At that time, Zai Tian was only four and Empress Dowager Ci Xi still attended to court affairs from behind a screen. In 1877 Emperor Guang Xu assumed the reins of government, however, the real power was still in Empress Dowager Ci Xi's hands. In 1889 when Emperor Guang Xu was 19, Ci Xi was forced to return the state power to Emperor Guang Xu. However, she still manipulated state affairs surreptitiously. She strangled the reform of 1895 and eventually betrayed Yi He Tuan as well.

Under the circumstances that foreign powers were at the city gate Empress Dowager Ci Xi knew clearly the crisis of the Qing rule. During the time when she escaped westward, she published two imperial edicts of "self-reproach" and "reform". In January 1901 she issued an imperial edict of reform. In April, the Qing government established a Political Supervising Office to plan a new administration and appointed Yi Kuang, Li Hongzhang, Ronglu and others all together six people as political supervising ministers. Some new policies such as reforming administrative organs, organizing and training new army as well as police, awarding business, establishing schools, abolishing the imperial examination system and encouraging students studying aboard, were issued in succession.

In 1905 the Qing court sent Zai Ze (1876-1928) and other four ministers to Europe to inspect politics there and announced its constitutional preparations, intending to keep popular feeling unruffled. In 1906 the Qing government declared its preparations to establish a National Consultative Assembly in Beijing and consultative councils in local areas. Kang Youwei and Liang Qichao aboard announced to replace the "Society of Protection of Emperor" with "National Constitutional Assembly". Moreover, they established. *Zheng Wen She* (Society of Political News) and sent its members to the homeland to work for the establishment of constitution at an early date. A domestic industrialist

Dyed ivory carving of Chinese cabbage, Qing Dynasty, 14. 2cm long, 6. 5cm wide, 2. 6cm thick

Filigree enamel fridge (2 pieces), Qing Dynasty, 76cm high, 72. 5cm long, 72. 5cm wide

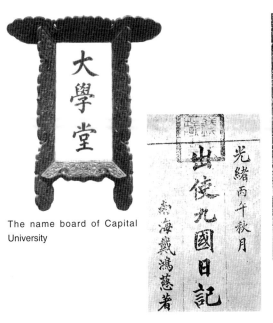

The name board of Capital University

Dai Hongci and Duan Fang's photo before their visit to foreign countries, Diary of Visiting Nine Countries published after Dai's return

Zhang Qian (1853-1926) set up the "Preparatory Constitutional Association" in Shanghai. Tang Hualong (1874-1918) created the "Society of Preparatory Constitutionalism" in Hubei and Tan Yankai (1880-1930) established the "Association of Constitutionalism" in Hunan. They operated publicly and demanded a quick practice of constitutionalism, thus formed a fairly influential group in society; known as "constitutionalists".

However, the "constitutional preparations" of the Qing court was just a fraud. Longing for a peaceful life in her old age, Empress Dowager Ci Xi took a perfunctory attitude and played for time. The Manchu nobility intended to restore the military as well as political power of the local government by the reform of the official system, which caused the constitutionalists to petition to convene a congress. In 1908 the Qing court issued an "Imperial Constitution" stipulating a nine-year preparatory period for setting up a constitutional government. In November Empress Dowager Ci Xi and Emperor Guang Xu died one after another. Puyi (1906-1967), who was not more than three, then succeeded to the throne with the reign title of Xuan Tong and his father Zai Feng, (1883-1951) Prince Chun acted as regent. Zai Feng, however, still adopted the tactics of fake establishment of

Shrine carved with figures and flowers, late Qing Dynasty (1851-1911 AD)

Gilded bronze chime clock, Emperor Qian Long of Qing Dynasty (1736-1795 AD)

constitutionalism and true centralization of power. In 1903 the constitutionalists dispatched three times representatives to Beijing for a petition. They demanded to set up a cabinet at once as well as to convene the congress and to reduce the nine-year preparatory period to five years. In May 1911 the court declared the establishment of the first cabinet and appointed Yi Kuang Prince Qing as the Prime Minister. But nine of thirteen ministers were the Manchus and seven were members of the imperial clan, so that people at that time called it "imperial cabinet". The constitutionalists were greatly disappointed at the cheating tactics of the Qing government and thus many of them joined the anti-Qing ranks.

Imperial Mausoleum of Qing Dynasty

第九篇

辉煌落日

13. Conventions and Variations--the Merging Customs

As a unique social organizational form, Banner System played an important role in the establishment of the Qing Dynasty and the unification of the whole nation. In order to maintain the characteristics of the Manchu Eight Banners, the Qing government prescribed that in the conquered areas all the people must cut their hair according to the customs of Manchu, that is to shave all the hair on the forehead and wear the other hair in a braid. They must change the costumes of Ming Dynasty and wear that of the Qing Dynasty. Due to people's fierce opposition, the Qing government had to change their policy: men must wear Manchu costumes while women may keep the old practice; government officials must have Manchu costumes while slaves may wear Han clothes. This led to a strange combination of Manchu and Han costumes.

The Qing Dynasty had a rigid hierarchy. As the rulers, Manchu nobles enjoyed privileges everywhere. In the late Qing Dynasty, Han women began to favor the cheongsam of Manchu and accept their hair style. The rulers adopted tolerate policies in many aspects, such as food, clothing, shelter, transport, marriage, funeral and festivals. The customs of marriage basically inherited that of the Ming Dynasty. Based on "six protocols" of Han, the royal wedding ceremony combined the customs of both Manchu and Han. These protocols included presenting gifts, wedding procession, drinking the nuptial cup and, especially emphasizing presenting gifts and wedding procession.

Qing people learned the essence of Manchu and Han cuisines and created the well-known

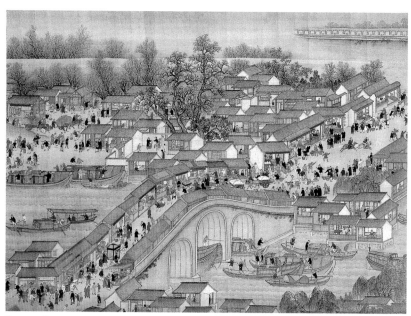

Emperor Kang Xi's Visit to Southern China, 12th chapter, partial

Man-Han Banquet. It first appeared in Jiangsu, Zhejiang and the surrounding areas, then was brought into the imperial palace and spread all over the nation. Having its embryonic form as early as the Yongzheng Period, it gradually developed through Qianlong and Jiaqing Periods and became a banquet of the highest standard and with the largest variety of dishes. It consists of two main parts, Manchu steamed bread and dishes with the traditional Han flavor. Since it includes both staple and non-staple food with Manchu and Han features, it's called Man-Han Banquet. It has 110 dishes in all and can be divided into 5 parts. The first three parts are delicacies from land and sea, the fourth are typical Manchu foods and the fifth are the famous dishes of *jiangnan* (areas south of the lower reaches of the Yangtze River).This feast is an integration of the north and south cuisines, which represents that Manchu cuisine features barbecue while Han cuisine features soups.

Qiqiao Festival, partial, Qing Dynasty, by Ding Guanpeng (1736-1795 AD), ink on paper, 28.7cm high, 384.5cm long

Shui Fang Yan Xiu: On July 7th when the Emperor is in Rehe, Empress Dowager, Empress, Concubine and princesses have a Qiqiao Festival

A pair of ivory fans, Qing Dynasty, 36.5cm high

The whole nation joining in the jubilation-Yangge, a popular rural folk dance

The whole nation joining in the jubilation-Five-Tone Big Drum

The utensils of the Qing largely followed the traditions of the previous dynasties especially Ming Dynasty. Creations were few but they had their unique characteristics. Before the Kangxi Period, the furniture remained almost the same as that of Ming, till Qianlong Period they formed a distinctive feature--with heavy materials and intricate decorations. Most of the furniture in the imperial palace had both Chinese and Western characteristics. The Western-style designs were carved or inlaid in the furniture of Chinese features. The porcelain made in Kangxi and Qianlong Periods were famous worldwide. The techniques of red porcelain and color pot were exquisite. In the Qing Dynasty, many western missionaries brought rare things into the imperial palace and officials' homes, such as chime clock, musical instrument, cross, microscope, snuff bottle, music box etc, most of which were made of glass, bronze and porcelain with delicate shapes.

In the Ming and Qing Dynasties, the prosperity of economy in Jiangnan gave birth to the great development of gardening, especially in Suzhou, the appearance of hundreds of garden architectural complex made this area the center of gardening art in Jiangsu province. They not only set good examples for gardens in other places but also influenced imperial gardens. There were many imperial gardens in the Qing Dynasty. The two seas to the north of the Forbidden City (generally called *tai ye chi*, namely

Civilian residential housing in Wan Nan

Stone memorial arch in Wan Nan

An ancient village in Wan Nan-Xidi Hongcun in Anhui province

The gardens in Suzhou, Jichang Garden

The gardens in Suzhou, Lion Forest, Yanyu Hall

the North Sea and Zhongnanhai) and Jingshan mountain to the west were attached gardens of the imperial palace. Changchuyuan, Jingmingyuan, Changchuyuan, Zizhuyuan, Diaoyutai, Wanchunyuan, Jingyiyuan, Leshanyuan, Nanhuayuan, Yuanmingyuan and Yiheyuan Gardens lay in the west outskirts of Beijing. Nanyuan situated in the south outskirts was the imperial hunting ground. Yuanmingyuan was a model combining Chinese and Western styles. It used to be a little garden of the imperial family in Ming Dynasty, then it was extended in Yongzheng Period, and had further development in Qianlong Period. It not only imitated many famous gardens in Suzhou and Hangzhou, but also appointed westerners to design and build European-style buildings. It was constantly extended during Jiaqin, Daoguang and Xianfeng Periods, and became a garden with plenty of rare treasures combining Chinese and Western architectures. So it was called "the King of Gardens". In the outskirts of Beijing, in the cities and vital communication lines of Hebei, Jiangsu, Zhejiang and the surrounding areas, numerous temporary dwelling places were built for emperors to pay homage at the imperial mausoleum and to travel for inspections. Some of them were well-known, such as the Hot Spring Xinggong (in east Tangshan of Changping, Beijing), Rehe Xinggong (north of Chengde,

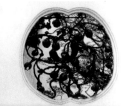

The gardens in Suzhou, the Master-of-Nets Gardens

Hebei), Great Xinggong (in Nanjing, Jiangsu) and Hangzhoufu Xinggong (in Hangzhou). Rehe Xinggong was the largest and the best-preserved ancient imperial temporary dwelling place. The private mansions of the princes, officials and wealthy people followed the quadrangle structure of Ming Dynasty. Nowadays there are still exquisite gardens all over the nation.

The water-side pavilion in the summer resort in Chengde, Hebei province

第九篇

辉煌落日

The superficial prosperity of Qing Dynasty put a premium on the extravagance and corruption. Lots of people were addicted to opium. The Opium War made the opium trade legal and this brought endless trouble to Chinese people.

The Taiping Revolution set off a strong fervor of "worshipping God". Temples were damaged, Buddha statues were destroyed and the God was worshipped. In Nanjing, Taiping Army called for establishing a new society, new stipulations of costume, shoes, hat, marriage and funeral ceremonies. They fought against the lavish marriage customs, forbade coffin burial. It had an importance of opposing the traditional secular ideas.

As the Western big powers designated their settlements, built residence and roads, set up business service and places for entertainment, more and more foreigners settled down in China. The western life style gradually infiltrated into the everyday life of the Chinese people. The Westernization Movement began in the 1860s opened some modern industries. The railway constructions, the development of telecommunication service, provided great convenience to politics, military affairs, business and civil use. After the Reform Movement of 1898, the educational system also was reformed. Modern schools and educational forms appeared, new-style books and newspapers prevailed and people's horizons were broadened. Therefore, the connection and communication between China and the world was enhanced.

Lotuses, by Zhu Da (1626-1705 AD)

Running script, Qing Dynasty, by Yi Bingshou, 172cm long, 62.8cm wide

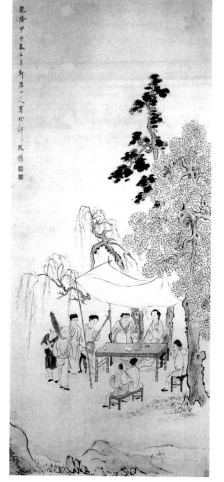

The Blind Storyteller, Qing Dynasty, By Hua Yan (1682-1756 AD), 133.5cm long, 60cm wide

Carpet made in Xinjiang

Crepe silk lined jacket with embroidery edges

Evening Banquet in Yihong Garden, the
illustration in A Dream of Red Mansions,
Qing, by unknown artist

Zhi Yanzhai's comments on the Story of the Stone in
Jiawu year of Emperor Qian Long

Zhu Xuezhai's copy of Strange Tales
from a Lonely Studio

The great warrior attendants of Buddha

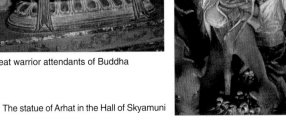

The statue of Arhat in the Hall of Skyamuni

Buying Chrysanthemum, the illustration of Strange Tales
from a Lonely Studio, Qing, by unknown artist

第九篇

辉煌落日

14. Sun Yat-sen and the Bourgeois Revolutionary Movement

Sun Yat-sen (1866-1925 AD)

Huang Xing (1874-1916 AD)

Sun Yat-sen (1866-1925), whose last name was Wen, styled himself Deming. He had an alias of Rixin, which was changed later to Yixian. As he once used an assumed name of Zhongshanqiao when he went into exile in Japan, he was well-known in his time with the name of Zhongshan. He was born in the village of Cuiheng in Xiangshan (present-day Zhongshan City),Guangdong Province. As a teenager he

studied in a private school for three years. At twelve he went to Honolulu where he attended secondary school. After he returned to China at the age of seventeen he studied medicine in Guangzhou and Hong Kong. In 1892 when he graduated from the Western Medicine Academy in Hong Kong, he began to practice in Guangzhou and Macao and actively participated in political activities in the meantime. In 1894 he went to Honolulu and established the *Xing Zhong* Hui (Society for the Revival of China). He proposed to "drive out the Manchus, restore China and establish a united government". Early the next year he established the General Headquarters of *Xing Zhong* Hui in Hong Kong. Shortly afterwards, *Xing Zhong* Hui prepared to stage an armed uprising on the Double Ninth Festival in Guangzhou. However, the uprising was crushed and Sun Yat-sen fled abroad. Then he set up in Yokohama the *Xing Zhong* Hui. In 1900 Sun Yat-sen dispatched Zheng Shiliang to stage an uprising in Huizhou where the insurgents grew to over twenty thousand. However, it was also crushed half a month later. Hereafter Sun Yat-sen became a generally acknowledged revolutionary leader.

In order to resist revolution, *Bao Huang Hui* actively propagated "protection of the emperor" and slandered revolution viciously, while the revolutionaries took up a pen and combated violently. Sun Yat-sen published the Pulic Notice to Fellow Countrymen and the Refutation of Bao Huang Bao. Zhang Taiyan (1869-1936) published the "Letter in Refutation of Kang Youwei's Views on Revolution". Zou Rong (1885-1905) wrote The Revolutionary Army. Chen Tianhua (1875-1905) wrote the *About Face*! and Alarm Bell. All of the books and articles mentioned above helped to spread the influence of democratic revolutionary ideas with which many small revolutionary groups were formed at home, such as the *Hua Xing Hui* (Society for the Revival of the Chinese Nation) organized by Huang Xing (1874-1916) and Song Jiaoren (1882-1913) in Hunan, t*he Kexue Buxi Suo* (Science Study Group) by Liu Jingan (1875-1911) and Zhang Nanxiang (1874-1968) in Hubei, *the Guang Fu Hui* (Restoration Society) by Cai Yuanpei (1868-1940), Zhang Taiyan, Xu Xilin (1873-1907), Tao Chengzhang (1878-1912) and Qiu Jin (1875-1907) in Zhejiang. These people actively expanded the membership by selecting candidates from the New Army and party members and organized anti-Qing uprisings, but none was successful.

In summer of 1905 when Sun Yat-sen came to Tokyo from Europe, he amalgamated parts of the membership of Hua xing Hui and other revolutionary bodies to form *the Zhongguo Tong Meng Hui* (Chinese Revolutionary League). It adopted the programme to "drive out the Manchus, restore China, establish a republic and equalize landownership", elected Sun Yat-sen as president and set up an executive group with the head of Huang Xing, and appraising group and a judicial group. Besides, it created the Min Bao (People's Journal). In its first issue Sun Yat-sen put forward the Principle of Nationalism, the Principle of Democracy and the Principle of People's Livelihood, which called for Chinese people's struggle for the overthrow of the Qing rule and the establishment of an independent republic. With its general headquarters in Tokyo, Tong Meng Hui established many branches in cities such as Shanghai, Hankou, Chongqin, Yantai, Hong Kong, and areas south beyond the South China Sea, Europe, America and Honolulu. The

Emperor Xuan Tong of Qing Dynasty, Aisin Gioro Puyi (1906-1967 AD) and his father Zai Feng (1883-1952 AD)

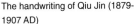

The handwriting of Qiu Jin (1879-1907 AD)

Revolutionary Army by Zou Rong

Sun Yat-sen and the members of Tong Meng Hui in Detroit, USA

revolutionaries vigorously carried out revolutionary activities and with *Min Bao* as their fortress, held an offensive debate with *the Xin Ming Cingbao* (New People's Journal) published by those who protected the emperor.

Meanwhile, Tong Meng Hui organized armed uprisings time and again, among them the famous ones erupted on the borders of Henan and Jiangxi, in Liling and in Pingxiang. Besides, it launched six uprisings in succession in coastal areas and border areas in the Southeast and Gangdong. Xu Xilin and Qiu Jin, who were members of Tong Meng Hui and who carried on revolution in the name of Guang Fu Hui also launched uprisings in secret in Anhui and Zhejiang. Some revolutionaries even acted independently for national salvation. They looked for every opportunity of political assassination, which caused all the high officials in the court to feel endangered. On April 27, 1911 (the 29th day of the 3rd lunar month), Tong Meng Hui once again staged the Guangzhou Uprising at Huanghuagang. However, it ended in defeat and the remains of the seventy-two martyrs were buried at Huanghuagang.

Local revolts also gained momentum every day, such as agitation against taxation and robbery of rice and the struggle for restoration of the rights of railways and mines was particularly vigorous. People in Jiangzhe opposed Britain to control the railway from Shanghai to Hangzhou and to Ningbo; people in Shanxi and Henan demanded to take railway rights from the British; and people in Yunnan resisted French to build the railway of Dianyue and people in Sichuan, Hubei, Hunan and Guangdong demanded restoration of railway rights along the line from Guangdong to Wuhan and that from Sichuan to Wuhan. The movement to protect railway rights was most vigorous in Sichuan. However, the local authorities dispatched army and police to suppress the petitioning people, causing the outraged civilians to take arms to organize the Protecting Railway Rights Army and launch armed uprisings.

The Qing government brought in troops from Hubei to suppress the revolts in Sichuan and thus the two secret societies in the Hubei New Army, the Wen Xue She (Liberty Association) and the Gong Jin Hui(March Together League)seized the opportunity to launch uprisings. They established uprising headquarters with Jiang Yiwu (1885-1913) as the commander-in-chief and Sun Wu (1880-1939) as the chief of staff. Besides, they sent people to Shanghai to escort the leaders of the Tong

Song Jiaoren (1882-1913 AD)

Min Bao of Tong Meng Hui and its forward

Tao Chengzhang (1st from left)-the leader of Guang Fu Hui, Xu Xilin (1st from right) and some friends

第九篇

輝煌落日

Li Yuanhong (1964-1928 AD)

Jiang Yiwu (1882-1913 AD), the leader of Wen Xue She, who organized Wuchang Uprising

Sun Wu, the leader of Gong Jin hui, who organized Wuchang Uprising

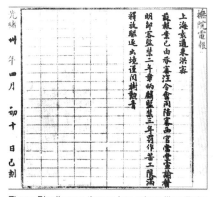

Zhang Binglin was thrown into prison illegally by Shanghai International Settlement Joint Trial Court in 1904. This is the secret telegram from Yuan Shuxun.

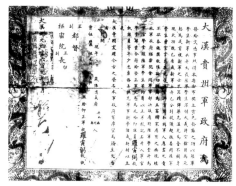

The Declaration of Guizhou military government

The handwriting of Sun Yat-sen on a card asking for help when he fell into imminent danger in London

The calligraphy sent to a Japanese friend by Sun Yat-sen

Meng Hui from Shanghai to Wuhan to discuss significant affairs. The uprising time was originally set on the Middle- Autumn Day of 1911 (October 6), however, it was delayed since more time was needed for preparations. But due to the accidental explosion of a bomb trial produced by Sun Wu in a French concession in Han Kou, the Qing troops in Wuhan searched and arrested the revolutionaries. A large number of the revolutionary leaders were arrested and executed and Jiang Yiwu was forced to flee. Seeing the situation was critical, the revolutionaries of the Eighth Battalion of the New Army were compelled to go ahead with the uprising on the night of October 10. Then all the other battalions rose in response. Having fought a bloody war against the Qing troops for a whole day, the insurrectionary army eventually captured Wuchang City. On October 12, Hankou and Hanyang were also occupied. Then on the recommendation of the insurrectionary army, Li Yuanhong, former brigade commander of the New Army, was elected as military governor and the Hubei Military Government was set up, which declared independence of Hubei. Shortly afterwards, many provinces such as Hunan, Shaanxi, Shanxi, Yunnan, Jiangxi, Guizhou declared independence in succession. As it was the year of Xinhai according to Chinese lunar calendar, the revolution of this year was known to historians as Revolution of Xinhai. In December when Sun Yat-Sen returned to China from abroad, the provincial delegates convened in Nanjing and elected him Provisional President and declared 1912 as the first year of the republic. On January 1, Sun Yat-sen took the oath of office and proclaimed the establishment of the provisional government of the Republic of China. On February 12, Emperor Puyi of the Qing Dynasty was forced to declare abdication, leading to the end of the Qing rule, as well as the autocratic monarchy that lasted for more than 2000 years.

The memorial of the Movement to Protect Railway Projects in autumn, Xinhai year

The tomb of 72 revolutionary martyrs in Huanghuagang, Guangzhou, Guangdong province

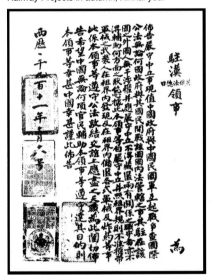

The neutrality note by foreign consuls in Wuhan during the Wuchang Uprising

The breakthrough of the office of governor-general of Hunan and Hubei during the Wuchang Uprising

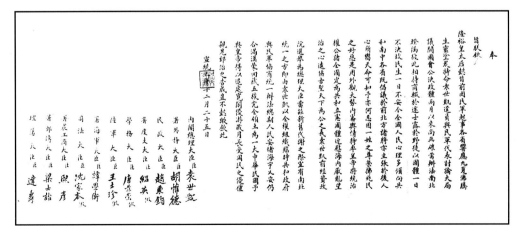

The imperial abdication edict Emperor Xuan Tong of Qing Dynasty, Aisin Gioro Puyi (1906-1967 AD)

212

Chapter 10

Tradition Awaited Renewal
--Republic of China

The Revolution of 1911 swept away the absolute monarchy.
The Republic of China was established, launching a scene that was unprecedented through thousands of years.
The old had been broken and the new was yet to be set up.
The road of history was never smooth, the independence and mightiness of the Chinese nation were indeed full of hardships!

Jiuzhaigou, Sichuan Province

Northern Government Beijing	Sun Wen (the interim President, assumed office in Nanjing, Jan.-Mar. 1912)	Yuan Shikai (the interim President, assumed office in Beijing, Mar. 1912-Oct. 1913)	Yuan Shikai (President, Oct. 1913-Jun. 1916)

| The military government of Republic of China (Guangzhou) | | | |

| National Government (Guangzhou -Nanjing) | Jiang Zhongzheng (Chairman of the National Government, Oct. 1928-Dec. 1931) | Lin Sen (Chairman of the National Government, Dec. 1931-Aug. 1943, the National Government changed its capital to Chongqing) | |

| ...nhong ...dent, ...July. ..7) | Feng Guozhang (President, Jun.1917-Oct. 1918) | Xu Shichang (President, Oct. 1918-Jun. 1922) | Li Yuanhong (President, Jun. 1922 -Jun. 1923) | Gai Lingwei (Premier and President, Jun.-Oct. 1923) | Cao Kun (President, Jan. 1923-Oct. 1924) | Huang Fu (Premier and President, Oct.-Nov. 1924) | Duan Qirui (temporary Nov. 1924-Apr. 1926) | Yan Huiqing (Premier and President May. -Jun. 1926) | Du XIgui (Premier and President Jun. -Sep. 1926) | Gu Weijun (Premier and President Oct.1926-Jun. 1927) | Zhang Zuolin (Marshal of military government, Jun. 1927-Jun. 1928) |

| Sun Wen (Marshal Sep. 1917-May. 1919) | Sun Wen (Marshal Apr.1921-Mar. 1923) | National Government (Guangzhou-Wuhan) | Wang Jingwei (the chairman of the National Government, Jul. 1925 - Sep. 1927) |

| ...ongzheng ...an of the ...ommission ...man of the ...ional ...nment, ...ep.1943) | Jiang Zhongzheng (Chairman of the National Government, Sep.1943-Dec. 1947 May. 1948) | Jiang Zhongzheng (Chairman of the National Government, May.1948-Apr. 1949) | Li Zongren (Vice President and Act President Jan.-Apr. 1949) | In April 1949, the Chinese People's Liberation Army conquered Nanjing. The National Government moved to Taiwan. |

1. The Seizure of State Power and Recovery of Monarchy

The first temporary Grand President of the Republic of China-Sun Yat-sen

On the New Year's Day of 1912, Nanjing Provisional Government declared its establishment. On January 4th, its first cabinet conference was held.

People of various circles in Ningbo, Jiangsu celebrated the establishment of Nanjing Provisional Government.

On November 16th, 1911, the Qing Dynasty established a Cabinet headed by Yuan Shikai, who held military power in his hands. Nanjing Provisional Government wished to win over Yuan Shikai through peaceful negotiation in the struggle against monarchy so as to make the emperor of the Qing Dynasty abdicate the throne and end the revolution as soon as possible. After forcing the emperor of the Qing Dynasty to abdicate on February 12th, 1912, Yuan Shikai was made the second temporary Grand President by Nanjing Provisional Government. However he refused to take the post under the pretence of the mutinies in Beijing. On the tenth of March, Yuan Shikai took the oath of office in Beijing and became the temporary Grand President. In April, Sun Yat-sen declared the removal of his position as the temporary Grand President, and the Provisional Government of the Republic was moved to Beijing.

Based on United League (*tong meng hui*), Sun Yat-sen, Huang Xing, Song Jiaoren and others established Kuomintang (the National People's Party) in state in Beijing. Sun Yat-sen was made director, while Song was in charge of practical Party affairs. In the national elections held in February 1913, Kuomintang won a majority of seats and gained the right to organize the parliament, which made Yuan upset and frightened. Soon after, when Song set out to the north from Shanghai, Yuan had him assassinated. Yuan Shikai raised lots of money from the banks of Britain, France, Germany, Japan and Russia and sent his troops southward to get rid of revolutionaries. Under the leadership of Sun Yat-

sen, Kuomintang launched the Second Revolution with the determination to suppress Yuan in virtue of armed forces. Li Liejun (1882-1946), Governor of Jiangxi first declared the independence of Jiangxi Province and launched a punitive expedition against Yuan in Hunan. This was followed by the independence of Nanjing by Huang Xing in Jiangsu. Later on, Anhui, Shanghai, Guangdong, Fujian, Hunan, Chongqing and other areas also declared independence one by one, joining in the rank of expeditions against Yuan. But these expeditions lasted no more than

Imprint of "the seal of the Republic of China"

Oath of the temporary Grand President signed by Sun Yat-sen

Sun Yat-sen's handwriting: "tianxia weigong"-referring to "World for Everyone"

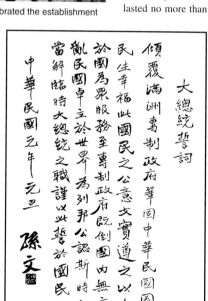

Yuan Shikai (1959-1916)

In 1912, Yuan Shikai took the oath of office as the temporary Grand President in Beijing.

Cai E (1859-1916), who was the first to launch military battle against Yuan and opposed Yuan's coming to the throne.

Yuan Shikai proclaimed himself as Emperor and held the ceremony of offering sacrifice to Heaven in the Temple of Heaven in Beijing.

two months before they declared failure.

After that, Yuan Shikai ordered the Kuomintang to dissolve and its members remove from parliament. Also, he suspended parliament and the provincial assemblies, abolished Provisional Constitution and forced the promulgation of a new constitution-the Constitution of the Republic of China, attempting to set up dictatorial rule, which, in effect, made him president for life. In 1915, Yuan Shikai accepted a few articles stating "to be further negotiated" in Item Five of Japan's 21 Demands, which aimed at swallowing up China. He instigated his subordinates to set up *chou an hui* (Society for the Preservation of Peace) as an organ to propagate the monarchical idea and made representatives from various provinces cast their ballots so as to reinstate the imperial system of government with himself as emperor. Yuan Shikai proclaimed himself the emperor of "Empire of China" on December 12th and named the next year as the year of "*hong xian*".

The restoration of monarchy by Yuan Shikai aroused people's strong opposition all over China. The peasant revolt led by Bai Lang in 1913 lasted over two years, covered five provinces and seized more than forty counties. Sun Yat-sen founded the Chinese Revolutionary Party in Tokyo, Japan and organized

After the failure of the Second Revolution against Yuan, Sun Yat-sen organized Chinese Revolutionary Party in Japan, which aimed at realizing civil rights, improving the people's livelihood, eradicating despotism and setting up a complete Republic of China.

armed forces to defeat Yuan at home in July, 1914. In December 1915, Li Liejun and others arrived in Kunming successively and organized Yunnan officers to fight against Yuan. On the 25th, Cai E declared the independence of Yunnan and launched *Huguo* Movement (the War of Guarding the Country) with *hu guo jun* (the Army of Guarding the Motherland). The provinces in the southwest and south gained independence one by one and established Military Office in Guangdong as an organization to connect various independent provinces. Being isolated by the majority including his subordinates, Yuan Shikai had to declare the end of the imperial system on March 22nd, 1916 and he died on June 6th. The farce of the imperial system of *hong xian* came to an end after 83 days' staging.

第十篇

传统待更新

2. Separate Regimes by Warlords

Li Yuanhong (1864-1928) took the post of the Grand President of Republic of China.

(1859-1919) (native of Hejian, Zhili), backed up by Britain and America, controlled Su (Jiangsu), Gan (Jiangxi), E (Hubei) and other provinces; and the *Feng* (Liaoning Province) Faction by Zhang Zuolin (native of Haicheng, Fengtian), supported by Japan, controlled the three provinces in the northeast. Besides, the *Jin* Faction by Yan Xishan seized Shanxi and Zhang Xun, who sought chances to help Pu Yi restore monarchy, stationed troops in Xuzhou. The southern warlords led by the military administrative office of *hu guo jun* consisted of the Dian Faction by Tang Jirao and *Gui* Faction by Lu Rongting.

Backed up by various foreign forces, different factions of warlords strove for the central regime, which led to constant transfer of regimes, frequent disasters of wars and great suffering of the people.

In August, 1916, Holding over the position of Grand President, Li Yuanhong declared the resumption of the Constitution of the Republic of China, convened the parliament and called off Guangdong Military Office. However, the military power of Beijing government was in reality held in the hands of Duan Qirui, then state premier. Being dissatisfied with the *Wan* Faction's power, Li Yuanhong ordered Duan Qirui be removed

Puyi's handwriting in his later years (1964), referring to "I have worked hard for four years to finish my book. I am performing meritorious services for the Party, the undertaking and the people to atone for my crimes."

Puyi (1906-1967), the last emperor of Qing. Feng Yuxiang launched Beijing Coup, Puyi left the Forbidden City in a flurry.

After the death of Yuan Shikai, Beijing government was still under the control of Beiyang (Northern) Warlords. Beiyang Warlords, divided into three branches, took up the north of China. The *Wan* (Anhui Province) Faction led by Duan Qirui (native of Hefei, Anhui Province) and supported by Japan, took over the control of Wan, Lu (Shandong Province), Zhe (Zhejiang), Min (Fujian), Shan (Shaanxi) and other provinces; the Zhi (Hebei Province) Faction by Feng Guozhang

Duan Qirui (1865-1936)

Zhang Zuolin (1875-1928)

Feng Guozhang (1859-1919)

Lu Rongting (1859-1928)

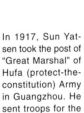

In 1917, Sun Yat-sen took the post of "Great Marshal" of Hufa (protect-the-constitution) Army in Guangzhou. He sent troops for the Northern Expedition so as to maintain the Provisional Constitution.

from his position, who, in response, got the *Wan* Faction and *Zhi* Faction to declare their independence and set up the general staffs of independent provinces in Tianjin so as to defeat Li Yuanhong. Li Yuanhong called for the help of Zhang Xun, a warlord from Xuzhou, who went to Beijing for reconcilement. Zhang Xun brought his Braid Army to Beijing and plotted the restoration of the Qing Dynasty with the warlords and veterans of the Qing court. On July 1st, 1917, Zhang Xun, Kang Youwei as well as others got Pu Yi, the abolished emperor of the Qing back to the throne.

The restoration of monarchy by Zhang Xun encountered strong opposition from the people all over China. Duan Qirui took a rally pledge in Machang, Tianjing, proclaiming himself General of the Army Against Zhang, and seized the opportunity to launch a battle against Zhang Xun in Beijing. Zhang Xun fled at the mere sight of the oncoming force. Pu Yi had to dethrone after the restoration which lasted only 12 days. Duan Qirui posed as a hero for the reestablishment of the Republic, took the position of State Premier once again. Under his leadership, the declaration of war against Germany in World War I was passed and large amounts of money was borrowed from Japan. Duan Qirui organized the so-called "*Can zhan jun*" (the army attending the war) so as to enlarge his power and strengthen his dictatorial rule. Meanwhile, he refused the recovery of the parliament and the Provisional Constitution.

In the middle of July, Sun Yat-sen arrived in Guangzhou and held "Unusual Parliament" with the parliament members. Also, he organized the military government with himself as "Great Marshal" in order to suppress Duan Qirui-the traitor of the Republic, which marked the start of *Hufa* Movement (Protect-the-constitution). The flame of Hufa movement spread to over ten provinces both in the south and north. The military government was split within itself and controlled by the Dian (Yunnan) and Gui (Guangxi) warlords, who changed the system of Great Marshal into that of Seven Leaders so as to squeeze out Sun Yat-sen. Full of indignation, Sun Yat-sen resigned. Soon after, the south and north reconciled and Hufa Movement ended in failure.

After that, Beijing Government was successively under the control of different warlords like *Wan*, *Zhi* and *Feng*. Colluding with the imperialists one by one, local warlords, compradors, and landowners held their own military forces and strove for more territories, bringing Chinese politics into a state of chaos.

Tang Jirao (1882-1927)

Zhang Xun (1854-1923)

Cao Kun (1862-1938)

Feng Yuxiang (1882-1948)

第十篇

传统待更新

3. New Culture Movement

Hu Shi (1891-1962)   Cai Yuanpei (1868-1940)   Chen Duxiu (1891-1942)   Li Dazhao (1889-1927)

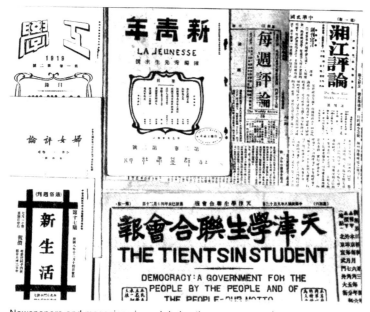

Newspapers and magazines issued during the New Culture Movement

On September 5th, 1915, Chen Duxiu (1891-1962) initiated the magazine *Youth* (named *New Youth* since the second issue), which advocated the revolution of ethics, politics, philosophy, religion and arts. The New Culture Movement therefore took root. In January 1917, Cai Yuanpei (1868-1940), appointed President of Beijing University, called for academic incorporation and absorption and invited Chen Duxiu to be dean of the School of Letters. So the newsroom of New Youth moved to Beijing from Shanghai. At that

time, Li Dazhao, Hu Shi, Qian Xuantong, Liu Bannong and other intellectuals of the New Culture Movement who worked as teachers in Beijing University also edited or wrote articles for New Youth. In December, 1918, Li Dazhao and Chen Duxiu started another magazine Weekly Review; Fu Sinian and Luo Jialun started *New Tide*.The main contents of the New Culture movement was democracy and science. Chen Duxiu published the article *To the Youth* in *New Youth*, which proposed the slogan of human rights and science and erected the banners of democracy and science for the first time. The New Culture Revolution called for democracy and opposed monocracy and warlord dictatorship; advocated science and opposed superstition and blindness; criticized the old formalities and morals represented by Confucius and proposed the elimination of Confucianism. Besides, they warmly discussed the problems concerning women's liberation, family, and marriage, and propagated the idea of equality between men and women as well as the individual liberation.

Another important part of the New Culture Movement was literature revolution, which advocated the writing of modern Chinese instead of those of classical style, supported new literature and opposed old literature. In January 1917, Hu Shi published *Suggestions on Improving Literature*, putting forward the watchword of literature improvement and advocating the writing of plain and substantial literature in place of hollow and affected old literature. In February of the same year, Chen Duxiu published *On Literature Revolution*, explicitly advancing the slogan of "Literature Revolution" and relating the revolution of literature to that of politics. The first issue of Volume 5 of *New Youth* (Jan.1918) adopted the vernacular Chinese and new punctuations. New poems also came out. In April, 1918, Lu Xun published "A Madman's Diary" in New Youth, which was the first story written in modern Chinese. Promoted and practiced by *New Youth*, new publications from various regions followed suit so that it became a trend to propagate new tide of thoughts through modern Chinese.

As the New Culture Movement broke the chains of the traditional dogmas, it was actually an unprecedented movement of mind emancipation. It preliminarily introduced the trend of western philosophy and social science as well as natural science so that people's mind got broadened and Chinese politics, ideology, science and culture were pushed forward tremendously.

4. May Fourth Movement and the Founding of The Communist Party of China (CPC)

After World War I, Paris Peace Conference was held among the winning countries in France. As one of the winners, China required an end to the privileges enjoyed by the imperialists and demanded the cancel of 21 demands signed by Yuan Shikai with Japan and reclaimed the rights enjoyed by Japan in Shandong Province, which were taken from Germany during the war. However, the Peace Conference, controlled by the imperialists, refused China's requirements and agreed to Japan's claim over Shandong Province. And Beijing Government was to sign on the peace treaty. When the news reached China, the whole country was angered.

On May Fourth, thousands of Beijing students headed by Beijing University held mass demonstrations in Tian'an Men Square, demanding the safeguarding of national sovereignty and eliminating traitors in the country. After the demonstrations, they burned the house Zhaojia Lou, the private residence of Cao Rulin and had a good beating of Zhang Zongxiang, then Minister stationed in Japan, who stayed there. Beijing government sent armed forces to suppress them and got 31 students and one citizen arrested. Strikes started among all the schools and universities in Beijing. The Student Association of all the schools equal or higher than secondary level was set up. The students held patriotic speeches on the streets, which propagated the boycotting of Japanese goods and promoting of Chinese products.

Later on, Beijing Government further arrested nearly 7000 Beijing students, which arouse greater indignation of the whole nation. Shanghai workers were the first to start strikes in support of the students and the merchants stopped business; trains, ships and city transports stopped working as well. Strikes of the workers, merchants and students also broke out in other cities, like Tianjin, Wuhan, Jiujiang, Nanjing and Hangzhou and the movement spread to over 150 cities in 22 provinces in good time. The struggle center shifted from Beijing to Shanghai and the workers, instead of the students, became the main force of the struggle. Then the students abroad and overseas Chinese also participated in the struggle.

Dread of the masses power, Beijing Government had to release the arrested students, dismiss Cao Rulin, Zhang Zongxiang and Lu Zongyu from office and refuse to sign the Paris Peace Treaty.

The May 4th Movement displayed the strength of the Chinese people and facilitated the development of the New Culture Movement. After 1919, various western social thoughts got widely disseminated in China and Marxism was brought to China with the victory of October Revolution in Russia. Li Dazhao and Chen Duxiu took to writing enthusiastically in the hope of propagating Marxism. Progressive publications came out in large numbers to introduce Marxism everywhere and Communist Groups aiming at propagating and studying Marxism also took shape one by one.

In August 1920, being helped by Communist International, China's first Communist group was set up in Shanghai and Chen Duxiu was elected its secretary. In October, Li Dazhao initiated the founding of Beijing Communist group. Later on, Communist groups were set up one after another in Wuhan, Changsha, Guangzhou, Jinan and so on. Besides, Paris Communist Group and Japan Communist Group were also set up abroad.

On July 23rd, 1921, the Communist Party of China held its First National Congress secretly in Shanghai. Present at the congress were representatives of the Communist groups at home and abroad. Malin, a representative from the Communist International also attended. The chief founders of the Party, Chen Duxiu and Li Dazhao, were both absent due to a crowded work schedule. In the middle of the congress it was raided by French policemen, so the last session of the congress was held on a painted pleasure boat in the Nanhu Lake in Jiaxing County, Zhejiang Province. The Communist Party of China was thus declared her founding and July 1st was stipulated as the birthday of the Party by the Central Committee of the Party in 1941.

In 1917, Duan Qirui Government declared war against Germany and participated in the war. In the picture, the Chinese soldiers in Qingdao were awaiting orders for setting out.

During the May Fourth Movement, Beijing students were making speeches in the street.

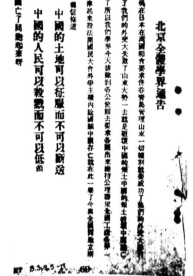

Announcement of the Whole Beijing Academic Circle

On May 7th, 1919, the arrested Beijing students regained freedom.

The extra of Xinshen Newspaper on the next day of May Fourth

Students of Jinan, Shandong were negotiating with the officers who were ordered to stop them

Dong Biwu, at the time of the First National Congress of the CPC

Li Da, at the time of the First National Congress of the CPC

Zhang Guotao, at the time of the First National Congress of the CPC

Malin, Representative of the Communist International

Mao Zedong (1893-1976), at the time of the First National Congress of the CPC

第十篇

传统待更新

The Communist Party of China declared its founding in a pleasure boat in the Nanhu Lake of Jiaxing County, Zhejiang Province

5. Northern Expedition War

The assembly room of the First National Congress of Kuomintang, in Guangzhou, on January 20th, 1924.

In 1919, Sun Yat-sen reformed the Chinese Revolutionary Party into Chinese Kuomintang. In 1922, Kuomintang held a conference in Shanghai, which reorganized Kuomintang. The First National Congress of Kuomintang was held in Guangzhou on February 20th, 1924. Sun Yat-sen, then prime minister, was presider of the congress. The Communist Party of China also attended the Congress. At this congress, Sun Yat-sen's Three People's Principles (*san min zhu yi*), namely, nationalism, democracy, and the people's livelihood, were explained in a new way and the Central Executive Board of Kuomintang was elected, which included the Communist Party of China. With the joint efforts of both parties, Guangdong Revolutionary Government was consolidated and large numbers of military and political intellectuals were trained.

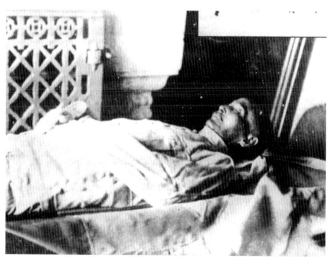

Remains of Sun Yat-sen and his will

Yan Xishan (1883-1960), Feng Yuxiang, Chiang Kai-shek and Li Zongren (1891-1969) fought unanimously against the same enemy in the Northern Expedition War and became enemies two years later, bringing forth a harsh war in the Central Plains.

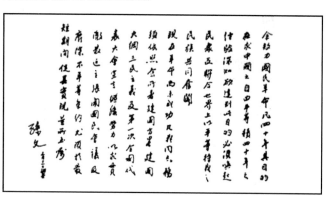

In November, 1924, at the invitation of Beijing Government, Sun Yat-sen went north despite of his illness in order to work out solutions of their problems. He proposed the holding of a national people's conference, the ending of warlords' rule, the abolishment of unequal treaties with the foreign countries and the resistance against the imperialist invasion. Unfortunately, he died of illnesses on March 12th of the following year in Beijing. Soon, Guangzhou National Government declared its founding and on the 6th, Guangzhou National Military Committee was formed to lead various forces of the National

Site of Huangpu Military College, in Huangpu, Guangzhou

Chiang Kai-shek (1887-1975). In July 1924, Huangpu Military College was founded and Chiang became President. Huangpu Military College is a cradle of the military talents of modern China.

Northern Expedition Army, marching in the triumphant songs

Liao Zhongkai (1877-1925), right hand of Sun Yat-sen, assassinated in Guangzhou, in 1925.

第十篇

传统待更新

Army. The National Army was formally organized in August. In the spring of 1926, Guangdong revolutionary bases became consolidated and the unification of Guangdong and Guangxi was realized, both of which paved the way for the Northern Expedition.

Then Beiyang Warlords were mainly made up of three branches: the first was the declining Zhi Faction led by Wu Peifu, who controlled Henan, Hunan, Hubei and areas including Zhili and Bao'an with a force of 200,000; the second was led by Sun Chuanfang, governor of Zhejiang, who disparted from the Zhi Faction and controlled Jiangsu, Zhejiang, Jiangxi, Anhui and Fujian with a force of 200,000; the third was the Feng Faction led by Zhang Zuolin, who, with 350,000 troops, occupied the northeast, Rehe, Qahar, Shandong, Beijing and Tianjin. The schedule of the Northern Expedition was made with the help of a Russian counselor Galens, Vasili Konstantinvich (1891-1969). The National Army originally had six corps with 100,000 troops and later on the Seventh Corps by Li Zongren in Guangxi and the Eighth Corps by Tang Shengzhi in Hunan also joined in.

On July 9th, 1926, with Chiang Kai-shek as its commander-in-chief, the National Army led an oath-taking rally in Guangzhou and then started the Northern Expedition officially by three routes. As a trailbreaker, the Independent Regiment led by Ye Ting had moved to Hunan as early as May. The First Corps of Northern Expedition launched attacks in Hunan and Hubei, defeating the main forces of Wu Peifu on the *ding si qiao* Bridge and *he sheng qiao* Bridge, and finally captured Wuhan; the Second Corps entered Jiangxi and seized Jiujiang, Nanchang and annihilated the main forces of Sun Chuanfang; the Third Corps advanced towards Fujian and

Zhejiang, and succeeded in capturing Fujian in December.

However, around the period of the Northern Expedition, disintegration took place within Kuomintang. Thus happened incidents like the murdering of Liao Zhongkai in 1925, Zhongshan Warship Incident in 1926 and the approval of the Resolution of Neatening the Party. In the early April 1927, anti-Communist conferences were secretly held in Shanghai. April 12th and July 15th saw the reactionary coup d'etats carried out respectively by Chiang Kai-shek in Shanghai and Wang Jingwei in Wuhan. Later on, the movement of "purging the Party" was unfolded on large scales, which marked the final break of the cooperation between the Communist Party of China and Kuomintang as well as the end of the Northern Expedition.

6. The Soviet Areas (Red Areas) and Kuomintang-controlled Areas (White Areas)

In April 1927, Nanjing National Government was set up with Chiang Kai-shek as Chairman. In July, Wuhan National Government, headed by Wang Jingwei, came into existence. Ning (Nanjing) and Han (Wuhan) confronted each other for legitimacy while the Feng faction led by Zhang Zuolin still held Beijing. In May of the same year, Nanjing Government Army launched the Northern Expedition by three routes. The Expedition army moved across the Changjiang River so that the Sun Chuanfang Faction and Zhang Zong Faction fled by way of Shandong. In August, having suffered failure in Northern Expedition and pressed by Wuhan Government, Chiang Kai-shek was forced to resign and move to Japan.

In September, the Central Special Committee of Kuomintang was set up in Shanghai. In November, Nanjing government, supported by the warlords of the Gui faction led by Li Zongren, defeated Tang Shengzhi who held forces in Wuhan. In January 1928, Chiang Kai-shek resumed his post as commander-in-chief of the National Revolutionary Army. He made himself a member of the Standing Committee of the Kuomintang and chairman of the Military Commission at the Fourth Plenary Session of its Second Central Executive Committee. On April 5th, Chiang Kai-shek led an oath-taking rally in Xuzhou and then launched another "Northern Expedition". Headed respectively by Chiang Kai-shek, Feng Yuxiang, Yan Xishan and Li Zongren as commander-in-chief of the four group armies, the Northern Expedition launched attacks against the Feng faction by four routes simultaneously. They aimed at defeating Zhang Zuolin who held Beijing. In June 1928, Zhang Zuolin, being defeated, left Beijing secretly and retreated to the northeast. However, he was killed in an explosion on a train at Huanggu Village near Shenyang by the Japanese imperialists. In August, the Expedition army captured Beijing. Having realized the Japanese imperialists' ambition of seizing the three provinces in the

In 1930, Nie Er, a musician (below), posed with his friend Zhang Genghou

northeast after the death of his father, Zhang Xueliang sent an open telegram in November, declaring he would "obey Nanjing government". The warlords in the provinces of the southwest also followed suit. Xinjiang and Rehe declared a "change of banner" as well. Thus Kuomintang expanded its rule to the whole country.

The Communist Party of China didn't remain silent at the rule of the Nanjing Government. On August 1st, 1927, Zhou Enlai and others led Nanchang Uprising, which fired the first shot against Kuomintang. The uprising army, being the elites of the National Revolutionary Army both politically and militarily, had a force of over 30,000 including the Officer and Initiator Corps led by Zhu De, the 15th Division of the Independent Regiment led by He Long, and the 24th Division of the 11th Army led by Ye Ting. After the seizure of Nanchang, the uprising army marched south

The stylish girl in the 1930s

Western ads swarmed into China in the 1930s

The assembly room where the congress of the Communist Party was held in the Soviet area for the first time. The one in the middle of the stage is Chairman Mao; the fourth from the right is Zhu De.

Qu Qiubai (1899-1935)

towards Guangdong, but suffered failure in eastern Guangdong. Then, part of the army joined the armed peasant forces and the other part, led by Zhu De and Chen Yi entered Hunan by way of the south of Jiangxi and northeast of Guangdong, carrying out guerrillas. On August 7th, 1927, a week after Nanchang Uprising, the CPC central Committee called an emergency conference at Hankou. At this conference, the Party decided to launch the Autumn-Harvest Uprising in Hunan, Hubei, Jiangxi, Guangdong and other provinces, centering on agrarian revolution. Also, a new Temporary Central Political Bureau was set up with Qu Qiubai (1899-1935) as general secretary.

After the August 7th Conference, Mao Zedong got to Hunan and established the field committee of Autumn-Harvest Uprising, which was the highest leading organ. On 9th, September, the uprising broke out on the Hunan-Jiangxi border. The uprising army seized counties like Liuyang and Liling, and planned to march into Changsha. However, due to lots of losses, it turned to the countryside. At the end of September, the troops arrived Sanwan Village, in Yongxin County, Jiangxi Province, where they got reorganized and the principle of Communist Party leadership over the army as well as the Soldier Committee was established so as to administer the army in a democratic way. In this way, a new people's army began to take shape both in politics and organization. After the reorganization, the troops advanced into *Jinggang* Mountains and set out to establish *Jinggang* Mountains base area. Later on, under the leadership of Fang Zhimin, peasant uprisings in Yiyang, Hengfeng, northeast of Jiangxi broke out, guerrilla warfare was carried out and the Worker-Peasant Democratic Government was set up. In November, the peasants in Hailufeng of Guangdong held three uprisings successively and set up Lufeng and Haifeng Worker-Peasant Democratic Governments respectively. In December, Zhang Tailei, Ye Ting and Ye Jianying led Guangzhou Uprising and occupied a large part of Guangzhou for a time. Between September 1927 and the summer of 1928, more than 100 armed uprisings took place all over China.

In May, 1928, the armies led by Zhu De and Chen Yi met the troops led by Mao Zedong in Jinggang Mountains, where they formed the Fourth Corps of the Chinese Workers' and Peasants' Red Army. In December, Peng Dehuai and Teng Daiyuan brought part of the 5th Corps, which participated in Pingjiang Uprising, to Jinggang Mountains. In January 1929, Mao Zedong, Chenyi and Zhu De led the main forces of the Fourth Corps of the Chinese Workers' and Peasants' Red Army to the south of Jiangxi and west of Fujian. In the early 1930, besides the central base area in southern Jiangxi-western Fujian, the worker-peasant armed regimes also included Hunan-western Hubei base area, Hubei-Henan-Anhui base area, Fujian-Zhejiang-Jiangxi base area, Hunan-Hubei-Jiangxi base area, Zuojiang-youjiang base area as well as Guangdong Hailufeng, Qiongya base areas and northern Shaanxi base area. The Red Army had developed into 13 corps with a population of 60,000 over 11 provinces. In November 1931, the First All-China Soviet Congress was convened in Ruijin, Jiangxi Province and it proclaimed the Provisional Central Government of the Chinese Soviet Republic. From then on, the Soviet areas and Kuomintang-controlled white areas coexisted.

The Kuomintang Government carried out a series of economic and cultural construction measures within their areas: taking back the administering power of railway from the foreigners, getting the railway state-owned, increasing the railways and roads and determining the customs independently. Besides, it promoted the currency reform and unified currency. All these activities facilitated the recovery and development of agriculture, industry and commerce, getting the Chinese national economy increased by 8.3% from 1929 to 1936 and leading to a prosperous scene. In 1934, Chiang Kai-shek set down to carrying out New Life Movement, declaring it as "a most fundamental and efficient movement to save and construct the country as well as rejuvenate the nation". The essential principle of the New Life Movement was "sense of propriety, justice, honesty and honor", requiring a "tidy, clean, simple, prompt and true" life, pursuing a militarized life full of arts and production. Chiang Kai-shek proclaimed himself as chairman of the New Life Movement Promoting Committee, whose branches spread all over the country.

The Chinese Soviet Republic was a state of the workers and peasants' democratic dictatorship. The aim of dictatorship lied in demolishing all the feudal remains, getting rid of the imperialist powers in China and unifying China. Mao Zedong was appointed chairman of the Central Executive Committee and Zhu De, chairman of the Revolutionary Military Committee. The Soviet government also established foreign affairs, financial, labor, education, internal affairs and judicatory committees, and stipulated *Outline of the Constitution of the Chinese Soviet Republic, Labor Law, Land Law, Marriage Law* and so on. The construction of the Soviet areas displayed a new prospect of China.

7. Long March

During 1929 and 1930, Nanjing Government defeated Li Zongren, Feng Yuxiang and Yan Xishan successively. After the wars, Chiang Kai-shek moved the forces that fought against Feng and Yan southward so as to encircle the central revolutionary base area of the Communist Party of China. Between 1930 and 1933, Nanjing National Government Army led by Chiang Kai-shek launched four military encirclements on the central base area in Jiangxi, all of which suffered failure. However, the Communist Party of China failed due to opportunism in the fifth military encirclement. As a result, the Red Army was forced to retreat from Jiangxi revolutionary base area in October, 1934 and started the Long March, a strategic transfer.

The procession of the Red Army in the Long March

More than 80,000 people took part in the Long March. The Chief of Staff was Liu Bocheng, the main force was the First Corps led by Lin Biao and the Third Corps by Peng Dehuai. The main forces of Central Red Army set out from Ruijin, went through southern Jiangxi, northern Guangdong and moved to southern Hunan so that it broke three lines of defense from the Government Army. In late November, it crossed the Xiangjiang River and broke the fourth blockage. In December, the Red Army arrived at the Hunan-Guizhou border, where Mao Zedong decided to give up the plan to the western Hunan-Hubei and, instead advance towards Guizhou, where the enemy's strength is relatively weak. Mao's decision protected the Red Army from being destructed completely.

In January 1935, the Red Army captured Zunyi, where the Communist Party of China convened an enlarged meeting of the Political Bureau, which established the leadership of Mao Zedong. In May, the Red Army crossed the Jinsha River and shook off the trace of Kuomintang Government Army. Then, the Red Army successfully went through Daliang Mountain,

where the Yi nationality inhabited. Then, after forcing its way across the Luding Bridge on the Dadu River and climbing over the perennially snow-clad Liupan Mountain, the Central Red Army arrived at *Maogong* of Sichuan Province in June and joined forces with the Fourth Front Army there. As the Red Army aimed at establishing Sichuan-Shaanxi base area in the north, the Central Committee of the Party decided to reorganize the First and Fourth Front armies into the Right Route Army and the Left Route Army and continued to march across the marshlands northward. The Central Committee followed the Fourth Front Army northward and arrived Banyou and Baxi, advancing towards the south of Gansu Province. Unfortunately, Zhang Guotao, leader of the Fourth Front Army opposed marching northwards and attempted to set up a new central committee and split the Red Army.

Under the leadership of Mao Zedong and Zhou Enlai, the First Corps and Third Corps of the Central Red Army continued its northward march. They seized Lazikou, climbed over Minshan Mountain and broke through the Weishui River blockade line. On October 19th, they arrived at Wuqizhen, Shaanxi Province and joined the 15th Corps of the Red Army. The northern Shaanxi guerrilla area was set up by Liu Zhidan and Xie Zichang. In late 1934, Xu Haidong led the 25 Corps of Hubei-Henan-Shandong Red Army away from Henan and got to northern Shaanxi in 1935, where his army joined the army led by Liu Zhidan, forming the 15 Corps. In 1936, led by He Long, the Second Front Army left Hunan-western Hubei and followed the Central Red Army. Later, he first joined forces with the Fourth Front Army led by Xu Xiangqian at the northwest of Sichuan and then with the First Front Army at Huining County and Jingning County in Gansu Province. The Long March ended triumphantly.

The Long March was a grave epic. The main forces crossed more than ten provinces within two years and covered 25,000 kilometers from south to north so that it's also called the 25,000 Long March. The Long March propagated theories and policies of the Communist Party of China and sowed the Chinese revolutionary seeds of fire, becoming a great push in Chinese revolution. The northern Shaanxi revolutionary base area, centered around Yan'an brought a new prospect for China.

8. September 19th Incident and December 9th Movement

Japanese militarists considered it a Japanese national policy to invade China. In 1927, Japanese Prime Minister Giichi Tanaka proposed the scheme of invading China and constantly caused lots of disturbances in China. On the night of September 18th, 1931, the Japanese troops dynamited a section of the South Manchuria Railway in Shenyang's northern suburb and falsely accused Chinese troops of the act. On this pretext the Japanese troops suddenly attacked Beidaying and the inner city of Shenyang. On the same day, the Japanese troops also occupied important cities like Andong (today's Dandong), Yingkou, Fushun, Fenghuangcheng, Anshan, Changchun and others. Since Kuomintang adopted a non-resistance policy towards Japanese imperialist aggression, the northeastern provinces all fell into the enemies' hands. In January of the same year, Japan declared the establishment of "*Country of Manchu*" in Changchun with Pu Yi as its "chief executive", which was in fact a puppet state controlled by the Japanese imperialists for colonial rule over the northeastern provinces. (In March 1934, "Manchuguo" was renamed as "*Manchu* Empire" with Pu Yi as emperor.) Since then, with the northeast as the base, Japan expanded its rule towards the northern China and made trouble in big cities along the sea such as Tianjin, Tanggu, Qingdao, Xiamen, Fuzhou and Shanghai. On January 28th, 1932, the Japanese troops launched an attack on Shanghai. The 19th Route Army and the Fifth Corps under the leadership of Cai Tingkai, Jiang Guangnai and Zhang Zhizhong started resisting the Japanese Army. Due to Chiang Kai-shek's non-resistance policy, the Chinese troops were defeated and kept retreating. Later on, China and Japan accepted internal intermediation and declared truce. In early January 1933, the Japanese troops occupied Shanhaiguan Pass and attacked Rehe. In March, Chengde was occupied too. Within eight days, north and south of the Great Wall, as well as all the important barriers along the Great Wall were occupied by the Japanese troops. The garrison led by He Zhuguo and Song Zheyuan resisted heroically at the Great Wall. After that, Tanggu Agreement was signed between China and Japan, in which the Kuomintang Government acquiesced in the "lawfulness" of the Japanese occupation of the three northeastern provinces and Rehe. Beijing and Tianjin was at stake.

In June 1935, Yoshijiro Umezu, commander of the Japanese forces in north China, under the pretext that two Japanolatry journalists were killed within the Japanese concession in

After the September 18th Incident, the invasive ambition of Japan came to exposure day by day, while Chiang Kai-shek, insisting on the tenet that internal stability comes before resisting foreign aggression, didn't fight against Japan actively, which aroused the widespread dissatisfaction all over China. In the picture, Chiang Kai-shek was meeting the Beijing repetition representatives in Nanjing.

Tianjin, forced He Yingqin, acting director of the Beiping branch of the Military Commission of the National Government, to sign the "He-Umezu Agreement", which demanded the withdrawal of the Northeast Army and the Central Army, closing the KMT party headquarters in Hebei Province, and banning any anti-Japanese activities in Hebei Province. The KMT Government continued the non-resistance policy and was ready to establish Hebei-Qahar Administrative Council so as to meet the Japanese requirement of "specialization of administration in northern China". At this grave national crisis, on December 9th, thousands of Beiping (Beijing) students presented a petition to He Yingqin, then representative of Nanjing Government in Jurentang, to protest the establishment of Hebei-Qahar Administrative Council, to oppose the so-called Anti-Communist for Self-defense Movement, and to require the cease of any civil war as well as the freedom of speeches, meetings, community-forming and publishing for the people. On the 16th, Beiping students staged another demonstration on a greater scale. Beiping authority ordered the police and troops to suppress the students. The Beiping students' patriotic act brought an immediate response from students across the country and won their support. *jiu guo hui* (organization for national salvation) of various circles were set up one by one, which demanded National Government stop the civil war and send troops to resist Japan. The Resist-Japan-and-Save-the-Nation Movement surged up over the country in short order.

Jiang Guangnai

Cai Tingkai (1892-1968), army corps commander of the 19th Route Army, who led the February 28th Songhu Resistance Battle

第十篇

传统待更新

9. Xi'an Incident

Zhang Xueliang (1901-2002)

Yang Hucheng (1893-1949)

Zhou Enlai (1898-1976)

In the summer of 1935, Chiang Kai-shek set up Northwest Anti-Communist Headquarter in Xi'an and proclaimed himself commander-in-chief, with Zhang Xueliang as vice commander-in-chief. He forced Zhang Xueliang's Northeast Army and Yang Hucheng's 17th Route Army, both stationed in Shaanxi, to suppress the Red Army. Under the influence of anti-Japanese national united front led by the Communist Party of China, Zhang Xueliang and Yang Hucheng stopped attacking the Red Army.

In June 1936, in answer to the call of

Resist-Japan-and Save-the Nation, Chen Jitang, Li Zongren and Bai Chongxi in Guangdong and Guangxi refused to follow the Nanjing Government. After solving the Guangdong-Guangxi Incident, Chiang Kai-shek flew to Xi'an twice to force the Northeast Army and Northwest Army to attack the Red Army. The patriotic youths in Xi'an held demonstrations, demanding the end of the civil war and resistance against Japan. However, Chiang Kai-shek turned a deaf ear to this.

On December 7th, Zhang Xueliang and Yang Hucheng tearfully advised Chiang Kai-shek to change his policy of civil war and carry out a nationwide resistance against Japan. But they only received harsh condemnation from Chiang. On the morning of December 12th, in accordance with Zhang and Yang's plan, the Northeast Army besieged Huaqingchi at Lintong in good time and retained Chiang. At the same time, the 17th Route Army led by Yang controlled Xi'an City and arrested Chencheng, Wei Lihuang and other senior officers of Kuomintang. Zhang and Yang instantly declared the abolishment of Northwest Anti-Communist Headquarter and established Northwest Anti-Japanese United forces Provisional Military Committee. And they issued an open telegram which put forward eight proposals, including the reorganization of the Nanjing Government, the end of civil war, the release of the leaders of Jiuguo Hui and political prisoners, the opening of people's patriotic movement, the safeguard of people's freedom in holding meetings and forming communities, the abeyance of Sun Yet-sen's will and the convening of meetings for the salvation of nation. Meanwhile, they telegrammed to the Central Committee of CPC, requiring representatives sent to Xi'an to negotiate ways of resisting Japan. Later, the Japanophile, led by He Yingqin, suggested attacking Xi'an, intending to instigate a large-scale civil war; while Song Ziwen and Kong Xiangxi, supported by Britain and America, maintained that the incident should be settled peacefully. On the 17th, headed by Zhou Enlai, representatives of the CPC Central Committee arrived in Xi'an and talked with Zhang and Yang sincerely, suggesting a peaceful settlement of the incident. On the 22nd, Song Ziwen and Song Meiling flew to Xi'an for negotiations with Zhang, Yang and CPC representatives. On the 24th, they reached a series of agreements, such as reorganization of the National Government, driving out the Japanophile, releasing patriotic leaders of Shanghai and all political offenders, safeguarding of people's rights of freedom, uniting the Communists to resist Japan and so on. Zhou Enlai met Chiang Kai-shek, who swore to carry out these agreements on his personality. On the 25th, Zhang Xueliang escorted Chiang Kai-shek back to Nanjing from Xi'an before things were settled appropriately so that he suffered long-standing imprisonment by Chiang Kai-shek later on.

The Xi'an Incident had great impact on the Chinese historical progress. It forced Chiang Kai-shek to end the ten-year civil war and start talks with the Communist Party on the cooperation for resistance against Japan. In 1937, the July 7th Incident and the August 13th Resistance War in Songhu broke out and the invasion of Japan towards China had been pressing. Understanding that they had no time to delay, the National Government declared resistance against Japan and issued orders of reorganizing the Red Army into the Eighth Route Army and New Fourth Route Army. The second cooperation between Kuomintang and the Communist Party of China was therefore established. Since then, China underwent a longstanding tough war of resistance, which lasted for eight years.

Zhang Xueliang at his later age

10. War of Resistance Against Japan

On the evening of July 7th, the Japanese troops conducted a military exercise near Lugouqiao without notice. On the excuse that a soldier was missing as a shot was heard in Wanping City, the Japanese asked for a search of Wanping Ciy. When they were refused, they bombarded Lugouqiao. The 29th Corps, led by Tong Linge, and Ma Zhi'an's regiment, rose to fight back. This started the nationwide War of Resistance Against Japan. In late July, the Japanese troops attacked Beiping and Tianjin, the Chinese garrison fought back heroically. General Tong Linge and Zhao Dengyu died a heroic death. Beiping and Tianjing all fell into the Japanese hands. On August 13th, the Japanese troops attacked Shanghai, which marked the outbreak of Songhu War. The Chinese army with more than 70 divisions, 700,000 soldiers fought against 300,000 Japanese troops for nearly three months. This battle annihilated about 50,000 Japanese and shattered the Japanese invaders' dream of demolishing China within three months.

Faced with the common foreign enemy, Kuomintang and the Communist Party cooperated with each other in fighting against the Japanese troops under the banner of united resistance against Japan. In September 1937, the Eighth Route Army, assisted by Yan Xishan's Jinsui Army, attacked the Japanese troops at *Pingxingguan* Pass and annihilated more than 1000 enemies, which was the first victory since the War of Resistance. In the middle of October, Xinkou Battle broke out and both sides were locked in a stalemate for over 20 days with nearly 20,000 Japanese troops wiped out. In November, Shanghai and Taiyuan were captured so that the National Government had to move to Chongqing. In December, the Japanese troops attacked Nanjing. After a fierce fight, Nanjing fell. Having slaughtered more than 300,000 people, the Japanese troops committed the crime of massacre to the immaculate people. The atrocious conduct of the Japanese troops aroused greater determination of the people to resist Japan. In March 1938, a fierce battle broke out at Tai'erzhuang (today's Zaozhuang City, Shandong) between both sides. With over 10,000 Japanese elites annihilated, the Chinese troops achieved a great victory in this battle. In May 1938, the Japanese troops occupied Hefei, and marched west to Wuhan in October. After a tenacious four-month resistance, 200,000 Japanese troops suffered casualties and more than 400,000 Chinese troops were lost. Wuhan fell.

After the occupation of Wuhan, the Japanese imperialists changed their strategy of invasion. On one hand, they adopted the policy of luring the Chinese army into surrender; on the other hand, they directed their main forces to the Eighth Route Army and New Fourth Army, which led to differentiation within the Kuomintang the

On December 13th 1937, the Japanese troops occupied Nanjing and shed blood in the whole city for more than 40 days, causing the death of over 300,000 Chinese people and soldiers.

The Japanese troops invaded Shanghai, bringing about the August 13th Incident and made the citizens flee from the calamity. Songhu Battle broke out.

The Japanese troops slaughtered the Chinese cruelly.

第十篇

传统待更新

National Government. In March 1940, Wang Jingwei went over to Japan and set up Nanjing Puppet Government.

Due to their exquisite equipment, the Japanese troops gained advantage over southern China and mid-south of China. The Chinese army retreated everywhere and the National Government had to move to southwest. Therefore, half of Chinese territory fell into the hands of Japan. In the occupied areas, the Japanese imperialists strengthened the puppet government; in the liberated areas led by the Communist Party, they conducted endless clear-out and cruel *san guang* (to kill all the people, burn all the villages and rob all the property) Policy. At that time, people lived a hard life and those who died from war, hunger and wandering were uncountable. However, the Chinese people never lose heart. Instead, they persevered with resistance. Thanks to both parties' hard fight in the bloody battles under the military disadvantages, victories of regional battles were achieved.

After the outbreak of the War of Resistance, large numbers of national industries also moved to the rear area with the battlefront moving westward from the south. Sichuan, especially Chongqing, became the biggest industrial center. Those moving industries included mining and metallurgy, mechanic manufacture, shipbuilding, electrical equipment, chemical materials, textile, and food processing. At the same time, agriculture and transportation industry in the rear also developed rapidly. The temporal economic prosperity in the rear supported the War of Resistance effectively. Among those that moved together with the National Government were many colleges and universities, Central Institute, Central Library, and cultural relics of the Imperial Palace. Numerous scientists made great contributions to the Resist-Japan-and-Save-the-Nation Movement and large numbers of excellent talents grew up in the tough environment.

During the War of Resistance, culture became another battlefront of the Resist-Japan-and-Save-the-Nation Movement. Literature, arts, drama, film and journalism were all employed as sharp weapons to unite the people and attack the enemy. The Save-the-Nation Community of Shanghai Literature and Arts Circle, the Resist-the-Enemy Community of Chinese dramatists, musicians, film-makers, cartoonists as well as the Third Office of the Political Bureau of Kuomintang Military Committee, led by Zhou Enlai and Guo Moruo, became powerful organs

The Central Inspection Group of the Kuomintang was surveying Yan'an and other places. The picture shows the time when the inspection group entered Yan'an City.

The Eighth Route Army under the leadership of the Chinese Communist Party were ready to set out.

The Chinese troops stormed into Tai'er Zhuang and fought hard in the bloody battle against the Japanese army.

The Japanese army made a surprise assault on Pearl Harbor and America declared war against Japan, leading to the Pacific War.

Guangdong and Neimeng were also reoccupied. The Eighth Route Army, New Fourth Army and local guerrillas all participated in the counterattack and occupied 950,000 square kilometers including the areas of north China, middle China and south China. The Japanese Puppet Army was forced to shrink to some isolate middle or large-scaled cities,

working for the propagating of resistance. Numerous cultural publishing concerning the War of Resistance and the Resist-Japan-and-Save-the-Nation Movement came out, composing the most splendid chapter in the history of Chinese modern culture.

During the War of Resistance, the CPC Government of the Shaanxi-Gansu-Ningxia Border Region with Yan'an as capital carried out the policy of anti-Japanese national united front, established various levels of assemblies and people's democratic government, conducted tax and interest reduction movement, unfolded Great Production Movement, set up Marxism-Lenism Academy, Yan'an Natural Science Institution, Anti-Japanese Military and Political College, Northern Shaanxi Public School and Lu Xun Art College. All these made Yan'an a model of Chinese anti-Japanese democratic base areas and rear headquarter of the War of Resistance against Japan.

In December 1941, Japan launched a surprise attack on Pearl Harbor, leading to the outbreak of the Pacific War. Britain and America declared war against Japan. The War of Resistance against Japan became an important part of the War of Global Anti- fascist. In March 1942, China sent the Expedition Army to Burma in support of the allied forces. In early 1943, the Japanese troops suffered defeats one after another in the Pacific War and insufficient economic supply from home. Though Japan was destined to be defeated, it struggled desperately in the Chinese War Zone. In April 1945, the Chinese Army launched a violent counterattack in the west of Guangxi and recaptured Liuzhou and Guizhou. Soon after, Hunan, Henan and Fujian,

Wang Jingwei (1883-1944), quisling for personal glory, established a puppet government in Nanjing and begot reviling from the people.

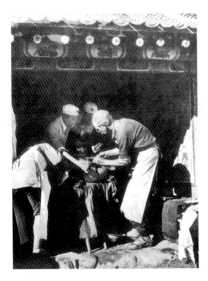

In 1937, Canadian doctor Henry Norman Bethune came to China with his medical team in support of the Chinese war of resistance. The picture shows Bethune was operating on the injured soldiers of the Eighth Route Army in the front.

The commander-in-chief Chiang Kai-shek and his chief of staff-American general Joseph Steve during the Second World War.

The Chinese Expedition army in Burma

Soldiers of "Flying Tiger Team" of the American air force, who volunteered to come to China in support of the Chinese war.

The Chinese army had made one victory after another since 1945, causing the Japanese army to disarm and surrender in succession.

On September 9th, 1945, Okamura Yasuji, commander-in-chief of the Japanese army, presented the Instrument of Surrender to He Yingqin, commander-in-chief of the Chinese land army.

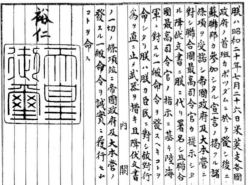

became a spent bullet. In August, America dropped atomic bombs on Hiroshima and Nagasaki. The Soviet government declared war against Japan and sent troops to northeastern China and Inner Mongolia. On August 15th, Japan's emperor Hirohito announced acceptance of the unconditional surrender. On September 2nd, representatives of the Japanese government signed the Instrument of Surrender with Chinese and American representatives. On September 9th, the surrender ceremony of the Chinese War Zone was held in Nanjing, marking the victorious end of an eight-year war of Resistance against Japan.

On August 14th, 1945, Japanese emperor signed the book of surrender. The Second World War declared its end.

第十篇

传统待更新

11. A Decisive Battle between Two Destinies

Mao Zedong and Chiang Kai-shek during the Chongqing Negotiation

After the War of Resistance, Kuomintang attempted to govern China. Kuomintang and the Communist Party of China still confronted each other. Under the mediation of Patrick Jay Hurley (1883-1963), then U.S. Ambassador to China, the two parties held negotiations in Chongqing in August 1945. The CPC Representatives included Mao Zedong, Zhou Enlai and Wang Ruofei; while the Kuomintang side included Wang Shijie, Zhang Zhizhong and Shao Lizi. On October 10th, both

sides signed "Summary of Conversations Between the Government and Representatives of the Communist Party of China", also known as the "October 10th Agreement", which was a resolution for the aim of peaceful settlement of the internal problems. However, it failed to settle the disputes between the two parties in nature.

In late 1945, American President Truman appointed General George Catlett Marshall (1880-1950) as the president's special representative to mediate the conflicts between Kuomintang and the Communist Party. In the spring of 1946, with the mediation of Marshall, the two parties reached an agreement concerning measures for preventing internal military conflicts and established Three-Person Military Group joined by Marshall, Zhang Qun (later changed to Zhang Zhizhong, Xu Yongchang), and Beiping Military Mediation and Execution Department made up by the representatives of three sides. In April, the National Government removed to Nanjing.

In June 1946, because of the perfidius Kuomintang, an all-out civil war broke out. In August, Marshall and U.S Ambassador John Leighton Stuart (1876-1962) issued a joint statement, declaring that their "mediation" had been a failure. After eight-month fighting, the National Government suffered grave losses in Zhejiang, Anhui, Shandong, Shanxi, Hebei and northeast. In July 1947, the National Government declared general mobilization of all people to "quell rebellion". It sent large numbers of forces to attack the CPC base areas in northern Shaanxi and Shandong, but all were defeated by the Northwest Field Army and East China Field Army of the CPC. In January 1948, The National Government was forced to adopt the policy of Divisional Defense. However, the Chinese People's Liberation Army (PLA) led by the Communist Party launched fiercer attacks.

In the second half of 1948, the Chinese civil war came to a decisive stage. In September, under the leadership of Chen Yi, the PLA captured Jinan. In October, led by Lin Biao, the PLA captured Jinzhou, Changchun and in December, seized Shenyang, hence recovering the whole northeastern area. In November, Chen Yi and Liu Bocheng's East China and Central Plains Field Army confronted Kuomintang Government Army led by Qiu Qingquan, Huang Bodao and Huang Wei in the Huaihai River area between Xuzhou and Bangbu. The fight between them lasted over two months and ended in the defeat of National Government Army. In December, the Fourth Field Army and North China Field Army of the CPC attacked Tianjin and captured it in January 1949, which enabled them to enter Beiping peacefully. In the

After the War of Resistance, social economy was ruined and factories employed lots of children workers. The picture shows the children workers in the Japanese cotton factory.

three campaigns- Liaoxi -Shenyang, Huaihai and Beiping-Tianjin, a total of over 1500,000 National Government troops were wiped out so that the Communist army won decisive victory. On January 21st, 1949, Chiang Kai-shek declared that he could not attend to business and asked Li Zongren to act for him. Though negotiations were held constantly between the two sides, their disputes were unable to be solved peacefully.

Meanwhile, economy in the Kuomintang-ruled areas collapsed completely. As a result of the colossal military expenditure, the financial deficit of the government and commodity prices soared sharply. The price rose by 60,000 times in July 1947, and at the end of the same year by 145,000 times. Also, industrial output value decreased sharply and agricultural production became stagnant day by day. All these made life harder for the common people and complaints were heard everywhere. The rule of Kuomintang was difficult to maintain.

On April 21st, 1949, a million PLA troops crossed the Changjiang River and captured Nanjing on the 23rd. In May, after the recovery of Hangzhou, Wuhan, Xi'an, Nanchang and Shanghai, the PLA marched on towards the southeast, northwest, south of China and west of China so that the National Government had to end its rule on the mainland and flee to Taiwan.

The boiling inflation in the Kuomintang-ruled area made people rush to buy daily commodities with bundles of bank notes.

During the civil war, the people in the liberated area supported the front actively. The picture shows the certificate for their glorious support on the front.

On January 31st, 1949, Beiping was liberated peacefully. The picture shows that the People's Liberation Army was holding the ceremony of "entering the city".

The People's Liberation Army took Nanjing and occupied the office of the president.

Chapter 11

Great Renewal of the Chinese Nation
--the People's Republic of China

A new China stands towering in the east of the world.

Advancing through exploration, full of twists and hardships, the spring of reform and opening-up came eventually.

China is marching towards a great renewal!

Tian'anmen, Beijing

1. The Birth of the People's Republic of China

On September 19th, 1949, Mao Zedong and other leaders of the Chinese Communist Party as well as the democrats posed before Qinian Hall of the Temple of Heaven. From the left: Su Yu, Liu Bocheng, Cheng Xingling, Li Mingyang, Li Minghao, Mao Zedong, Chen Mingren, Zhang Yuanji, Chen Yi, Cheng Qian.

In December 1949, the first plenary session of the Chinese People's Political Consultation Conference opened in Beiping. Among those who attended the conference were representatives of the Communist Party of China, various democratic parties and people's organizations, the Chinese People's Liberation Army, various local areas and minor nationalities, overseas Chinese and non-Party democrats. The conference passed the *Organizational Law of the Chinese People's Political Consultative Conference, Organizational Law of Central People's Government of the People's Republic of China* and *Common Programme of the Chinese People's Political Consultative Conference.* And it elected the first National Committee of the CPPCC, with Mao Zedong as chairman, and the Central People's Government Council with Mao Zedong as chairman, Zhu De, Liu Shaoqi, Soong Ching Ling, Li Jishen, Zhang Lan and Gao Gang as vice-chairman and 56 members including Chen Yi and others. The session chose Beiping as the capital of the People's Republic of China, renaming it Beijing, and adopted the Christian era as the chronological system of the People's Republic of China, *March of the Volunteers* as the national anthem and a flag with five

Seal of the Central People's Government of the People's Republic of China

300,000 Beijing people and soldiers declared the founding of a new China ceremoniously on Tian'anmen Square at 3 p.m on the afternoon of October 1st, 1949. The picture shows that Mao Zedong was reading the Proclamation of the Central People's Government of the People's Republic of China, declaring the establishment of the People's Republic of China.

Mao Zedong (1893-1976)

Zhu De (1886-1976)

stars on a field of red as the national flag.

At 2 p.m. on October 1st, the Central People's Government Council held its first conference and declared its accession in Qinzheng Palace of Zhongnanhai, Beijng. It appointed Lin Boqu secretary of the Central People's Government Council, Zhou Enlai premier and foreign minister of the Government Administration Council of the Central People's Government, Mao Zedong chairman of the Revolutionary Military Commission, Zhu De commander-in-chief of the Chinese People's Liberation Army, Shen Junru president of the Supreme People's Court, and Luo Ronghuan chief procurator of the Supreme Procuratorial Office. The conference decided to accept *Common Programme of the Chinese People's Political Consultative Conference* as the administrative policy and declared to governments of all the countries that the Central People's Government of the People's Republic of China was the only lawful government standing for the people of the People's Republic of China and wished to establish diplomatic relations with any government of foreign countries who would obey the principles of equality and mutual benefits, respecting territories and sovereignty. At 3 p.m. 300,000 people of Beijing assembled on Tian'anmen Square to participate in the inauguration ceremony. After Lin Boqu announced the beginning of the ceremony, the national song was played. Then Chairman Mao Zedong proclaimed to the world the birth of the People's Republic of China. After that, the military show of navy, land and air forces began. Zhu De, commander-in-chief of the People's Liberation Army, proclaimed the order of the PLA General Headquarter. After the ceremony, grand marches of the people were held.

At the beginning of new China, battles continued. Chiang Kai-shek's army still controlled large areas of Guangdong, Guangxi, Sichuan, Guizhou, Yunnan and Xikang, considerable parts of Shaanxi, Hunan and Hubei. At the end of 1949, the PLA occupied all the areas except Tibet. In October 1951, the PLA entered Tibet peacefully. Hence after, except Taiwan and the adjoining islands, actual unification of the mainland was realized.

On May 24th, 1951, Mao Zedong, chairman of the Central People's Government, held a banquet to celebrate the signing of the Agreement on the Ways to Liberate Tibet Peacefully. The picture shows Mao Zedong at the banquet. The first on the left is Apei Awangjinmei, the third is Banchan E'erdeni Quejijianzan.

第十一篇　在探索中前进

2. Resisting America in Support of Korea

The peasants joined the army enthusiastically, forming the stretcher teams and transportation teams for the front.

Peng Dehuai, commander of the Chinese People's Volunteer Army and political commissioner was surveying in the front of Korea.

In August 1945, when Japan declared unconditional surrender, American and Soviet armies divided Korea at the 38th parallel, the north of which was Democratic People's Republic of Korea while the south was Korean People's Republic. On June 25, 1950, the Korean War broke out. On June 27th, American President Truman declared entering the war and sent the 7th Fleet of the Navy to the Taiwan Channel so as to prevent the PLA from liberating Taiwan. On July 7th, United Nations Security Council approved America to gather 15 nations including Britain, France, South Africa and others in order to form United Nations Command. Truman appointed MacArthur Commander-in-Chief of United Nations Command. From the middle of September, UN Command launched over 50,000 troops including warships and planes and landed

The Chinese People's Volunteer Army charged at the American positions under the covering fire.

Inchon. These troops crossed the 38th parallel in early October, occupied Pyongyang and started flames of war along the Yalu River, bombed Andong of China (today's Dandong) and other places, posing a serious threat to the safety of China.

Sensing the grave situation, North Korean Party and government asked the CPC and Chinese government for military aid. On October 8th, the Central Committee of the CPC made the strategic policy of entering the Korean War so as to support Korea in their resistance against America and protecting the homeland. Mao Zedong, chairman of the Chinese People's Military Committee, demanded the northeast frontier forces to be renamed the Chinese People's Volunteer Army with Peng Dehuai as commander-in-Chief and political commissioner. On the 19th, the Chinese People's Volunteer Army crossed the Yalu River by three routes and resisted with the Korean people. Thus started the mass movement of aiding Korea to resist America and protect homeland all over China in short order. To support the front, youths of proper age joined the Chinese People's Volunteer Army enthusiastically; the masses of various circles donated planes and cannons one after another; all the lines were devoted to production and strictly practiced thrift.

The War of Resisting America in support of Korea lasted for two years and nine months. In June, 1951, Sino-Korean armies organized five big battles which counterattacked strategically and harvested five victories with 230,000 enemy troops wiped out and American invaders driven to the 38th parallel from the Yalu River and the Kum River. America had to accept the suggestion of holding truce talks. On July 10th, the first session of truce talks was held at Kaesong.

After that, negotiations and battles went side by side on the Korean battlefield. From July to September, the US troops launched large-scale "Summer Offensive" and "Fall Offensive", adopting the so-called "Strangling War Strategy". Making use of landform, Sino-Korean troops dug trenches and combined defensive positions with mobile war. In this way, they stabilized their front line around the 38th parallel with the accumulation of small victories. On October 14th, US troops attacked Sino-Korean troops violently at Heartbreak Ridge northeast of Taeu-san. On the position of 3.7 square kilometer, US troops deployed 60,000 troops, 3,000 planes and 200 tanks, dropped 1,900,000 bombs and launched over 900 attacks in all, chopping the top of the mountain by two meters. However, the Volunteer Army held fast to their post for 43 days and nights and annihilated 25,000 enemy troops. From June to July 1953, Sino-Korean troops launched Kumsong Counterattack, which wiped out over 120,000 enemies. America had to sign the Korean Armistice Agreement at Panmunjom on July 27th. To sign a defeated truce agreement was the first in American history. Although China also suffered grave costs in the war, the victory over America enhanced the Chinese People's national confidence and pride, greatly increased the international prestige of China and further consolidated and strengthened China's independent status.

3. Economical Recovery and Systematical Neatening

In 1952, steel output reached 13,490,000, 46.2% more than the highest annual output in the old China, 753,8% more than that of 1949. The picture shows then Anshan Steel Factory.

In 1952, electricity of over 7,2 billion kilowatt-hours was generated, 168.8% of that of 1949 and 121.7% of that of the year with the most electricity in old China.

In 1952, the grain output of the whole country reached 327.8 billion jin, which was 44.8% more than that of 1949 and 9.3% more than that of the year with the highest annual output in old China.

Between 1949 and 1952, the old railway of over 10,000 kilometers was repaired and 1,320 kilometers of new railway was built. About 24,500 kilometers of railway was open to traffic throughout the whole country.

After the birth of the People's Republic of China, the new government's task was shifted to economic construction. Among the 60 articles of *Common Programme of the Chinese People's Political Consultative Conference*, 16 were concerned about economy. Among the 31 departments of the Central Government, 16 dealt with economy. The fundamental guidelines of national economic construction were: attention to both public and private interests, mutual interests for labor and capital, mutual help between urban and rural areas, communication at home and abroad. The People's Government controlled energy supply and production of many productive materials through confiscation of bureaucratic capital, control of important departments that were vital to national economy such as finance, transportation, communications and so on.

While capitalist economy was allowed existence and appropriate development, activities were carried out to strike the speculator's forestallment for huge profits, adjust the relationship between the public and private interests, expand the processing order and product purchase to private industries so as to bring private industries into the orbit of national plan. Capitalists must respect the leading power of the working class and the workers must put forward practical requirements so as to achieve mutual interests between labor and capital. Meanwhile, the relationship between production and sale was adjusted to facilitate capitalist planning.

In June 1950, *Agrarian Reform Law of the People's Republic of China* was issued. From that winter on, land reform movement was carried out in far-reaching new liberated areas. The land reform would abolish the landlord ownership and remove the economic basis of feudalistic system. By the end of 1952, all over China except Xinjiang, Tibet and Taiwan, 300,000,000 peasants who had no or few land had been distributed a land of 740,000,000 *mu* and numerous productive materials as well as other properties, and were exempted from taxes of 70-billion-*jin* (half a kilogram) grains. Masses of peasants were liberated in word and in deed.

In October 1950, the CPC Central Committee issued *Direction on Suppressing Counterrevolutionary Activities* and carried out the movement aiming at suppressing counterrevolution. This movement focused on bandits, secret agents, local tyrants and leaders of reactive parties and communities. Through this movement, the counterrevolutionary forces left on the mainland by Kuomintang reactionaries were wiped out in substance and rampant bandit gangs as well as the gangdom forces in the cities were basically eliminated so that the Chinese social order obtained unprecedented stability.

In June 1950, the CPC Central Committee proposed that three years would be spent in achieving the basic straightening-up of national financial and economic state. The outbreak of Korean War and embargo laid on China by countries headed by the USA posed great pressure to economic recovery and construction. While working hard to stabilize internal markets, the Central Government spared no chance to carry out economic construction. Agriculturally, it started construction of irrigation works to prevent disasters and facilitate production; industrially, it laid emphasis on the development of transportation, production of electric power, coal and steel. With the recovery and development of industry and agriculture, the state of national finance was obviously improved and the cultural and living standards of the people attained visible melioration.

In October 1951, the CPC Central Committee put forward the guideline of "better troops and simpler administration, increase production and practice thrift" and the Chinese People's Political Consultative Conference also called on people all over the country to carry out the patriotic movement of putting on production and practicing economy. In order to overcome the serious three evils- "corruption, waste and bureaucratism" among the rank of cadres, the CPC Central Committee called for "*san fan*" movement (three anti's, e.g. attacks against corruption, waste and bureaucratism) all over China. During this movement, some criminals who committed large quantities of embezzlement were dealt with accordingly. For instance, Liu Qingshan, Zhang Zishan and others in Hebei were sentenced to death. The other big grafters and graft blocs were captured one after another. The government office staffs that were punished due to the commitment of "three evils" to some degree covered 4.5%.

Meanwhile, "*wu fan*" movement (five anti's) was carried out among the industrial and commercial circle. The "*wu fan*" movement was directed to the five evils- "bribery, tax evasion, cheating in government contracts, thefts of economic intelligence, and stealing of state assets". In the course of this campaign, large numbers of shocking evils committed by unlawful capitalists were uncovered.

The "*san fan*" and "*wu fan*" movement had stricken a blow on the unlawful conducts of capitalists, set up clean and simple social mode and guaranteed the accomplishment of the recovery of the national economy.

On June 28th, 1950, the Central People's Government issued Agrarian Reform Law of the People's Republic of China, which received warm support from masses of peasants.

Prostitutes regained a new life through education and reform. Some joined the team of the hygiene and epidemic prevention, who were injecting vaccine to the country children.

The People's Government took in the vagrants. The picture shows that the vagrants and beggars were being sent to the South China Reform School.

On April 30th ,1950, the CPC Central Committee issued Marriage Law, which abolished the arranged marriages, practiced equality between men and women as well as freedom of marriage. The picture shows that Beijing citizens were listening to the broadcasting of Marriage Law.

Smoking sets and gambling devices taken over by People's Government.

In March 1953, the Central People's Government issued Election Law of the National People's Congress and Local People's Congresses of the Republic of China, stipulating that women enjoy the same right of electing and being elected. The picture shows Lu Lanfen, director of women's union of Qifei Village, Yi Minority Municipality of Mile County, Yunnan, was elected delegate of the Village People's Congress and congratulated by the electorates.

4. Independent Foreign Policy

Mao Zedong and Ho Chi Minh

Led by Premier Zhou Enlai, Chinese delegation attended Bandung Conference.

According to the *Common Programme* approved at the Chinese People's Political Consultative Conference, new Chinese government carried out the foreign policy of "Leaning to One Side", that's, leaning to the socialist countries. The day after the birth of new China, the Soviet Union decided to establish diplomatic relations with China. Later on, Bulgaria, Romania, Hungary, Mongolia, Korea, Poland, Democratic Germany, Albania, Vietnam, Burma, Indonesia, Sweden, Denmark and Switzerland established diplomatic relations with China successively. Pakistan, Britain, Sri Lanka, Norway, Afghanistan, Finland and Holland recognized the People's Republic of China one by one. By the end of October 1950, there had been 25 nations which recognized new China, among which 17 established formal diplomatic relations with China.

In December 1949, headed by Mao Zedong, Chinese CPC Political Delegation visited Moscow. In February 1950, China and Soviet Union signed the *Treaty of Friendship,*

Alliance and Mutual Assistance. The treaty prescribed that both countries should develop and consolidate economic and cultural relations in accordance with the principles of "equality, mutual interests, mutual respect for sovereignty and integrity of territory, non-interference of internal affairs". In 1953, the *Pact on Assisting Chinese Government in Developing National Economy* was signed by China and Soviet Union.

Faced with formidable pressure from the western camp, Chinese government maintained independent and peaceful foreign policy so that a comparatively favorable international environment was gained for economic construction of new China, capital and technology for internal construction were strived for from the international assistance. After the ceasefire of Korean War, in order to settle the problem concerning the unification of Korea and the peace of Indochina, the delegation led by Premier and Foreign Minister Zhou Enlai attended the Conference of Ministers of Foreign Affairs from April to July 1954 in Geneva. 23 countries including China, Soviet Union, USA, Britain, France, Democratic Korean People's Republic and Democratic Vietnam Republic attended the conference. This was the first important international conference that new China attended.

During the conference, Zhou Enlai visited India and Burma on invitation. On June 28th and 29th

1954, the joint statement of premiers of Sino-India and Sino-Burma reached consensus on the five principles- "mutual respect for territory and sovereign, mutual non-aggression, mutual non-interference, equality and mutual interests, and peaceful coexistence" as fundamental principles guiding the relationship between the Sino-India, Sino-Burma relationship. The five principles of peaceful coexistence, recognized and praised by the international public opinion, brought forth far-reaching influence for international relationship and facilitated the unity of all the nations in Asia and played an important role in the maintenance of Asia and world peace.

In April 1955, with the soaring national liberation movement in Asia and Africa, Asia-Africa Conference convened at Bandung, Indonesia with 29 nations from Asia and Africa taking part. Premier Zhou Enlai proposed the guideline of "seeking common points while reserving difference" and called on all the nations to put aside differences and strengthen the unity and cooperation so as to achieve the common interest of fighting against colonists. This conference released the *Final Communique of the Asia-Africa Conference*, which put forward common proposals on developing and strengthening economic and cultural cooperation among all the nations, safeguarding human rights and rights of independence, settling issues concerning the people on the adjunctive land and on promoting world peace and cooperation. Meanwhile, based on the five principles, another ten principles were put forward as guidelines for the establishment of friendly relationship among all the nations in Asia and Africa. Asia-Africa Conference was the first one held by Asian and African nations without the participation of western countries since World War II. During this conference, China displayed its prominent role in international affairs.

After Bandung Conference, the relationship between China and Asian-African nations was constantly strengthened, and visits were frequently exchanged among the leaders. By the end of the 60s, there had been leaders from 22 Asian-African nations visiting China. Chinese national leaders also visited many Asia-African regions. More than 20 nations in Asia, Africa and Latin America established diplomatic relations with China. In January 1964, China and France established formal

Mao Zedong and Asia-African youths

diplomatic relations and soon after, commercial representatives were sent to each other between China and Italy, China and Austria, which stroke a heavy blow to America's isolation policy on China.

When Khrushchev came into power in 1956, the Sino-Soviet relationship changed dramatically. In 1958, Khrushchev proposed establishing joint fleets with China and long wave radio, attempting to control China. To maintain Chinese sovereignty and national dignity, Mao Zedong offered a flat refusal. In June 1959, Soviet government unilaterally broke the agreement on new technology of national defense signed by both sides in October 1957 and refused to offer the sample of atomic bombs as well as the technological materials of A-bomb-making. In July 1960, the Soviet government delivered a note to the Chinese government, unilaterally deciding to recall their technicians from China and abolish various agreements and contracts concerning cooperation on economy and technology, which brought a large number of constructing projects to a halt, resulting in grave suffering of the Chinese economy.

After the 22nd Congress of the Soviet Communist Party, Soviet Communist leaders, magazines as well as communist leaders in many other countries influenced by Soviet Communist Party delivered numerous resolutions, announcement and articles to attack the Communist Party of China, stirring up the wave of anti-China and instigating the open Sino-Soviet dispute. In 1964, Khrushchev drop the reins of government and Brezhnev, the successor, didn't change the policy towards China at all. After the 23rd Congress of the Soviet Communist Party in 1966, Sino-Soviet relationship broke off. Since the early 1960s, conflicts as to military ones had constantly broken out along the Sino-Soviet borders. The gravest were the invasions of Soviet tanks on *Zhenbao* Island from January 1967 to March 1969, which led to blooding clashes by Soviet frontier guards. Chinese frontier guards were forced to counterattack and drive away the invaders.

5. Progress and Twists

In February 1956, the CPC Central Committee and State Department decided to establish Committee of National Science Programming. The picture shows Zhou Enlai and those in charge of the Committee of National Science Programming, such as Li Fuchun, Nie Rongzhen, among the scientific workers.

In 1952, the CPC Central Committee proposed an elementary accomplishment of "transition to socialism" within ten or fifteen years from 1953 on. In September 1954, the first National People's Congress passed the Constitution of the People's Republic of China, which stipulated that "the general task of the country during the transition period is to realize socialist industrialization of the nation step by step, to accomplish socialist reform of agriculture, handicraft industry, capitalist industry and commerce step by step". In 1955, the CPC National Congress adopted Resolution on First Five-Year Plan for Development of National Economy and the First

During the first Five-Year Plan for development of national economy, the Soviet Union sent over 3,000 experts to China in assistance of Chinese development. In the picture, Soviet experts were studying engineer designing with technicians of Angang Steel Factory.

第十一篇

在探索中前进

Five-Year Plan was completed a year ahead of time. By 1957, a group of key enterprises were put into production, such as the big rolling mill and seamless steel tube factory of Angang, the first truck producer of China- Changchun Auto Corporation, the first plane factory and machine tool factory. Besides, Wuhan Changjiang Bridge was completed and the railways of Qingzang and Kangzang were open to traffic. Agriculture and light industry also attained large-scale development. All these led to evident improvement of the people's living standard.

Meanwhile, the government carried out socialist reform on the private ownership of productive materials. In the countryside, Mutual Assistance and Cooperation Movement was carried out far and wide from 1949-1952 in the areas where land reform had been practiced. After the publication of the general line, cooperation movement entered the stage of preliminary agricultural cooperation. From 1955 on, cooperation movement arrived at the stage of senior agricultural production cooperation of complete socialist nature. By the end of 1956, the agricultural socialist reform had been fundamentally fulfilled.

The reform of capitalist industry and commerce was conducted through peaceful redemption. From 1953 to the summer of 1955, the elementary form of national capitalism was practiced, and from then on to 1956 came the stage of adopting the senior form of national capitalism. Following the policy of employing, limiting and reforming capitalist industry and commerce, joint state-private ownership was practiced among the capitalist industry and commerce so that the transition from private capitalist ownership to socialist public ownership was realized and capitalists were changed into laborers earning their own living. In this way, exploiting class and system were wiped out and the Chinese society realized the transition from New Democratism to Socialism.

During this period, far-reaching studies and criticism were carried out in the field of ideology so as to study Marxism, Mao Zedong Thought, propagate dialectic materialism and historical materialism and criticize historical mentalism as well as metaphysics. The works of Marx and Selected Works of Mao Zedong (volume1-3) were published one by one. In 1951, criticism on the film *Story of Wuxun* was conducted and then followed by the criticisms on Yu Pingbo's Studies of "*Dream of the Red Mansion*" and on Hu Feng's literary thought. These criticisms widely propagated historical materialism in the intellectual and cultural circles and educated many old-fashioned intellectuals. However, they were conducted in the form of political condemnation instead of democratic ideological

After November 1955, joint state-private ownership of national capitalist industry and commerce came to a climax. The picture shows that people were celebrating the joint state-private ownership among all walks of life in front of Yong'an Company, Shanghai.

endeavor and literary criticism. What's worse, they mistakenly defined the differences on literary thought as the battle between revolution and counterrevolution so that the literary and educational undertaking of new China suffered serious damage.

In 1956, Chairman Mao Zedong suggested "the booming of a hundred flowers" in art and literary circles and "contending of a hundred schools of thought" in the academic world should be adopted as guidelines to develop science and prosper art and literature, which received warm support from the intellectual circles all over China. Shortly after that, the undertaking of art, literature and science all took on a vigorous scene. Meanwhile, in view of expanding democratic construction of politics, the Communist Party of China put forward the guideline of "longstanding coexistence and mutual supervision" between the power of national leaders and various democratic parties, suggested a proper settlement of the internal conflicts among the people and mobilization of every active element for the construction of socialism.

In April 1957, the Central Committee of the CPC issued Instructions on Rectification Movement, which aimed at conducting an ideological movement of criticism and self-criticism in accordance with the existent bureaucratism, subjectivism, commandism as well as the backward ideology of some cadres within the party. Non-Party people were also welcome to take part in this movement to help the CPC with the rectification and free airing of their views was encouraged. The people out of the Party put forward well-meaning views like "the Party is in place of political power and differentiation between the Party and political power is wanting, construction of law should be improved, importance should be attached to bringing the out-of-the-Party people into play" and so on. But a few rightists took the chance to launch violent attacks on the Communist Party. Therefore, the rectification movement was turned into an "anti-rightist" campaign. As the Communist Party overestimated class struggle and rightists' attack, the anti-rightist campaign was seriously expanded and carried out all over China. However it ended with more than 550,000 people being mistakenly defined as rightists, among whom half were dismissed from their post and considerable numbers of people were forced to labor under supervision.

At a gathering for anti- "right" struggle in the Ministry of Communications, Minister Zhang Bojun was criticized.

6. The Great Leap Forward and People's Commune Movement

As a result of the great victory achieved in social reform and economic construction, blind pride and the leftist feeling of eagerness in final accomplishment turned out within the Party. Meanwhile, the Chineses leaders spurred by the slogan of "Catching up with Britain and exceeding America within 15 years", put forward by Soviet Union in 1957, proposed the idea of catching Britain or surpassing America in 15 years. In March 1958, Mao Zedong proposed the general line of "going all out, aiming high and achieving greater, faster, better, and more economical results to build socialism" at Chengdu Conference, which displayed his notion of building socialist China at a great speed. This proposal, taken as a general line of the CPC, proclaimed that China was at a great time when "one day is equal to twenty years". Soon after, the Great Leap Forward Movement was unfolded in all walks of life.

The Great Leap Forward Movement began from blind and unilateral pursuit of productive speed in industry and agriculture, especially the high speed and high index of steel production. On May 12, 1958, the People's Daily issued the editorial, titled "*Develop local industry with greater, faster, better and more economical results*". Then industry was set up in various provinces, local regions, counties, villages, communes and teams, not letting pass of offices and schools. In August 1958, the CPC Central Committee demanded that 10.57million tons of steel should be produced in 1958, double that of 1957. People's Daily published an editorial, calling on all the people to produce steel. Manpower, material resources and financial resources were organized everywhere in the way of mass movement to build converters and blast furnaces for steel-making. Meanwhile, the grain output claimed by various regions grew higher and pompous competitions boasting "satellite speed" were prevailing. Slogans like "how courageous you are, how much output you will yield", "whatever you think of, you will turn them into reality" came out as well. The Great Leap Forward Movement led to serious aftermath, causing national economy falling in confusion and the proportion of different departments to be extremely unbalanced.

In April 1958, according to Mao Zedong's suggestion, the CPC Central Committee issued *Advice on Befittingly Incorporating Small Agricultural Production Cooperatives into Big Cooperatives*. The mass of some incorporated and expanded agricultural production cooperatives spontaneously adopted names such as "Communist Commune", "Big Commune" and so on. In early August, 1958, after the survey in Hebei, Henan, Shandong and other palaces, Mao Zedong established the name "People's Commune". Then the CPC Central Committee passed Resolution on Establishing People's Communes in Rural Areas, which sparked the spread of People's Communes. From the summer of 1958 on, over 74,000 agricultural production cooperatives were reformed into 26,000 People's Communes, realizing People's communization within a few months.

The People's Communes were "big and public" (*yi da er gong*) with high degree of public ownership. Though the establishment of People's Communes played a certain role in the construction of irrigation works and productive cooperation, generally speaking, they were divorced from the reality of the Chinese countryside. In the People's Communes, the spirit of "communization" (*gong chan feng*), of falsification and embellishment (*fu kua feng*) and of blind command and forced instructions prevailed, inflicting serious damage to the agricultural production. Although the CPC Central Committee had tried to correct the problems popping up in the Great Leap Forward Movement and the People's Commune Movement, the struggle against Right-Opportunism, started at Lushan Conference in 1959, stroke a blow on the correct views presented by Peng Dehuai and others. In this way, not only did the leftist errors keep spreading in economic work but also the theory of expanded class struggle attained further development so that the inner-Party democracy was destroyed and the arbitrary rule by Mao Zedong as well as personality cult were fostered. By 1960, national economy slumped into an extremely difficult situtation. Cornered in this situation, the Communist Party undertook a readjustment on national economy which lasted for five years from 1961-1965 so that the crisis of national economy was tided over and national economy and various undertakings made greater achievements once more.

245

第十一篇 在探索中前进

Starting from the summer and autumn of 1958, more than 26,000 People's Communes were established. 12,000,000 peasants' household joined the Communes. The picture shows the people in Ningxiang County of Hunan Province were celebrating the establishment of People's Communes.

The Spring Flower Agricultural Commune in Yanta District of Xi'an, Shaanxi was frescoing the picture of "Great Leap Forward"-Get High Mountains to Lower Their Heads, Water to Make Way for Us.

The People's Communes set up large numbers of public dining halls, which were free for all the people. The picture displays the public dinning hall in Longshan Commune, Fanshun County, Guangdong Province.

In December 1958, workers of Shanghai Hudong Dockyard were celebrating the finishing of their task of steel production. Ministry of Metallurgy announced that national steel output had doubled, reaching 10,730,000 ton. In fact, only 8,000,000 ton was qualified, covering 3/4 of the "doubling" goal.

Homemade blast furnaces were densely spread over the barren hillocks of Wulidun, suburb of Xinyang City of Henan Province during the Movement of Steel-making.

In 1965, the missile developed by China on her own was successfully sent up.

On October 16th, 1964, the first atomic bomb of China was successfully exploded. The picture shows the mushroom cloud after the explosion of the atomic bomb.

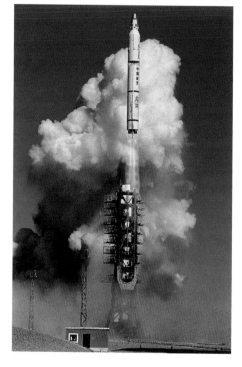

7. The Cultural Revolution

On August 18th, 1966, Mao Zedong was among the Red Guards.

The ten-year Cultural Revolution was launched and led by Mao Zedong in person. The criticism of the historical play *Hai Rui's Resignation From His Post* started from November 1965, which directly initiated the prelude of the Cultural Revolution. In May 1966, the enlarged conference of Political Bureau of CPC Central Committee adopted *Circular of CPC Central Committee* (known as May 16th Circular) and *Decision Concerning the Great Proletarian Cultural Revolution*. Then, imputations were cast on Peng Zhen, Luo Ruiqing, Lu Dingyi and Yang Shangkun, mistaken struggle were conducted against Liu Shaoqi and Deng Xiaoping. Newly-founded "Central Cultural Revolution Group" took most of the central power. From then on, the individual leadership guided by Mao Zedong's leftist error took the place of group leadership of the CPC Central Committee. The "Central Cultural Revolution Group" headed by Lin Biao and Jiang Qing put lots of efforts into cultivating the personality cult of Mao Zedong. Meanwhile, they employed the enthusiasm of personality cult to enhance their social status and influence,

conspiring to seize the national top leadership. This complicated the nature of the Cultural Revolution.

From August to November of 1966, on eight occasions at Tiananmen Square, Mao Zedong reviewed the Red Guards from all over China, whose number reached up to 13 million. Numerous young students turned their worship and craze for Mao Zedong into indignation and attacks on "revisionism" and "bourgeois headquarters". The party and governmental organs were widely stricken and became paralyzed or half-paralyzed, large numbers of cadres were criticized and fought, experts and scholars were put on the hat of "Reactive Learned Authority", enduring the name of "*niu gui she shen*" (ox ghost, snake demon).

In April 1969, the Ninth Congress of the Communist Party of China adopted Lin Biao's political report, which led to the swelling of the ambition of the Lin Biao Bloc. However, as the speeding up of their scheme of seizing state power was seen through by Mao Zedong, Lin Biao tried to escape abroad in a flurry by plane and died in a crash at Undurkhan in Mongolia.

In September 1976, Mao Zedong died. In October, Hua Guofeng, Ye Jianying and Li Xiannian and other members of the Central Committee Political Bureau convened a conference at which a decision was made to arrest the "Gang of Four". The "Gang of Four" met their end and the Cultural Revolution proclaimed its close.

The Cultural Revolution was a catastrophic decade for the Chinese nation, resulting in tremendous damage of splendid Chinese cultural heritage. Flowers withered away on the stage of art, only leaving the so-called eight "Revolutionary Sample Dramas". With the rising of the Red Guards, the enrollment of colleges and universities terminated and secondary school graduates of three years had been kept in stock by 1968. By the end of the same year, at the call of Mao Zedong, urban youths were mobilized to go "up to the mountains and down to the villages" (*shang shan xia xiang*). Large numbers of young students were sent to the country or frontier farms to take up agricultural labor.

Zhang Zhixin (1930-1975), native of Tianjin. She joined the Communist Party in 1955 and was a graduate from the Chinese People's University. She was also a cadre of Liaoning Provincial Publicizing Department of the CPC. During the "Cultural Revolution", she was prisoned in 1970 and cruelly killed on April 4th, 1975 as the result of her frequent criticism on the "left" error of Party leaders.

Propagandist poster of "Revolutionary Sample Dramas"

On February 22nd, 1968, Xinhua News Agency broadcast Mao Zedong's call that "young intellectuals shall go to the countryside for reeducation from the poor and middle peasants", which brought about the movement of "young intellectuals going up to the mountains and down to the villages". During the ten years after that, 16,230,000 young intellectuals all over the country went up to the mountains and down to the villages for reeducation from the poor and middle peasants.

Late in the "Cultural Revolution", Mao Zedong's "Direction of May 7th" was carried out everywhere and "May 7th" Cadre School was established. Large numbers of cadres, teachers, experts and artists were sent to take up labor in the country. The picture shows that teachers of Beijing University and Qinghua University were working in the "May 7th" Cadre School on Poyang Lake of Jiangxi.

On June 17th, 1967, the first Chinese hydrogen bomb was successfully exploded.

On April 24th, 1970, China successfully sent up the first man-made earth satellite.

On December 29, 1968, Nanjing Changjiang Bridge was completed and opened to traffic.

8. Thawing of Sino-American and Sino-Japanese Relationship and Recovery of China's Lawful Seat in the United Nations

Between February 21 and 28, 1972, American President Nixon visited China. The picture shows Premier Zhou Enlai was meeting Nixon.

On February 21st, 1972, Mao Zedong met Nixon.

On September 20th, 1972, Mao Zedong met Japanese Prime Minister Kakuei Tanaka.

By the end of the 1960s, in the world structure characterized by the contending for hegemony between America and Soviet Union, China became a power attended by both America and Soviet Union. However, China hoped to get rid of the confrontation with the two superpowers.

In November 1969, Nixon became President of America, who started to ease up Sino-US relations. On October 1st, 1970, Mao Zedong met American writer Edgar Snow at the platform of *Tian'anmen* and explicitly expressed that President Nixon would be welcome to China. In April 1971, China invited American Ping-pong team, which was attending the 31st World Ping-Pong Tournament in Japan to China, unfolding the "Ping-pong Diplomacy". From July 9th to 11th 1971, Dr. Kissinger, National Security Advisor to President Nixon visited China secretly. On July 16th, the Sino-US governments issued a communique, announcing President Nixon's future visit to China. This news shocked the whole world. At 11:40 a.m. February 21st, 1972, American President Nixon arrived in Beijing. On the afternoon of the same day, Mao Zedong met Nixon, which ended the isolation between China and America over 20 years. On July 28th, Sino-US issued *Joint Communique* , confirming: first, both sides should conduct the Sino-US relations based on the five principles of peaceful coexistence; second, both sides shouldn't seek hegemony in the Asia-Pacific region; third, all the Chinese on both sides of the Taiwan srait should be recognized one as China and Taiwan is part of China. The US government didn't raise objection to that stand. Since then, Sino-US relations started the process of normalization.

From October 18th to 25th 1971, the 26th General Assembly of United Nations, by overwhelming majority vote, passed the resolution on resumption of all legitimate rights of the People's Republic of China in the United Nations. On November 15th, 1971, a Chinese delegation, headed by Qiao Guanhua and Huanghua, attended the 26th the UN General Assembly session and took up the duty of a permanent member of UN Security Council.In April 1974, a Chinese delegation, headed by Deng Xiaoping attended the 6th Special Session of the UN General Assembly and explained the theory of "three worlds", announcing that "China is not now, and will never be a superpower".

Meanwhile, after a long period of hovering, Sino-Japanese relations became normalized with Japanese Prime Minister Kakuei Tanaka' visits to China in September 1972.

On January 31st, 1979, Vice Premier Deng Xiaoping held a grand reception in the Chinese Liaison Office in America.

9. Start of Reform and Opening-up

Masses of every circle held gatherings to celebrate the shattering of "Gang of Four".

Deng Xiaoping (1900-1996), general designer of Chinese reform and opening-up

After the Cultural Revolution, the erroneous guideline "two whatevers" (namely, "support whatever policy decisions Chairman Mao made and follow whatever instructions Chairman Mao issued") prevented the vast historical problems from being solved thoroughly and the newly-rising problems in reality from being tackled correctly. In May 1977, Deng Xiaoping demanded the eradication of the errors of "two whatevers". On May 1st, 1978, the Party School of Central Committee issued the article "*Practice is the Sole Criterion of Testing Truth*" in the magazine *Theoretical Trends*, and it was republished in *Guangming Daily*, *Xinhua News Agency*, *People's Daily* and the *PLA's Daily*. Numerous newspapers and magazines all over China conducted a warm debate, which facilitated the emancipation of people's mind.

The Third Plenum of the Eleventh National Party Congress Central Committee was convened from December 12th to 22nd, 1978. This congress summarized historical experience obtained since the founding of new China, made decisions on many major issues, corrected the erroneous conclusion concerning Peng Dehuai, Tao Zhu, Bo Yibo, Yang Shangkun and others and started the first step towards overall construction and opening-up to the world. In February 1980, the Fifth Plenum of the Eleventh National Party Congress decided to rehabilitate Liu Shaoqi. Meanwhile, the Central Committee conducted overall reverse of wronged and false

cases, carried out various policies on a full scale and rehabilitated those wrongly charged as rightists, which created preconditions for shifting the pivot of the Party's work to economic construction.

In the summer of 1977, Anhui and Sichuan carried out explorations and tests on the system of household responsibility for management (*bao gan dao hu*) and for output (*bao chan dao hu*) in the agricultural production, which resulted in evident increase of agricultural product. The Fourth Plenum of the Eleventh CPC National Congress formally approved *Decisions on Some Questions Concerning Acceleration of Agricultural Development (draft)*, deciding to lay emphasis on the reform of economic system in the rural areas and on the implementation of the household responsibility system. By 1982, over 90 % of the productive teams had set up various forms of household production responsibility system. Beginning from 1983, the system of People's Commune was reformed so as to increase the variety of occupations in the rural areas and facilitate the integration of agriculture, industry and commerce. Township enterprises emerged as a new force. The Zhujiang River Delta, lower reaches of the Changjiang River and coastal areas in southeastern China all displayed the new system of rural economic structure characterized by multi-economy.

In 1981, the government decided to take Shashi in Hubei, Changzhou in Jiangsu, Chongqing

Members of Hanjiawan Production Team, Chang'an County, Shaanxi Province, were receiving the contracts of household contract responsibility.

第十一篇

在探索中前进

in Sichuan and other cities as the pilot cities for comprehensive economic reform in central cities. Among the pilot cities were also Beijing, Tianjin, Shanghai and Guangzhou.

In July 1979, economic zones were established in Shenzhen, Zhuhai and Shantou of Guangdong Province, Xiamen of Fujian Province as the window and experimental fields of China's opening-up. In 1984, the CPC Central Committee and State Council decided to open Hainan Island and fourteen coastal cities, including Dalian, Qinhuangdao, Tianjin, Yantai, Lianyungang, Nantong, Shanghai, Ningbo, Wenzhou, Fuzhou, Guangzhou, Zhanjiang and Beihai. In 1985, China further opened the Changjiang River Delta, the Zhujiang River Delta, the Xia (Xiamen) Zhang (Zhangzhou) Quan (Quanzhou) Delta in southern Fujian, Jiaodong Peninsula and Liaodong Peninsula. In this way, Chinese closed economy gradually moved to open economy and evidently attained greater economic strength.

Zhongguancun Road, Beijing

New looks of Pudong, Shanghai

In 1980, Shenzhen Economic Zone was found. In the past 20 years, Shenzhen has become an international business city with strong capacities of handy industry, finance and ocean shipping. The picture shows the new looks of Shenzhen City.

10. The Return of Hong Kong and Macao

Since the practice of reform and opening-up, China has maintained independent and peaceful diplomacy, securing a favorable international environment for economic construction. China has maintained and developed friendly relations with many countries, actively taken part in the activities of the UN and other international organizations, pushed forward the peaceful settlement of regional conflicts and worked hard for the establishment of a new international political and economic order. In 1985, China declared disarmament of 1 million and promised it would never be the first to employ nuclear weapons under any condition and never use nuclear weapons to the nations that had no nuclear weapons.

After the first Opium War, Hong Kong of China was occupied by Britain and taken as its colony, which was the testimony of China's humiliation. Therefore, taking over the sovereignty of Hong Kong at a proper time had long been the firm stand of new Chinese government. In September 1982, the British

The ceremony of taking-over Hongkong between China and Britain on July 1st, 1997, Hongkong

Prime Minister Margaret Thatcher visited China. Deng Xiaoping, director of the CPC Central Committee consultative committee talked about the future of Hong Kong with her and explicitly brought forward the scenario of "One Country, Two Systems". After that, while meeting foreign guests and Hong Kong personages, Deng Xiaoping illuminated the idea for many times that Taiwan and Hong Kong could maintain capitalism, with the mainland continuing its socialist system after the unification and the People's Republic of China would be the only one that could stand for China in the world. In May 1984, the formula of "One Country, Two System" was formally brought forward at the Second Session of the Sixth National People's Congress and was made a lawful national policy, which facilitated the settlement of Hong Kong and Macao issues.

According to the "One Country, Two system" principle, Sino-British government reached initiated *Joint Declaration of the Government of the United Kingdom of Great Britain and Northern Ireland and the Government of the People's Republic of China* on the question of Hong Kong on September 26th, 1984 in Beijing, declaring that China would restore its sovereignty over Hong Kong from July 1st, 1997 on and British government would return Hong Kong to China on the same day. The People's Republic of China was to set up Hong Kong Special Administrative Region, managed by the Hong Kong natives without touching

the current society, economic system, lifestyle and law. These guidelines should be in effect for 50 years since the establishment of Hong Kong Special Administrative Region. In November, the Eighth Session of the Sixth National People's Congress approved the *Sino-British Joint Declaration* and both sides exchanged books of approval of the *Sino-British Joint Declaration*.

Delegations of Chinese and Portuguese government started talks on the question of Macao in June 1986. After four rounds of talks, both sides initiated *Joint Declaration of the Government of Republic of Portugal and the Government of the People's Republic of China*, declaring the People's Republic of China would take over the sovereignty over Macao on December 20th, 1999 and establish the PRC Macao Special Administrative Region. Macao today enjoys a high degree of autonomy, except that foreign affairs and national defense are administered by the central People's government. On April 14th, *the Joint Sino-Portuguese Declaration* was formally signed in Beijing.

On July 1st, 1997 and December 20th, 1999, Hong Kong and Macao returned to China and Hong Kong, Macao Special Administrative Regions were established respectively, signifying a new important step towards China's unification.

On October 1st, 2000, almost a year since its return to China, Macao Government held the ceremony of flag-raising in Gold Lotus Park to celebrate Chinese National Day.

11. Marching towards Grand Revival of the Chinese Nation

In the early days of 1992, Deng Xiaoping made a significant tour to the south. The picture shows Deng Xiaoping in Wuchang.

During the critical period of Chinese socialist construction of modernization, Deng Xiaoping, then aged 88, inspected Wuhan, Shenzhen, Zhuhai, Shanghai as well as other places and made important speeches all the way from January 28th to February 21st 1992. He pointed out that the pace of reform and opening-up must be sped up; plan and market were not the essential difference between socialism and capitalism; the nature of socialism lay in the emancipation and development of productive forces; the extermination of exploitation, elimination of polarization and ultimate achievement of common affluence. In October 1992, the Fourteenth CPC National Congress explicitly advanced the idea that the objective of reforming the Chinese economic system was to set up socialist market economy. Thus the theory of building socialism with Chinese characteristics was formed to a full scale. Chinese economy picks up speed and attains sustained development once again.

In 1992, the Fifth Session of the Seventh National People's Congress adopted *Resolution on Three Gorges Project* and announced its official launching on December 14th, 1994. The Three Gorges is 192 kilometers long, stretching from Baidicheng of Chongqing City upstream to Nanjin Pass of Yichang, Hubei Province downstream. It's made up of Qutang, Wuxia and Xiling Gorges. Being capable of controlling floods, making electricity and facilitating navigation, the Three Gorges Dam Project is a gigantic project that harvests comprehensive benefits. It can prevent the destructive disasters along the Jingjiang River (a

section of the Changjiang River) and will become the largest water and power station in China or even in the world after its completion. It will greatly improve the navigation conditions of the Changjiang River so that the 10,000 tons fleets will be able to sail to Chongqing City directly from Wuhan. The first batch of generators will begin to generate power in 2003 and the entire project is to be completed by 2009.

After June 1998, heavy storm rains covered both the south and north of China, causing sharp rise of the water levels of the Changjiang River. Jiangxi, Hubei, Hunan, Chongqing, Sichuan, Inner Mongolia, Heilongjiang and other provinces suffered floods. Jiang Zemin, Li Peng, Zhu Rongji and other leaders of the Party and government went to the anti-flood battlefields in person to direct the anti-flood and disaster relief. Millions of soldiers and people took strict precautions against the floods and sturdily defended the levees so that they won the victory of the anti-flood battle. During the severe flood disasters, all the Chinese people were concerned with the disaster areas. They relieved the people in the flood-stricken areas in various forms, which demonstrated the great cohesion and staunch fighting spirit of the Chinese nation.

In 1998, a financial crisis that shocked the whole world broke out in Asia. As a large responsible nation, China sustained the value of Renminbi and contributed for the tiding-over of Asian financial crisis. Meanwhile, Chinese economy maintained the annual growth rate of 7% that has been attained continuously for many years and displayed an evident increase of comprehensive national strength.

In June 1999, China started the splendid project of Grand Development of Western Regions, which will optimize the local distribution of productive forces, shorten the local developmental gap and speed up the overall economic development of China.

On July 13th, 2001, Beijing won the bid for hosting the 2008 Olympic Games at the 112th session of the International Olympic Committee in Moscow and the victory fully demonstrated the world's confidence on China's future development.

China was accepted by the World Trade Organization officially on December 11th, 2001. China's entry into WTO has not only facilitated China's reform and opening-up but also built up the confidence on global economic development.

On July 13th, 2001, the International Olympic Committee announced that China was elected to hold the Olympic Game in 2008. Peolpe all over the country is excited by the news.

On November 12th, 2001, Shi Guangsheng, Minister of Ministry of Foreign Economy and Trade, signed on the agreement concerning China's entry to WTO on behalf of the government of the People's Republic of China.

Under the leadership of the Central Committee with Jiang Zemin at the core, the Chinese people are marching towards the grant revival of the Chinese nation with big strides.

Chronologie

Chine	Relations	Occident
v. 2205-1767 (?) av. J.-C. Dynastie des Hsia dans la Chine du Nord (vallée du Fleuve jaune)		2775 1re dynastie d'Ur 2723-2563 IVe dynastie égyptienne : les pyramides
1766-1112 (?) av. J.-C. Dynastie des Chang, puis des Yin		1580 Fondation du Nouvel Empire en Égypte 1180 Guerre de Troie
1111-771 av. J.-C. Dynastie des Tcheou occidentaux		1029-974 Règne de David
770-256 Dynastie des Tcheou orientaux Confucius 551-478 av. J.-C. Lao-tseu (Ve s. av. J.-C.)	Hérodote (484-425) : première mention de la Chine	753 Fondation de Rome
453-221 av. J.-C. Période des Royaumes combattants		443 Apogée de Périclès 399 Mort de Socrate 376-323 Campagnes d'Alexandre
Première unification de l'empire 221-206 av. J.-C. Dynastie des Ts'in fondée par Ts'in Che Houang-ti		219-201 Deuxième Guerre punique
206 av.-9 apr. J.-C. Dynastie des Han antérieurs ou occidentaux 9-23 Usurpation de Wang Mang 23-220 Dynastie des Han postérieurs ou orientaux	97 apr. J.-C. Échec de la première ambassade chinoise venue en Occident	59-50 av. J.-C. Conquête de la Gaule par César Naissance de Jésus-Christ (antérieure de 4 ou 5 ans au début de l'ère chrétienne) 70 Destruction de Jérusalem
105 Invention du papier	166 Marchands syriens en Chine	161-180 Marc-Aurèle
Morcellement 220-280 Les Trois Royaumes		
Brève restauration de l'unité 265-316 Dynastie des Tsin		275 Invasion des Francs en Gaule
Invasions et morcellement 316-589 Chine du Nord : invasions des Huns, des Proto-Mongols et des Turcomans. Chine du Sud : succession de dynasties chinoises	498 Fondation de l'Église nestorienne en Perse 555 Introduction de la soie à Constantinople depuis la Chine	330 Fondation de Constantinople 380 Le christianisme seule religion licite dans l'Empire romain 451 Invasion des Huns 476 Fin de l'empire d'Occident 496 Conversion de Clovis
Unification 589-618 Dynastie des Souei 618-907 Dynastie des T'ang. Capitale : Tch'ang-ngan	638 Fondation d'une Église nestorienne en Chine 851 *Relation de la Chine et de l'Inde*	622 L'Hégire 632 Mort de Mahomet 732 Charles Martel arrête l'invasion arabe à Poitiers 800 Charlemagne couronné empereur à Rome
Morcellement 907-960 Les cinq dynasties dans le Nord		
Unification 960-1126 Dynastie des Song		987 Hugues Capet roi de France 1095 Prédication de la 1re croisade 1099 Prise de Jérusalem par les croisés
Séparation du Nord et du Sud 1115-1234 Dynastie Kin de race toungouse dans le Nord 1127-1279 Dynastie Song dans le Sud, capitale : Hang-tcheou	1245-1246 Voyage de Jean du Plan Carpin 1253 Voyage de Guillaume de Rubrouck 1260 Voyage de Nicolo et Mafeo Polo	1187 Prise de Jérusalem par Saladin 1204 Prise de Constantinople par les croisés (4e croisade) 1216 5e croisade 1226-1270 Règne de saint Louis 1230 Invasion mongole en Europe
Unification 1280-1368 Dynastie mongole des Yuan, capitale : Pékin	1272-1295 Voyage de Marco Polo 1287 Voyage de Rabban Cauma en Europe 1293-1328 Séjour de Montcorvin à Pékin 1314-1328 Voyage d'Odoric de Pordenone	1291 Les croisés expulsés de Terre sainte 1309 La papauté en Avignon 1329 Début de la guerre de Cent Ans 1365 Début des conquêtes de Tamerlan
1368-1644 Dynastie nationale des Ming, capitale : Nankin, puis Pékin	1498 Vasco de Gama arrive à Calicut 1517 Ambassade portugaise à Canton 1557 Les Portugais s'installent à Macao 1580 Le P. Ricci arrive à Macao	1453 Prise de Constantinople par les Turcs 1492 Premier voyage de Christophe Colomb 1516 Avènement de Charles Quint 1521 Excommunication de Luther 1539 Organisation de la Compagnie de Jésus
1592-1597 Expédition japonaise en Corée		1589-1610 Règne d'Henri IV
1644-1912 Dynastie mandchoue des Ts'ing, capitale : Pékin 1667-1722 Règne de K'ang-hi 1735-1796 Règne de K'ien-long 1851-1864 Révolte des T'ai-p'ing 1862 L'impératrice Ts'eu-hi régente	1685 Jésuites français envoyés à Pékin par Louis XIV 1704 Condamnation des « rites chinois » par le pape 1792-1793 Ambassade anglaise de lord Macartney 1839 Première guerre de l'opium 1857-1860 Seconde guerre de l'opium, sac de Pékin 1869 Début de l'ère Meiji au Japon 1884-1885 Guerre franco-chinoise (Indochine)	1661 Début du règne personnel de Louis XIV 1685 Révocation de l'Édit de Nantes 1715 Mort de Louis XIV, la Régence 1764 Dissolution de la Compagnie de Jésus en France 1773 Suppression de l'ordre des jésuites par le pape 1789 Réunion des états généraux en France 1793 Exécution de Louis XVI 1804 Napoléon Ier empereur des Français 1830 Avènement de Louis-Philippe 1852 Napoléon III empereur
1895 La Chine vaincue par le Japon en Corée 1898 Tentative de réforme (K'ang Yeou-wei) 1908 Mort de l'impératrice Ts'eu-hi	1897-1898 Développement des concessions étrangères à Chang-hai 1900-1901 Guerre des « Boxeurs » 1904-1905 Les Russes vaincus par les Japonais	
1911 La République chinoise 1921 Fondation du parti communiste chinois 1925 Mort de Sun Yat-sen, Tchang Kai-chek lui succède 1937 Invasion japonaise		1914-1918 Première Guerre mondiale 1917 Révolution d'octobre en Russie 1939-1945 Seconde Guerre mondiale 1945 Fondation de l'O.N.U.
1949 La République populaire de Chine 1950 Traité d'alliance sino-soviétique 1956-1957 Les Cent Fleurs 1958 Le Grand Bond en avant 1959-1961 Année de disette 1960 Rupture sino-soviétique 1966-1968 La Révolution culturelle 1976 Mort de Chou En-lai, puis de Mao Tse-tong	1950 Guerre de Corée 1964 La France reconnaît la Chine populaire 1971 Admission de la Chine à l'O.N.U.	1953 Mort de Staline 1954 Défaite de Dien Bien Phu 1956 Khrouchtchev dénonce les fautes de Staline au XXe congrès du P.C.U.S. Les troupes soviétiques à Budapest 1958 De Gaulle président de la République 1968 Intervention soviétique en Tchécoslovaquie 1969 Retraite de De Gaulle

The List of World Heritage Sites in China

No.	Name	Dynasty	Place	Description	Page
1	The Palace Museum	Ming and Qing	Beijing	The imperial palace of Ming and Qing Dynasties	153
2	The Great Wall	Ming	China	From Jiayu Pass in the west to Shanhai Pass in the east, known as the "seventh wonder of the world", added to the list of the World Cultural Heritage Sites in December, 1987	148
3	Potala Palace, Jokhang Monastery	Yuan	Northwestern outskirts of Lhasa, Tibet Autonomous Region	A palace-style architectural complex, the essence of ancient Tibetan architectural art	143
4	Qinshihuang's Mausoleum And Terra-cotta Army	Qin	Xi'an city, Shanxi Province	The most important archaeological finding in the 20th century, enjoyed the fame as the "eighth wonder of the world"	52
5	The Mogao Graves at Dunhuang	Tang	Mingsha Mountain, Dunhuang, Gansu Province	Buddhist Grave temple dug from the Sixteen States to Yuan Dynasty. It is the largest treasure-house of Buddhist Art in the world	86
6	Jiuzhaigou Valley Scenic Area	Republic of China	Jiuzhaigou County, Aba Tibetan Autonomous Prefecture, Sichuan Province	Regarded as "magic mountains and holy waters" by the local Zang people, called "heaven on earth" by Easterners, compared to "fairy land" by Westerners	212
7	The Summer Palace of Beijing	Qing	Beijing	One of the largest imperial gardens in the world	172
8	The Temple of Heaven of Beijing	Ming	Beijing	During the Ming and Qing Dynasties, emperors came to the temple to worship the God of Heaven, pray for a good harvest, pray for rain in Summer and snow in Winter	152
9	The Taishan Mountain Scenic Area	Qin and Han	Tai'an, Shandong Province	Also called "Eastern Sacred Mountain", "Daizong" and "Daiyue", in the list of Cultural and Natural Heritage	48
10	The Lushan Mountain Scenic Area	Song	North of Jiangxi Province	Known to the world for its "majesty, grotesqueness, precipitousness and Beauty"	137
11	Pingyao Ancient City	Ming	Pingyao, Shandong Province	Built in the Western Zhou Dynasty, well-preserved look of Ming and Qing Dynasties	155
12	Chengde Summer Resorts and Surrounding Temples	Qing	Chengde, Hebei Province	Consists of imperial palace, gardens and marvelous temple complex	183
13	Zhoukoudian: Home of the Peking Man	Remote antiquity	Zhoukoudian County, Fangshan District, Beijing	The richest and most systematic relics of the Old Stone Age in the world	8
14	Lijiang Ancient City	Yuan	Lijiang Naxi Autonomous County, Yunnan Province	Built in the end of Song and the beginning Yuan, palace, gardens, business districts and official mansions were well-preserved	131
15	Suzhou Classical Gardens	Qing	Suzhou, Jiangsu Province	Combining architectural, natural and artificial beauty, delicate and elegant, with distinct characteristics	204
16	Dazu Rock Carvings	Song	Dazu County	Statues scatter around the county, the best preserved rock carving arts	129
17	Ancient Buildings on the Wudang Mountain	Northern and Southern	Danjiangkou City, northwestern Hubei Province	Also called "Taihe Mountain" and "Xuanyue Mountain", the well-known sacred Taoist place, famous for the marvelous Taoist temples	79
18	The Longmen Grottoes	Northern Wei and Tang	Luoyang, Henan Province	Built in Northern Wei through Eastern and Western Wei, Northern Qin, Sui, Tang and Song Dynasties. Together with Mogao Grottoes in Dunhuang, Gansu and Yungang Grottoes in Datong, Shanxi are called the Three Great Grottoes of China	96
19	Imperial Mausoleum of Ming and Qing Dynasties	Ming and Qing	Nanjing, Beijing and Anlu in Hubei Province, Zunhua in Hebei Province	It has 18 imperial tombs of Ming and 15 tombs of Qing, with great scale and complete structure	201
20	Qufu, Confucius's Mansion, Temple and Cemetery	Spring and Autumn Period, Warring States Period	Qufu, Shandong Province	Largest Confucius' Temple, the residence of Confucius' descendants and the family graveyard	42
21	Dujiang Weirs and Qingchengshan Mountain	Warring States Period	Dujiangyan City, Sichuan Province	Built by the prefecture chief Li Bin and his son in Shu. Qingchengshan Mountain is ancient and peaceful	32
22	Ancient Villages in Southern Anhui-Xidi and Hongcun	Qing	Yixian County, Anhui Province	It has 3600 well-preserved ancient civilian residences	203
23	The Huanglong Scenic Area	Three Kingdoms	Songfan County, Sichuan Province	With unique landscapes, rich resources, original ecosystem, well-preserved, known as "Jasper Lake on earth"	70
24	The Huangshan Mountain Scenic Area and Historic Interest Area	Song and Yuan	Huangshan City, Anhui Province	Enjoys the fame of "the Greatest Mountain of China", on the list of the World Cultural and Natural Heritage Sites	144
25	Wulingyuan Scenic and Historic Interest Area	Northern and Southern Dynasties	Zhangjiajie City, Hunan Province	With precipitous mountains, strange peaks, beautiful rivers, peaceful valleys and pretty caves	82
26	The Emei Mountains and LeshanGiant Buddha	Tang	Emeishan City and Leshan city, Sichuan Province	One of the China's four famous Buddhist Mountains. Leshan Giant Buddha is also referred to as Lingyun Giant Buddh. Built in Tang Dynasty, 71m high, the highest Buddha in the world	113
27	The Wuyishan Mountain Scenic Area	Southern Song	Wuyishan City, Fujian Province	With changeable sceneries. It is the center of Chinese southeastern culture, called "Dao Nan Li Ku"	133
28	The Yugang Grottoes	Northern Wei	Datong City, Shanxi Province	Built in Northern Wei, extends 1km from east to west. It has 53 caves and 51000 statues in all. Majestic and solemn	81